T0329402

CAMBRIDGE LIBRARY COLLECTION

Books of enduring scholarly value

British and Irish History, Nineteenth Century

This series comprises contemporary or near-contemporary accounts of the political, economic and social history of the British Isles during the nineteenth century. It includes material on international diplomacy and trade, labour relations and the women's movement, developments in education and social welfare, religious emancipation, the justice system, and special events including the Great Exhibition of 1851.

A History of Political Economy

Living most of his life in Dublin, John Kells Ingram (1823–1907) published papers on Shakespeare, geometry, differential calculus, and Mexican antiques, held professorial chairs in English Literature and Greek, and in 1843 wrote 'The Memory of the Dead', a celebrated Irish nationalist hymn. He helped to found the Dublin Statistical Society in 1847, and from the 1860s began to write papers such as 'Work and the Workman', reflecting his adherence to the positivist sociology of Auguste Comte. He saw economics as an integral part of sociology which, through practical application, could contribute towards the betterment of humanity. Published in 1888, *A History of Political Economy* was hugely successful, being translated into ten languages. In it, Ingram expands on the historicist rejection of laissez-faire and free trade as being universally correct, and promotes the notion that the state can play a constructive role in improving the lives of its people.

Cambridge University Press has long been a pioneer in the reissuing of out-of-print titles from its own backlist, producing digital reprints of books that are still sought after by scholars and students but could not be reprinted economically using traditional technology. The Cambridge Library Collection extends this activity to a wider range of books which are still of importance to researchers and professionals, either for the source material they contain, or as landmarks in the history of their academic discipline.

Drawing from the world-renowned collections in the Cambridge University Library and other partner libraries, and guided by the advice of experts in each subject area, Cambridge University Press is using state-of-the-art scanning machines in its own Printing House to capture the content of each book selected for inclusion. The files are processed to give a consistently clear, crisp image, and the books finished to the high quality standard for which the Press is recognised around the world. The latest print-on-demand technology ensures that the books will remain available indefinitely, and that orders for single or multiple copies can quickly be supplied.

The Cambridge Library Collection brings back to life books of enduring scholarly value (including out-of-copyright works originally issued by other publishers) across a wide range of disciplines in the humanities and social sciences and in science and technology.

A History of
Political Economy

JOHN K. INGRAM

CAMBRIDGE
UNIVERSITY PRESS

CAMBRIDGE UNIVERSITY PRESS

Cambridge, New York, Melbourne, Madrid, Cape Town,
Singapore, São Paolo, Delhi, Mexico City

Published in the United States of America by Cambridge University Press, New York

www.cambridge.org
Information on this title: www.cambridge.org/9781108053020

© in this compilation Cambridge University Press 2013

This edition first published 1888
This digitally printed version 2013

ISBN 978-1-108-05302-0 Paperback

HISTORY OF

POLITICAL ECONOMY

A HISTORY

OF

POLITICAL ECONOMY

BY

JOHN KELLS INGRAM, LL.D.

FELLOW OF TRINITY COLLEGE, DUBLIN

EDINBURGH: ADAM & CHARLES BLACK

MDCCCLXXXVIII

CONTENTS.

——◆——

PREFATORY NOTE.

THE object of the following pages is rather to exhibit the historic development of economic thought in its relations with general philosophic ideas than to give an exhaustive account of economic literature. An attempt has, however, been made, so far as was consistent with the main design, to notice all the really important works on the science. Readers who desire more detailed information are referred to the under-mentioned books on the history of Political Economy, all of which have been more or less, and some very largely, used in the preparation of the present work.

GENERAL HISTORIES.—*Histoire de l'Économie Politique en Europe depuis les anciens jusqu'à nos jours*, by Jerôme Adolphe Blanqui (1837–38); of which there is an English translation by Emily J. Leonard (1880). *Histoire de l'Économie Politique*, by Alban de Villeneuve-Bargemont (Brussels, 1839; Paris, 1841); written from the Catholic point of view. *View of the Progress of Political Economy in Europe since the Sixteenth Century*, by Travers Twiss, D.C.L. (1847). *Die geschichtliche Entwickelung der National Oekonomik und ihrer Literatur*, by Julius Kautz (2d ed. 1860); a valuable work, marked by philosophical breadth, and exhibiting the results of extensive research, but too declamatory in style; the book sadly wants an index. *Kritische Ge-schichte der National-ökonomie und des Socialismus,* by Emile Dühring (1871; 3d ed. 1879); characterised by its author's usual sagacity, but also by his usual perverseness and depre-ciation of meritorious writers in his own field. *Guida allo studio dell' Economia Politica,* by Luigi Cossa (1876 and 1878; Eng. trans. 1880). *Geschichte der Nationalökonomik,* by H. Eisenhart (1881); a vigorous and original sketch. And, lastly, a brief but excellent history by H. von Scheel in the *Handbuch der politischen Oekonomie* (a great encyclo-pædia of economic knowledge in all its extent and applica-tions; edited by Gustav Schönberg, 1882; 2d ed., enlarged and improved, 1886). To these histories proper must be added *The Literature of Political Economy,* by J. R. M'Culloch (1845), a book which might with advantage be re-edited, supplemented where imperfect, and continued to our own time. Some of the biographical and critical notices by Eugène Daire and others in the *Collection des principaux Économistes* will also be found useful, as well as the articles in the *Dictionnaire de l'Économie Politique* of Coquelin and Guillaumin (1852–53; 3d ed. 1864), which is justly described by Jevons as "on the whole the best work of reference in the literature of the science."

SPECIAL HISTORIES.—*Italy.*—*Storia della Economia Pub-blica in Italia, ossia Epilogo critico degli Economisti Italiani,* by Count Giuseppe Pecchio (1829), intended as an appendix to Baron Custodi's collection of the *Scrittori classici Italiani di Economia Politica,* 50 vols., comprising the writings of Italian economists from 1582 to 1804. There is a French translation of Pecchio's work by Leonard Gallois (1830). The book is not without value, though often superficial and rhetorical.

Spain.—Storia della Economia Politica in España (1863), by M. Colmeiro ; rather a history of economy than of economics—of policies and institutions rather than of theories and literary works.

Germany.—Geschichte der Nationalökonomik in Deutschland (1874), by Wilhelm Roscher ; a vast repertory of learning on its subject, with occasional side-glances at other economic literatures. *Die neuere Nationalökonomie in ihren Hauptrichtungen,* by Moritz Meyer (3d ed. 1882) ; a useful handbook dealing almost exclusively with recent German speculation and policy.

England.—Zur Geschichte der Englischen Volkswirthschaftslehre, by W. Roscher (1851–52).

The reader is also advised to consult the articles in the ninth edition of the Encyclopædia Britannica which relate to the principal writers on political economy, especially those on Petty, Quesnay, Turgot, Smith, Say, and Ricardo. The present work, it should be stated, is for the most part a reproduction of the article " Political Economy," which appeared (1885) in volume xix. of the Encyclopædia Britannica.

TRINITY COLLEGE, DUBLIN,
March 15, 1888.

OUTLINES

OF THE

HISTORY OF POLITICAL ECONOMY.

———◆———

CHAPTER I.

INTRODUCTORY.

In the present condition of Political Economy, the production
of new dogmatic treatises on the subject does not appear to be
opportune.   There are many works, accessible to every one,
in which, with more or less of variation in details, what
is known as the "orthodox" or "classical" system is expounded.   But there exists in England and other countries wide-
spread dissatisfaction with that system, and much difference
of opinion with respect both to the method and the doctrines
of Economic Science.   There is, in fact, good reason to
believe that this department of social theory has entered on
a transition stage, and is destined ere long to undergo a considerable transformation.   But the new body of thought
which will replace, or at least profoundly modify, the old,
has not yet been fully elaborated. The attitude of mind
which these circumstances seem to prescribe is that of pause
and retrospection. It is thought that our position will be
rendered clearer and our further progress facilitated by
tracing historically, and from a general point of view, the

A

course of speculation regarding economic phenomena, and contemplating the successive forms of opinion concerning them in relation to the periods at which they were respectively evolved. And this is the task undertaken in the following pages.

Such a study is in harmony with the best intellectual tendencies of our age, which is, more than anything else, characterised by the universal supremacy of the historical spirit. To such a degree has this spirit permeated all our modes of thinking, that with respect to every branch of knowledge, no less than with respect to every institution and every form of human activity, we almost instinctively ask, not merely what is its existing condition, but what were its earliest discoverable germs, and what has been the course of its development? The assertion of J. B. Say[1] that the history of Political Economy is of little value, being for the most part a record of absurd and justly exploded opinions, belongs to a system of ideas already obsolete, and requires at the present time no formal refutation.[2] It deserves notice only as reminding us that we must discriminate between history and antiquarianism: what from the first had no significance it is mere pedantry to study now. We need concern ourselves only with those modes of thinking which have prevailed largely and seriously influenced practice in the past, or in which we can discover the roots of the present and the future.

When we thus place ourselves at the point of view of history, it becomes unnecessary to discuss the definition of Political Economy, or to enlarge on its method, at the outset. It will suffice to conceive it as the theory of social wealth, or to accept provisionally Say's definition, which makes it

[1] " Que pourrions-nous gagner à recueillir des opinions absurdes, des doctrines décriées et qui meritent de l'être? Il serait à la fois inutile et fastidieux." Écon. Pol. Pratique, IXme Partie. The "cependant" which follows does not really modify this judgment.

[2] See Roscher's Geschichte der National-œkonomik in Deutschland, Vorrede.

the science of the production, distribution, and consumption of wealth. Any supplementary ideas which require to be taken into account will be suggested in the progress of our survey, and the determination of the proper method of economic research will be treated as one of the principal results of the historical evolution of the science.

The history of Political Economy must of course be distinguished from the economic history of mankind, or of any separate portion of our race. The study of the succession of economic facts themselves is one thing; the study of the succession of theoretic ideas concerning the facts is another. And it is with the latter alone that we are here directly concerned. But these two branches of research, though distinct, yet stand in the closest relation to each other. The rise and the form of economic doctrines have been largely conditioned by the practical situation, needs, and tendencies of the corresponding epochs. With each important social change new economic questions have presented themselves; and the theories prevailing in each period have owed much of their influence to the fact that they seemed to offer solutions of the urgent problems of the age. Again, every thinker, however in some respects he may stand above or before his contemporaries, is yet a child of his time, and cannot be isolated from the social medium in which he lives and moves. He will necessarily be affected by the circumstances which surround him, and in particular by the practical exigencies of which his fellows feel the strain. This connection of theory with practice has its advantages and its dangers. It tends to give a real and positive character to theoretic inquiry; but it may also be expected to produce exaggerations in doctrine, to lend undue prominence to particular sides of the truth, and to make transitory situations or temporary expedients be regarded as universally normal conditions.

There are other relations which we must not overlook in tracing the progress of economic opinion. The several branches of the science of society are so closely connected that the history of no one of them can with perfect rationality be treated apart, though such a treatment is recommended—indeed necessitated—by practical utility. The movement of economic thought is constantly and powerfully affected by the prevalent mode of thinking, and even the habitual tone of sentiment, on social subjects generally. All the intellectual manifestations of a period in relation to human questions have a kindred character, and bear a certain stamp of homogeneity, which is vaguely present to our minds when we speak of the spirit of the age. Social speculation again, and economic research as one branch of it, is both through its philosophic method and through its doctrine under the influence of the sciences which in the order of development precede the social, especially of the science of organic nature.

It is of the highest importance to bear in mind these several relations of economic research both to external circumstance and to other spheres of contemporary thought, because by keeping them in view we shall be led to form less absolute and therefore juster estimates of the successive phases of opinion. Instead of merely praising or blaming these according to the degrees of their accordance with a predetermined standard of doctrine, we shall view them as elements in an ordered series, to be studied mainly with respect to their filiation, their opportuneness, and their influences. We shall not regard each new step in this theoretic development as implying an unconditional negation of earlier views, which often had a relative justification, resting, as they did, on a real, though narrower, basis of experience, or assuming the existence of a different social order. Nor shall we consider all the theoretic positions now occupied as definitive; for the practical system of life which they tacitly assume is itself susceptible of change, and destined, without doubt, more or less to undergo it. Within the limits of a sketch like the present these considerations cannot be fully worked out; but an effort will be made to keep them in view, and to mark the relations here indicated, wherever their influence is specially important or interesting.

The particular situation and tendencies of the several thinkers whose names are associated with economic doctrines have, of course, modified in a greater or less degree the spirit or form of those doctrines. Their relation to special predecessors, their native temperament, their early training, their religious prepossessions and political partialities, have all had their effects. To these we shall in some remarkable instances direct attention; but, in the main, they are, for our present purpose, secondary and subordinate. The *ensemble* must preponderate over the individual; and the constructors of theories must be regarded as organs of a common intellectual and social movement.

The history of economic inquiry is most naturally divided into the three great periods of (1) the ancient, (2) the mediæval, and (3) the modern worlds. In the two former, this branch of study could exist only in a rudimentary state. It is evident that for any considerable development of social theory two conditions must be fulfilled. First, the phenomena must have exhibited themselves on a sufficiently extended scale to supply adequate matter for observation, and afford a satisfactory basis for scientific generalisations; and secondly, whilst the spectacle is thus provided, the spectator must have been trained for his task, and armed with the appropriate aids and instruments of research, that is to say, there must have been such a previous cultivation of the simpler sciences as will have both furnished the necessary data of doctrine and prepared the proper methods of investigation. Sociology requires to use for its purposes theorems which belong to the domains of physics and biology, and which it must borrow from their professors; and, on the logical side, the methods which it has to employ—deductive, observational, comparative—must have been previously shaped in the cultivation of mathematics and the study of the inorganic world or of organisms less complex than the social. Hence it is plain that, though some laws or tendencies of society must have been forced on men's attention in every age by practical exigencies which could not be postponed, and though the questions thus raised must have received some empirical solution, a really scientific sociology must be the product of a very advanced stage of intellectual development. And this is true of the economic, as of other branches of social theory. We shall therefore content ourselves with a general outline of the character of economic thought in antiquity and the Middle Ages, and of the conditions which determined that character.

CHAPTER II.

ANCIENT TIMES.

THE earliest surviving expressions of thought on economic subjects have come down to us from the Oriental theocracies. The general spirit of the corresponding type of social life consisted in taking imitation for the fundamental principle of education, and consolidating nascent civilisation by heredity of the different functions and professions, or even by a system of castes, hierarchically subordinated to each other according to the nature of their respective offices, under the common supreme direction of the sacerdotal caste. This last was charged with the traditional stock of conceptions, and their application for purposes of discipline. It sought to realise a complete regulation of human life in all its departments on the basis of this transmitted body of practical ideas. Conservation is the principal task of this social order, and its most remarkable quality is stability, which tends to degenerate into stagnation. But there can be no doubt that the useful arts were long, though slowly, progressive under this régime, from which they were inherited by the later civilisations,—the system of classes or castes maintaining the degree of division of labour which had been reached in those early periods. The leading members of the corporations which presided over the theocracies without doubt gave much earnest thought to the conduct of industry, which, unlike war, did not imperil their political pre-eminence by developing a rival class. But, conceiving life as a whole, and making its regulation their primary aim, they naturally considered most the social reactions which industry is fitted to exercise. The moral side of economics is the one they habitually contemplate, or (what is not the same) the economic side of morals. They abound in those warnings against greed and the haste to be rich which religion and philosophy have in all ages seen to be necessary. They insist on honesty in mutual dealings, on just weights and measures, on the faithful observance of contracts. They admonish against the pride and arrogance apt to be generated by riches, against undue prodigality and self-indulgence, and enforce the duties of justice and beneficence towards servants and inferiors. Whilst, in accordance with the theological spirit, the personal acquisition of wealth is in general thesis represented as determined by divine wills, its dependence on individual diligence and thrift is emphatically taught. There is indeed in the fully developed theocratic systems a tendency to carry precept, which there differs little from command, to an excessive degree of minuteness,—to prescribe in detail the time, the mode, and the accompaniments of almost every act of every member of the community. This system of exaggerated surveillance is connected with the union, or rather confusion, of the spiritual and temporal powers, whence it results that many parts of the government of society are conducted by direct injunction or restraint, which at a later stage are intrusted to general intellectual and moral influences.

The practical economic enterprises of Greek and Roman antiquity could not, even independently of any special adverse influences, have competed in magnitude of scale or variety of resource with those of modern times. The unadvanced condition of physical science prevented a large application of the less obvious natural powers to production, or the extensive use of machinery, which has acquired such an immense development as a factor in modern industry. The imperfection of geographical knowledge and of the means of communication and transport were impediments to the growth of foreign commerce. These obstacles arose necessarily out of the mere immaturity of the industrial life of the periods in question. But more deeply rooted impediments to a vigorous and expansive economic practical system existed in the characteristic principles of the civilisation of antiquity. Some writers have attempted to set aside the distinction between the ancient and modern worlds as imaginary or unimportant, and, whilst admitting the broad separation between ourselves and the theocratic peoples of the East, to represent the Greeks and Romans as standing on a substantially similar ground of thought, feeling, and action with the Western populations of our own time. But this is a serious error, arising from the same too exclusive pre-occupation with the cultivated classes and with the mere speculative intellect which has often led to an undue disparagement of the Middle Ages. There is this essential difference between the spirit and life of ancient and of modern communities, that the former were organised for war, the latter during their whole history have increasingly tended to be organised for industry, as their practical end and aim. The profound influence of these differing conditions on every form of human activity must never be overlooked or forgotten. With the military constitution of ancient societies the institution of slavery was essentially connected. Far from being an excrescence on the contemporary system of life, as it was in the modern West Indies or the United States of America, it was so entirely in harmony with that life that the most eminent thinkers regarded it as no less indispensable than inevitable. It does, indeed, seem to have been a temporary necessity, and on the whole, regard being had to what might have taken its place, a relative good. But it was attended with manifold evils. It led to the prevalence amongst the citizen class of a contempt for industrial occupations; every form of production, with a partial exception in favour of agriculture, was branded as unworthy of a free man, —the only noble forms of activity being those directly connected with public life, whether military or administrative. Labour was degraded by the relegation of most departments of it to the servile class, above whom the free artisans were but little elevated in general esteem. The producers being thus for the most part destitute of intellectual cultivation and excluded from any share in civic ideas, interests, or efforts, were unfitted in character as well as by position for the habits of skilful combination and vigorous initiation which the progress of industry demands. To this must be added that the comparative insecurity of life and property arising out of military habits, and the consequent risks which attended accumulation, were grave obstructions to the formation of large capitals, and to the establishment of an effective system of credit. These causes conspired with the undeveloped state of knowledge and of social relations in giving to the economic life of the ancients the limitation and monotony which contrast so strongly with the inexhaustible resource, the ceaseless expansion, and the thousandfold variety of the same activities in the modern world. It is, of course, absurd to expect incompatible qualities in any social system; each system must be estimated according to the work it has to do. Now the historical vocation of the ancient civilisation was to be accomplished, not through industry, but through war, which was in the end to create a condition of things admitting of its own elimination and of the foundation of a régime based on pacific activity.

THE GREEKS.

This office was, however, reserved for Rome, as the final result of her system of conquest; the military activity of Greece, though continuous, was incoherent and sterile, except in the defence against Persia, and did not issue in the accomplishment of any such social mission. It was, doubtless, the inadequacy of the warrior life, under these conditions, to absorb the faculties of the race, that threw the energies of its most eminent members into the channel of intellectual activity, and produced a singularly rapid evolution of the æsthetic, philosophic, and scientific germs transmitted by the theocratic societies.

In the *Works and Days* of Hesiod, we find an order of thinking in the economic sphere very similar to that of the theocracies. With a recognition of the divine disposing power, and traditional rules of sacerdotal origin, is combined practical sagacity embodied in precept or proverbial saying. But the development of abstract thought, beginning from the time of Thales, soon gives to Greek culture its characteristic form, and marks a new epoch in the intellectual history of mankind.

The movement was now begun, destined to mould the whole future of humanity, which, gradually sapping the old hereditary structure of theological convictions, tended to the substitution of rational theories in every department of speculation. The eminent Greek thinkers, while taking a deep interest in the rise of positive science, and most of them studying the only science—that of geometry—then assuming its definitive character, were led by the social exigencies which always powerfully affect great minds to study with special care the nature of man and the conditions of his existence in society. These studies were indeed essentially premature; a long development of the inorganic and vital sciences was necessary before sociology or morals could attain their normal constitution. But by their prosecution amongst the Greeks a noble intellectual activity was kept alive, and many of those partial lights obtained for which mankind cannot afford to wait. Economic inquiries, along with others, tended towards rationality; Plutus was dethroned, and terrestrial substituted for supernatural agencies. But such inquiries, resting on no sufficiently large basis of practical life, could not attain any considerable results. The military constitution of society, and the existence of slavery, which was related to it, leading, as has been shown, to a low estimate of productive industry, turned away the habitual attention of thinkers from that domain. On the other hand, the absorption of citizens in the life of the state, and their pre-occupation with party struggles, brought questions relating to politics, properly so called, into special prominence. The principal writers on social subjects

are therefore almost exclusively occupied with the examination
and comparison of political constitutions, and with the search
after the education best adapted to train the citizen for public
functions. And we find, accordingly, in them no systematic or
adequate handling of economic questions,—only some happy
ideas and striking partial anticipations of later research.

In their thinking on such questions, as on all sociological
subjects, the following general features are observable.

1. The individual is conceived as subordinated to the state,
through which alone his nature can be developed and completed, and to the maintenance and service of which all
his efforts must be directed. The great aim of all political
thought is the formation of good citizens; every social question is studied primarily from the ethical and educational
point of view. The citizen is not regarded as a producer, but
only as a possessor, of material wealth; and this wealth is not
esteemed for its own sake or for the enjoyments it procures,
but for the higher moral and public aims to which it may be
made subservient.

2. The state, therefore, claims and exercises a controlling
and regulating authority over every sphere of social life,
including the economic, in order to bring individual action
into harmony with the good of the whole.

3. With these fundamental notions is combined a tendency
to attribute to institutions and to legislation an unlimited
efficacy, as if society had no spontaneous tendencies, but
would obey any external impulse, if impressed upon it with
sufficient force and continuity.

Every eminent social speculator had his ideal state, which
approximated to or diverged from the actual or possible,
according to the degree in which a sense of reality and a
positive habit of thinking characterised the author.

The most celebrated of these ideal systems is that of Plato.
In it the idea of the subordination of the individual to the
state appears in its most extreme form. Within that class of
the citizens of his republic who represent the highest type of

life, community of property and of wives is established, as
the most effective means of suppressing the sense of private
interest, and consecrating the individual entirely to the public
service. It cannot perhaps be truly said that his scheme was
incapable of realisation in an ancient community favourably
situated for the purpose. But it would soon be broken to
pieces by the forces which would be developed in an industrial
society. It has, however, been the fruitful parent of modern
Utopias, specially attractive as it is to minds in which the
literary instinct is stronger than the scientific judgment, in
consequence of the freshness and brilliancy of Plato's exposition and the unrivalled charm of his style. Mixed with what
we should call the chimerical ideas in his work, there are
many striking and elevated moral conceptions, and, what is
more to our present purpose, some just economic analyses. In
particular, he gives a correct account of the division and combination of employments, as they naturally arise in society.
The foundation of the social organisation he traces, perhaps,
too exclusively to economic grounds, not giving sufficient
weight to the disinterested social impulses in men which tend
to draw and bind them together. But he explains clearly how
the different wants and capacities of individuals demand and
give rise to mutual services, and how, by the restriction of
each to the sort of occupation to which, by his position,
abilities, and training, he is best adapted, everything needful
for the whole is more easily and better produced or effected.
In the spirit of all the ancient legislators he desires a self-
sufficing state, protected from unnecessary contacts with
foreign populations, which might tend to break down its
internal organisation or to deteriorate the national character.
Hence he discountenances foreign trade, and with this view
removes his ideal city to some distance from the sea. The
limits of its territory are rigidly fixed, and the population is
restricted by the prohibition of early marriages, by the ex-
posure of infants, and by the maintenance of a determinate
number of individual lots of land in the hands of the citizens

who cultivate the soil.   These precautions are inspired more
by political and moral motives than by the Malthusian fear
of failure of subsistence.   Plato aims, as far as possible, at
equality of property amongst the families of the community
which are engaged in the immediate prosecution of industry.
This last class, as distinguished from the governing and
military classes, he holds, according to the spirit of his age, in
but little esteem ; he regards their habitual occupations as
tending to the degradation of the mind and the enfeeblement
of the body, and rendering those who follow them unfit for
the higher duties of men and citizens.   The lowest forms of
labour he would commit to foreigners and slaves.   Again, in
the spirit of ancient theory, he wishes (*Legg.*, v. 12) to banish
the precious metals, as far as practicable, from use in internal
commerce, and forbids the lending of money on interest,
leaving indeed to the free will of the debtor even the repay-
ment of the capital of the loan.   All economic dealings he
subjects to active control on the part of the Government, not
merely to prevent violence and fraud, but to check the growth
of luxurious habits, and secure to the population of the state
a due supply of the necessaries and comforts of life.

    Contrasted with the exaggerated idealism of Plato is the
somewhat limited but eminently practical genius of Xenophon.
In him the man of action predominates, but he has also a large
element of the speculative tendency and talent of the Greek.
His treatise entitled *Œconomicus* is well worth reading for the
interesting and animated picture it presents of some aspects of
contemporary life, and is justly praised by Sismondi for the
spirit of mild philanthropy and tender piety which breathes
through it.   But it scarcely passes beyond the bounds of
domestic economy, though within that limit its author
exhibits much sound sense and sagacity.   His precepts for
the judicious conduct of private property do not concern us
here, nor his wise suggestions for the government of the
family and its dependants.   Yet it is in this narrower sphere
and in general in the concrete domain that his chief excellence

lies; to economics in their wider aspects he does not contribute much. He shares the ordinary preference of his fellow-countrymen for agriculture over other employments, and is, indeed, enthusiastic in his praises of it as developing patriotic and religious feeling and a respect for property, as furnishing the best preparation for military life, and as leaving sufficient time and thought disposable to admit of considerable intellectual and political activity. Yet his practical sense leads him to attribute greater importance than most other Greek writers to manufactures, and still more to trade, to enter more largely on questions relating to their conditions and development, and to bespeak for them the countenance and protection of the state. Though his views on the nature of money are vague, and in some respects erroneous, he sees that its export in exchange for commodities will not impoverish the community. He also insists on the necessity, with a view to a flourishing commerce with other countries, of peace, of a courteous and respectful treatment of foreign traders, and of a prompt and equitable decision of their legal suits. The institution of slavery he of course recognises and does not disapprove; he even recommends, for the increase of the Attic revenues, the hiring out of slaves by the state for labour in the mines, after branding them to prevent their escape, the number of slaves being constantly increased by fresh purchases out of the gains of the enterprise. (*De Vect.*, 3, 4.)

Almost the whole system of Greek ideas up to the time of Aristotle is represented in his encyclopædic construction. Mathematical and astronomical science was largely developed at a later stage, but in the field of social studies no higher point was ever attained by the Greeks than is reached in the writings of this great thinker. Both his gifts and his situation eminently favoured him in the treatment of these subjects. He combined in rare measure a capacity for keen observation with generalising power, and sobriety of judgment with ardour for the public good. All that was original or significant in the political life of Hellas had run its course before his time or under his own eyes, and he had thus a large basis of varied experience on which to ground his conclusions. Standing outside the actual movement of contemporary public life, he occupied the position of thoughtful spectator and impartial judge. He could not, indeed, for reasons already stated, any more than other Greek speculators, attain a fully normal attitude in these researches. Nor could he pass beyond the sphere of what is now called statical sociology; the idea of laws of the historical development of social phenomena he scarcely apprehended, except in some small degree in relation to the succession of political forms. But there is to be found in his writings a remarkable body of sound and valuable thoughts on the constitution and working of the social organism. The special notices of economic subjects are neither so numerous nor so detailed as we should desire. Like all the Greek thinkers, he recognises but one doctrine of the state, under which ethics, politics proper, and economics take their place as departments, bearing to each other a very close relation, and having indeed their lines of demarcation from each other not very distinctly marked. When wealth comes under consideration, it is studied not as an end in itself, but with a view to the higher elements and ultimate aims of the collective life.

The origin of society he traces, not to economic necessities, but to natural social impulses in the human constitution. The nature of the social union, when thus established, being determined by the partly spontaneous partly systematic combination of diverse activities, he respects the independence of the latter whilst seeking to effect their convergence. He therefore opposes himself to the suppression of personal freedom and initiative, and the excessive subordination of the individual to the state, and rejects the community of property and wives proposed by Plato for his governing class. The principle of private property he regards as deeply rooted in man, and the evils which are alleged to result from the corresponding social ordinance he thinks ought really to be attributed either to the imperfections of our nature or to the vices of other public institutions. Community of goods must, in his view, tend to neglect of the common interest and to the disturbance of social harmony.

Of the several classes which provide for the different wants of the society, those who are occupied directly with its material needs—the immediate cultivators of the soil, the mechanics and artificers—are excluded from any share in the government of the state, as being without the necessary leisure and cultivation, and apt to be debased by the nature of their occupations. In a celebrated passage he propounds a theory of slavery, in which it is based on the universality of the relation between command and obedience, and on the natural division by which the ruling is marked off from the subject race. He regards the slave as having no independent will, but as an " animated tool " in the hands of his master ; and in his subjection to such control, if only it be intelligent, Aristotle holds that the true wellbeing of the inferior as well as of the superior is to be found. This view, so shocking to our modern sentiment, is of course not personal to Aristotle ; it is simply the theoretic presentation of the facts of Greek life, in which the existence of a body of citizens pursuing the higher culture and devoted to the tasks of war and government was founded on the systematic degradation of a wronged and despised class, excluded from all the higher offices of human beings and sacrificed to the maintenance of a special type of society.

The methods of economic acquisition are divided by Aristotle into two, one of which has for its aim the appropriation of natural products and their application to the material uses of the household ; under this head come hunting, fishing, cattle-rearing, and agriculture. With this primary and " natural " method is, in some sense, contrasted the other to which Aristotle gives the name of " chrematistic," in which an active exchange of products goes on, and money comes into operation as its medium and regulator. A certain measure of this " non-natural " method, as it may be termed in opposition to the preceding and simpler form of industrial life, is accepted by Aristotle as a necessary extension of the latter, arising out of increased activity of intercourse, and satisfying real wants. But its development on the great scale, founded on the thirst for enjoyment and the unlimited desire of gain, he condemns as unworthy and corrupting. Though his views on this subject appear to be principally based on moral grounds, there are some indications of his having entertained the erroneous opinion held by the physiocrats of the eighteenth century, that agriculture alone (with the kindred arts above joined with it) is truly productive, whilst the other kinds of industry, which either modify the products of nature or distribute them by way of exchange, however convenient and useful they may be, make no addition to the wealth of the community.

He rightly regards money as altogether different from wealth, illustrating the difference by the story of Midas. And he seems to have seen that money, though its use rests on a social convention, must be composed of a material possessing an independent value of its own. That his views on capital were indistinct appears from his famous argument against interest on loans, which is based on the idea that money is barren and cannot produce money.

Like the other Greek social philosophers, Aristotle recommends to the care of Governments the preservation of a due proportion between the extent of the civic territory and its population, and relies on ante-nuptial continence, late marriages, and the prevention or destruction of births for the due limitation of the number of citizens, the insufficiency of the latter being dangerous to the independence and its superabundance to the tranquillity and good order of the state.

THE ROMANS.

Notwithstanding the eminently practical, realistic, and utilitarian character of the Romans, there was no energetic exercise of their powers in the economic field; they developed no large and many-sided system of production and exchange. Their historic mission was military and political, and the national energies were mainly devoted to the public service at home and in the field. To agriculture, indeed, much attention was given from the earliest times, and on it was founded the existence of the hardy population which won the first steps in the march to universal dominion. But in the course of their history the cultivation of the soil by a native yeomanry gave place to the introduction, in great numbers, of slave labourers acquired by their foreign conquests; and for the small properties of the earlier period were substituted the vast estates—the *latifundia*—which, in the judgment of Pliny, were the ruin of Italy.[1] The industrial arts and commerce (the latter, at least when not conducted on a great scale) they regarded as ignoble pursuits, unworthy of free citizens; and this feeling of contempt was not merely a prejudice of narrow or uninstructed minds, but was shared by Cicero and others among the most liberal spirits of the nation.[2] As might be expected from the want of speculative originality among the Romans, there is little evidence of serious theoretic inquiry on economic subjects. Their ideas on these as on other social questions were for the most part borrowed from the Greek thinkers. Such traces of economic thought as do occur are to be found in (1) the philosophers, (2) the writers *de re rustica*, and (3) the jurists. It must, however, be admitted that many of the passages in these authors referred to by those who assert the claim of the Romans to a more prominent place in the history of the science often contain only obvious truths or vague generalities.

[1] "Locis, quæ nunc, vix seminario exiguo militum relicto, servitia Romana ab solitudine vindicant."—Liv. vi. 12. "Villarum infinita spatia." Tac. *Ann.* iii. 53.

[2] "Opifices omnes in sordida arte versantur; nec enim quidquam ingenuum habere potest officina." Cic. *de Off.* i. 42. "Mercatura, si tenuis est, sordida putanda est: sin magna et copiosa, multa undique apportans multisque sine vanitate impertiens, non est admodum vituperanda."—*Ibid.* "Quæstus omnis Patribus indecorus visus est." Liv. xxi. 63.

In the philosophers, whom Cicero, Seneca, and the elder
Pliny sufficiently represent (the last indeed being rather a
learned encyclopædist or polyhistor than a philosopher), we
find a general consciousness of the decay of industry, the
relaxation of morals, and the growing spirit of self-indulgence
amongst their contemporaries, who are represented as deeply
tainted with the imported vices of the conquered nations.
This sentiment, both in these writers and in the poetry and
miscellaneous literature of their times, is accompanied by a
half-factitious enthusiasm for agriculture and an exaggerated
estimate of country life and of early Roman habits, which are
principally, no doubt, to be regarded as a form of protest
against existing abuses, and, from this point of view, remind
us of the declamations of Rousseau in a not dissimilar age.
But there is little of large or just thinking on the prevalent
economic evils and their proper remedies.　Pliny, still further
in the spirit of Rousseau, is of opinion that the introduction
of gold as a medium of exchange was a thing to be deplored,
and that the age of barter was preferable to that of money.
He expresses views on the necessity of preventing the efflux
of money similar to those of the modern mercantile school—
views which Cicero also, though not so clearly, appears to
have entertained.　Cato, Varro, and Columella concern themselves more with the technical precepts of husbandry than
with the general conditions of industrial success and social
well-being.　But the two last named have the great merit of
having seen and proclaimed the superior value of free to slave
labour, and Columella is convinced that to the use of the
latter the decline of the agricultural economy of the Romans
was in a great measure to be attributed.　These three writers
agree in the belief that it was chiefly by the revival and reform
of agriculture that the threatening inroads of moral corruption
could be stayed, the old Roman virtues fostered, and the
foundations of the commonwealth strengthened.　Their attitude is thus similar to that of the French physiocrats invoking the improvement and zealous pursuit of agriculture alike

against the material evils and the social degeneracy of their time. The question of the comparative merits of the large and small systems of cultivation appears to have been much discussed in the old Roman, as in the modern European world; Columella is a decided advocate of the *petite culture*. The jurists were led by the coincidence which sometimes takes place between their point of view and that of economic science to make certain classifications and establish some more or less refined distinctions which the modern economists have either adopted from them or used independently. They appear also (though this has been disputed, Neri and Carli maintaining the affirmative, Pagnini the negative) to have had correct notions of the nature of money as having a value of its own, determined by economic conditions, and incapable of being impressed upon it by convention or arbitrarily altered by public authority. But in general we find in these writers, as might be expected, not so much the results of independent thought as documents illustrating the facts of Roman economic life, and the historical policy of the nation with respect to economic subjects. From the latter point of view they are of much interest; and by the information they supply as to the course of legislation relating to property generally, to sumptuary control, to the restrictions imposed on spendthrifts, to slavery, to the encouragement of population, and the like, they give us much clearer insight than we should otherwise possess into influences long potent in the history of Rome and of the Western world at large. But, as it is with the more limited field of systematic thought on political economy that we are here occupied, we cannot enter into these subjects. One matter, however, ought to be adverted to, because it was not only repeatedly dealt with by legislation, but is treated more or less fully by all Roman writers of note, namely, the interest on money loans. The rate was fixed by the laws of the Twelve Tables; but lending on interest was afterwards (B.C. 341) entirely prohibited by the Genucian Law. In the legislation of Justinian, rates were sanctioned varying from four to eight per cent. according to the nature of the case, the latter being fixed as the ordinary mercantile rate, whilst compound interest was forbidden. The Roman theorists, almost without exception, disapprove of lending on interest altogether. Cato, as Cicero tells us, thought it as bad as murder ("Quid fenerari? Quid hominem occidere?" *De Off.* ii. 25); and Cicero, Seneca, Pliny, Columella all join in condemning it. It is not difficult to see how in early states of society the trade of money-lending becomes, and not unjustly, the object of popular odium; but that these writers, at a period when commercial enterprise had made considerable progress, should continue to reprobate it argues very imperfect or confused ideas on the nature and functions of capital. It is probable that practice took little heed either of these speculative ideas or of legislation on the subject, which experience shows can always be easily evaded. The traffic in money seems to have gone on all through Roman history, and the rate to have fluctuated according to the condition of the market.

Looking back on the history of ancient economic speculation, we see that, as might be anticipated *a priori*, the results attained in that field by the Greek and Roman writers were very scanty. As Dühring has well remarked, the questions with which the science has to do were regarded by the ancient thinkers rather from their political than their properly economic side. This we have already pointed out with respect to their treatment of the subject of population, and the same may be seen in the case of the doctrine of the division of labour, with which Plato and Aristotle are in some degree occupied. They regard that principle as a basis of social classification, or use it in showing that society is founded on a spontaneous co-operation of diverse activities. From the strictly economic point of view, there are three important propositions which can be enunciated respecting that division: —(1) that its extension within any branch of production makes the products cheaper; (2) that it is limited by the extent of the market; and (3) that it can be carried further in manufactures than in agriculture. But we shall look in vain for these propositions in the ancient writers ; the first alone might be *inferred* from their discussions of the subject. It has been the tendency especially of German scholars to magnify unduly the extent and value of the contributions of antiquity to economic knowledge. The Greek and Roman authors ought certainly not to be omitted in any account of the evolution of this branch of study. But it must be kept steadily in view that we find in them only first hints or rudiments of general economic truths, and that the science is essentially a modern one. We shall indeed see hereafter that it could not have attained its definitive constitution before our own time.

CHAPTER III.

THE MIDDLE AGES.

THE Middle Ages (400–1300 A.D.) form a period of great significance in the economic, as in the general, history of Europe. They represent a vast transition, in which the germs of a new world were deposited, but in which little was fully elaborated. There is scarcely anything in the later movement of European society which we do not find there, though as yet, for the most part, crude and undeveloped. The mediæval period was the object of contemptuous depreciation on the part of the liberal schools of the last century, principally because it contributed so little to literature. But there are things more important to mankind than literature; and the great men of the Middle Ages had enough to do in other fields to occupy their utmost energies. The development of the Catholic institutions and the gradual establishment and maintenance of a settled order after the dissolution of the Western empire absorbed the powers of the thinkers and practical men of several centuries. The first mediæval phase, from the commencement of the fifth century to the end of the seventh, was occupied with the painful and stormy struggle towards the foundation of the new ecclesiastical and civil system; three more centuries were filled with the work of its consolidation and defence against the assaults of nomad populations; only in the final phase, during the eleventh, twelfth, and thirteenth centuries, when the unity of the West was founded by the collective action against impending Moslem invasion, did

it enjoy a sufficiently secure and stable existence to exhibit
its essential character and produce its noblest personal types.
The elaboration of feudalism was, indeed, in progress during
the whole period, showing itself in the decomposition of
power and the hierarchical subordination of its several grades,
the movement being only temporarily suspended in the second
phase by the salutary dictatorship of Charlemagne.   But not
before the first century of the last phase was the feudal system
fully constituted.   In like manner, only in the final phase
could the effort of Catholicism after a universal discipline be
carried out on the great scale—an effort for ever admirable,
though necessarily on the whole unsuccessful.

No large or varied economic activity was possible under the
full ascendency of feudalism.   That organisation, as has been
abundantly shown by philosophical historians, was indispensable for the preservation of order and for public defence, and
contributed important elements to general civilisation.   But,
whilst recognising it as opportune and relatively beneficent,
we must not expect from it advantages inconsistent with its
essential nature and historical office.   The class which pre-
dominated in it was not sympathetic with industry, and held
the handicrafts in contempt, except those subservient to war
or rural sports.   The whole practical life of the society was
founded on territorial property ; the wealth of the lord consisted in the produce of his lands and the dues paid to him in
kind ; this wealth was spent in supporting a body of retainers
whose services were repaid by their maintenance.   There
could be little room for manufactures, and less for commerce ;
and agriculture was carried on with a view to the wants of
the family, or at most of the immediate neighbourhood, not
to those of a wider market.   The economy of the period was
therefore simple, and, in the absence of special motors from
without, unprogressive.

In the latter portion of the Middle Ages several circumstances came into action which greatly modified these conditions.   The Crusades undoubtedly produced a powerful

economic effect by transferring in many cases the possessions
of the feudal chiefs to the industrious classes, whilst by
bringing different nations and races into contact, by enlarging
the horizon and widening the conceptions of the populations,
as well as by affording a special stimulus to navigation, they
tended to give a new activity to international trade.   The
independence of the towns and the rising importance of the
burgher class supplied a counterpoise to the power of the land
aristocracy; and the strength of these new social elements
was increased by the corporate constitution given to the
urban industries, the police of the towns being also founded
on the trade guilds, as that of the country districts was on the
feudal relations.   The increasing demand of the towns for the
products of agriculture gave to the prosecution of that art a
more extended and speculative character; and this again led
to improved methods of transport and communication.   But
the range of commercial enterprise continued everywhere
narrow, except in some favoured centres, such as the Italian
republics, in which, however, the growth of the normal habits
of industrial life was impeded or perverted by military ambition, which was not, in the case of those communities, checked
as it was elsewhere by the pressure of an aristocratic class.

   Every great change of opinion on the destinies of man
and the guiding principles of conduct must react on the
sphere of material interests; and the Catholic religion had a
powerful influence on the economic life of the Middle Ages.
Christianity inculcates, perhaps, no more effectively than the
older religions the special economic virtues of industry, thrift,
fidelity to engagements, obedience to rightful authority; but
it brought out more forcibly and presented more persistently
the higher aims of life, and so produced a more elevated way
of viewing the different social relations.   It purified domestic
life, a reform which has the most important economic results.
It taught the doctrine of fundamental human equality,
heightened the dignity of labour, and preached with quite
a new emphasis the obligations of love, compassion, and

forgiveness, and the claims of the poor. The constant presentation to the general mind and conscience of these ideas,
the dogmatic bases of which were scarcely as yet assailed by
scepticism, must have had a powerful effect in moralising life.
But to the influence of Christianity as a moral doctrine was
added that of the Church as an organisation, charged with
the application of the doctrine to men's daily transactions.
Besides the teachings of the sacred books, there was a mass
of ecclesiastical legislation providing specific prescriptions for
the conduct of the faithful. And this legislation dealt with
the economic as with other provinces of social activity. In
the *Corpus Juris Canonici*, which condenses the result of
centuries of study and effort, along with much else is set out
what we may call the Catholic economic theory, if we understand by theory, not a reasoned explanation of phenomena,
but a body of ideas leading to prescriptions for the guidance
of conduct. Life is here looked at from the point of view
of spiritual wellbeing; the aim is to establish and maintain
amongst men a true kingdom of God.

The canonists are friendly to the notion of a community
of goods from the side of sentiment ("Dulcissima rerum
possessio communis est"), though they regard the distinction
of *meum* and *tuum* as an institution necessitated by the fallen
state of man. In cases of need the public authority is justified
in re-establishing *pro hac vice* the primitive community. The
care of the poor is not a matter of free choice; the relief
of their necessities is *debitum legale*. *Avaritia* is idolatry;
cupiditas, even when it does not grasp at what is another's,
is the root of all evil, and ought to be not merely regulated
but eradicated. Agriculture and handiwork are viewed as
legitimate modes of earning food and clothing; but trade is
regarded with disfavour, because it was held almost certainly
to lead to fraud : of agriculture it was said, " Deo non dis-
plicet ; " but of the merchant, " Deo placere non potest." The
seller was bound to fix the price of his wares, not according
to the market rate, as determined by supply and demand,

but according to their real value (*justum pretium*). He must
not conceal the faults of his merchandise, nor take advantage of the need or ignorance of the buyer to obtain from
him more than the fair price. Interest on money is forbidden ; the prohibition of usury is, indeed, as Roscher says,
the centre of the whole canonistic system of economy, as
well as the foundation of a great part of the ecclesiastical
jurisdiction. The question whether a transaction was or was
not usurious turning mainly on the intentions of the parties,
the innocence or blameworthiness of dealings in which money
was lent became rightfully a subject of determination for the
Church, either by her casuists or in her courts.[1]

The foregoing principles point towards a noble ideal, but by
their ascetic exaggeration they worked in some directions as
an impediment to industrial progress. Thus, whilst, with the
increase of production, a greater division of labour and a larger
employment of borrowed capital naturally followed, the laws
on usury tended to hinder this expansion. Hence they were
undermined by various exceptions, or evaded by fictitious
transactions. These laws were in fact dictated by, and adapted
to, early conditions—to a state of society in which money
loans were commonly sought either with a view to wasteful
pleasures or for the relief of such urgent distress as ought
rather to have been the object of Christian beneficence. But
they were quite unsuited to a period in which capital was
borrowed for the extension of enterprise and the employment
of labour. The absolute theological spirit in this, as in other
instances, could not admit the modification in rules of conduct
demanded by a new social situation ; and vulgar good sense
better understood what were the fundamental conditions of
industrial life.

When the intellectual activity previously repressed by the
more urgent claims of social preoccupations tended to revive
towards the close of the mediæval period, the want of a

---

[1] Roscher, *Geschichte der N.O. in Deutschland*, pp. 5, sqq.

rational appreciation of the whole of human affairs was felt, and was temporarily met by the adoption of the results of the best Greek speculation. Hence we find in the writings of St. Thomas Aquinas the political and economic doctrines of Aristotle reproduced with a partial infusion of Christian elements. His adherence to his master's point of view is strikingly shown by the fact that he accepts (at least if he is the author of the *De Regimine Principum*)[1] the Aristotelian theory of slavery, though by the action of the forces of his own time the last relics of that institution were being eliminated from European society.

This great change—the enfranchisement of the working classes—was the most important practical outcome of the Middle Ages. The first step in this movement was the transformation of slavery, properly so called, into serfdom. The latter was, by its nature, a transitory condition. The serf was bound to the soil, had fixed domestic relations, and participated in the religious life of the society; and the tendency of all his circumstances, as well as of the opinions and sentiments of the time, was in the direction of liberation. This issue was, indeed, not so speedily reached by the rural as by the urban workman. Already in the second phase serfdom is abolished in the cities and towns, whilst agricultural serfdom does not anywhere disappear before the third. The latter revolution is attributed by Adam Smith to the operation of selfish interests, that of the proprietor on the one hand, who discovered the superior productiveness of cultivation by free tenants, and that of the sovereign on the other, who, jealous of the great lords, encouraged the encroachments of the villeins on their authority. But that the Church deserves a share of the merit seems beyond doubt—moral impulses, as often happens, conspiring with political and economic motives. The serfs were treated best on the ecclesiastical estates, and the members of the priesthood, both by their doctrine and by

---

[1] On this question see Jourdain, "Philosophie de S. Thomas," vol. I, pp. 141–9, and 400.

their situation since the Northern conquests, were constituted patrons and guardians of the oppressed or subject classes.

Out of the liberation of the serfs rose the first lineaments of the hierarchical constitution of modern industry in the separation between the entrepreneurs and the workers. The personal enfranchisement of the latter, stimulating activity and developing initiative, led to accumulations, which were further promoted by the establishment of order and good government by the civic corporations which grew out of the enfranchisement. Thus an active capitalist class came into existence. It appeared first in commerce, the inhabitants of the trading cities importing expensive luxuries from foreign countries, or the improved manufactures of richer communities, for which the great proprietors gladly exchanged the raw produce of their lands. In performing the office of carriers, too, between different countries, these cities had an increasing field for commercial enterprise. At a later period, as Adam Smith has shown, commerce promoted the growth of manufactures, which were either produced for foreign sale, or made from foreign materials, or imitated from the work of foreign artificers. But the first important development of handicrafts in modern Europe belongs to the fourteenth and fifteenth centuries, and the rise of manufacturing entrepreneurs is not conspicuous within the Middle Ages properly so called. Agriculture, of course, lags behind; though the feudal lords tend to transform themselves into directors of agricultural enterprise, their habits and prejudices retard such a movement, and the advance of rural industry proceeds slowly. It does, however, proceed, partly by the stimulation arising from the desire to procure the finer objects of manufacture imported from abroad or produced by increased skill at home, partly by the expenditure on the land of capital amassed in the prosecution of urban industries.

Some of the trade corporations in the cities appear to have been of great antiquity; but it was in the thirteenth century that they rose to importance by being legally recognised and regulated. These corporations have been much too absolutely condemned by most of the economists, who insist on applying to the Middle Ages the ideas of the eighteenth and nineteenth centuries. They were, it is true, unfitted for modern times, and it was necessary that they should disappear; their existence indeed was quite unduly prolonged. But they were at first in several respects highly beneficial. They were a valuable rallying-point for the new industrial forces, which were strengthened by the rise of the *esprit de corps* which they fostered. They improved technical skill by the precautions which were taken for the solidity and finished execution of the wares produced in each locality, and it was with a view to the advancement of the industrial arts that St. Louis undertook the better organisation of the trades of Paris. The corporations also encouraged good moral habits through the sort of spontaneous surveillance which they exercised, and they tended to develop the social sentiment within the limits of each profession, in times when a larger public spirit could scarcely yet be looked for.

CHAPTER IV.

MODERN TIMES: FIRST AND SECOND PHASES.

THE close of the Middle Ages, as Comte has shown, must be placed at the end, not of the fifteenth but of the thirteenth century. The modern period, which then began, is filled by a development exhibiting three successive phases, and issuing in the state of things which characterises our own epoch.

I. During the fourteenth and fifteenth centuries the Catholico-feudal system was breaking down by the mutual conflicts of its own official members, whilst the constituent elements of a new order were rising beneath it. On the practical side the antagonists matched against each other were the crown and the feudal chiefs ; and these rival powers sought to strengthen themselves by forming alliances with the towns and the industrial forces they represented. The movements of this phase can scarcely be said to find an echo in any contemporary economic literature.

II. In the second phase of the modern period, which opens with the beginning of the sixteenth century, the spontaneous collapse of the mediæval structure is followed by a series of systematic assaults which still further disorganise it. During this phase the central temporal power, which has made a great advance in stability and resources, lays hold of the rising elements of manufactures and commerce, and seeks, whilst satisfying the popular enthusiasm for their promotion, to use them for political ends, and make them subserve its own strength and splendour by furnishing the treasure necessary for military success. With this practical effort, and the social tendencies on which it rests, the Mercantile school of political economy, which then obtains a spontaneous ascendency, is in close relation. Whilst partially succeeding in the policy we have indicated, the European Governments yet on the whole necessarily fail, their origin and nature disqualifying them for the task of guiding the industrial movement; and the discredit of the spiritual power, with which most of them are confederate, further weakens and undermines them.

III. In the last phase, which coincides approximately with the eighteenth century, the tendency to a completely new system, both temporal and spiritual, becomes decisively pronounced, first in the philosophy and general literature of the period, and then in the great French explosion. The universal critical doctrine, which had been announced by the Protestantism of the previous phase, and systematised in England towards the close of that phase, is propagated and popularised, especially by French writers. The spirit of individualism inherent in the doctrine was eminently adapted to the wants of the time, and the general favour with which the dogmas of the social contract and *laisser faire* were received indicated a just sentiment of the conditions proper to the contemporary situation of European societies. So long as a new coherent system of thought and life could not be introduced, what was to be desired was a large and active development of personal energy under no further control of the old social powers than would suffice to prevent anarchy. Governments were therefore rightly called on to abandon any effective direction of the social movement, and, as far as possible, to restrict their intervention to the maintenance of material order. This policy was, from its nature, of temporary application only; but the negative school, according to its ordinary spirit, erected what was merely a transitory and exceptional necessity into a permanent and normal law. The unanimous European movement towards the liberation of effort, which sometimes rose to the height of a public passion, had various sides, corresponding to the different aspects of thought and life; and of the economic side the French physiocrats were the first theoretic representatives on the large scale, though the office they undertook was, both in its destructive and organic provinces, more thoroughly and effectively done by Adam Smith, who ought to be regarded as continuing and completing their work.

It must be admitted that with the whole modern movement serious moral evils were almost necessarily connected. The general discipline which the Middle Ages had sought to institute and had partially succeeded in establishing, though on precarious bases, having broken down, the sentiment of duty was weakened along with the spirit of *ensemble* which is its natural ally, and individualism in doctrine tended to encourage egoism in action. In the economic field this result is specially conspicuous. National selfishness and private cupidity increasingly dominate; and the higher and lower industrial classes tend to separation and even to mutual hostility. The new elements—science and industry—which were gradually acquiring ascendency bore indeed in their bosom an ultimate discipline more efficacious and stable than that which had been dissolved; but the final synthesis was long too remote, and too indeterminate in its nature, to be seen through the dispersive and seemingly incoherent growth of those elements. Now, however, that synthesis is becoming appreciable; and it is the effort towards it, and towards the practical system to be founded on it, that gives its peculiar character to the period in which we live. And to this spontaneous nisus of society corresponds, as we shall see, a new form of economic doctrine, in which it tends to be absorbed into general sociology and subordinated to morals.

It will be the object of the following pages to verify and illustrate in detail the scheme here broadly indicated, and to point out the manner in which the respective features of the several successive modern phases find their counterpart and reflection in the historical development of economic speculation.

First Modern Phase.

The first phase was marked, on the one hand, by the spontaneous decomposition of the mediæval system, and, on the other, by the rise of several important elements of the new order. The spiritual power became less apt as well as less able to fulfil its moral office, and the social movement was more and more left to the irregular impulses of individual energy, often enlisted in the service of ambition and cupidity. Strong governments were formed, which served to maintain material order amidst the growing intellectual and moral disorder. The universal admission of the commons as an element in the political system showed the growing strength of the industrial forces, as did also in another way the insurrections of the working classes. The decisive prevalence of peaceful activity was indicated by the rise of the institution of paid armies—at first temporary, afterwards permanent—which prevented the interruption or distraction of labour by devoting a determinate minority of the population to martial operations and exercises. Manufactures became increasingly important; and in this branch of industry the distinction between the entrepreneur and the workers was first firmly established, whilst fixed relations between these were made possible by the restriction of military training and service to a special profession. Navigation was facilitated by the use of the mariner's compass. The art of printing showed how the intellectual movement and the industrial development were destined to be brought into relation with each other and to work towards common ends. Public credit rose in Florence, Venice, and Genoa long before Holland and England attained any great financial importance. Just at the close of the phase, the discovery of America and of the new route to the East, whilst revolutionising the course of trade, prepared the way for the establishment of colonies, which contributed powerfully to the growing preponderance of industrial life, and pointed to its ultimate universality.

It is doubtless due to the equivocal nature of this stage, standing between the mediæval and the fully characterised modern period, that on the theoretic side we find nothing corresponding to such marvellous practical ferment and expansion. The general political doctrine of Aquinas was retained, with merely subordinate modifications. The only special economic question which seems to have received particular attention was that of the nature and functions of money, the importance of which began to be felt as payments in service or in kind were discontinued, and regular systems of taxation began to be introduced.

Roscher,[1] and after him Wolowski, have called attention to Nicole Oresme, who was teacher of Charles V., King of France, and died Bishop of Lisieux in 1382. Roscher pronounces him a great economist.[2] His *Tractatus de Origine, Natura, Jure, et Mutationibus Monetarum* (reprinted by Wolowski, 1864) contains a theory of money which is almost entirely correct according to the views of the nineteenth century, and is stated with such brevity, clearness, and simplicity of language as show the work to be from the hand of a master.

Second Modern Phase: Mercantile System.

Throughout the first modern phase the rise of the new social forces had been essentially spontaneous; in the second they became the object of systematic encouragement on the part of Governments, which, now that the financial methods of the Middle Ages no longer sufficed, could not further their military and political ends by any other means than increased taxation, implying augmented wealth of the community. Industry thus became a permanent interest of European Governments, and even tended to become the principal object of their policy. In natural harmony with this state of facts,

---

[1] *Comptes rendus de l'Académie des Sciences morales et politiques*, lxii. 435, sqq.

[2] *Geschichte der N.O. in Deutschland*, p. 25.

the mercantile system arose and grew, attaining its highest development about the middle of the seventeenth century.

The Mercantile doctrine, stated in its most extreme form, makes wealth and money identical, and regards it therefore as the great object of a community so to conduct its dealings with other nations as to attract to itself the largest possible share of the precious metals. Each country must seek to export the utmost possible quantity of its own manufactures, and to import as little as possible of those of other countries, receiving the difference of the two values in gold and silver. This difference is called the balance of trade, and the balance is favourable when more money is received than is paid. Governments must resort to all available expedients—prohibition of, or high duties on, the importation of foreign wares, bounties on the export of home manufactures, restrictions on the export of the precious metals—for the purpose of securing such a balance.

But this statement of the doctrine, though current in the text-books, does not represent correctly the views of all who must be classed as belonging to the Mercantile school. Many of the members of that school were much too clear-sighted to entertain the belief, which the modern student feels difficulty in supposing any class of thinkers to have professed, that wealth consists exclusively of gold and silver. The mercantilists may be best described, as Roscher [1] has remarked, not by any definite economic theorem which they held in common, but by a set of theoretic tendencies, commonly found in combination, though severally prevailing in different degrees in different minds. These tendencies may be enumerated as follows:—(1) Towards over-estimating the importance of possessing a large amount of the precious metals; (2) towards an undue exaltation (a) of foreign trade over domestic, and (b) of the industry which works up materials over that which provides them; (3) towards attaching too high a value to a dense population as an element of national strength; and (4)

---

[1] *Geschichte der N.O. in Deutschland*, p. 228, sqq.

towards invoking the action of the state in furthering artificially the attainment of the several ends thus proposed as
desirable.

If we consider the contemporary position of affairs in Western
Europe, we shall have no difficulty in understanding how these
tendencies would inevitably arise. The discoveries in the
New World had led to a large development of the European
currencies. The old feudal economy, founded principally on
dealings in kind, had given way before the new "money
economy," and the dimensions of the latter were everywhere
expanding. Circulation was becoming more rapid, distant
communications more frequent, city life and movable property
more important. The mercantilists were impressed by the
fact that money is wealth *sui generis*, that it is at all times in
universal demand, and that it puts into the hands of its possessor the power of acquiring all other commodities. The
period, again, was marked by the formation of great states, with
powerful Governments at their head. These Governments
required men and money for the maintenance of permanent
armies, which, especially for the religious and Italian wars,
were kept up on a great scale. Court expenses, too, were
more lavish than ever before, and a larger number of civil
officials was employed. The royal domains and dues were
insufficient to meet these requirements, and taxation grew with
the demands of the monarchies. Statesmen saw that for their
own political ends industry must flourish. But manufactures
make possible a denser population and a higher total value of
exports than agriculture ; they open a less limited and more
promptly extensible field to enterprise. Hence they became
the object of special Governmental favour and patronage,
whilst agriculture fell comparatively into the background.
The growth of manufactures reacted on commerce, to which a
new and mighty arena had been opened by the establishment
of colonies. These were viewed simply as estates to be worked
for the advantage of the mother countries, and the aim of
statesmen was to make the colonial trade a new source of

public revenue. Each nation, as a whole, working for its own power, and the greater ones for predominance, they entered into a competitive struggle in the economic no less than in the political field, success in the former being indeed, by the rulers, regarded as instrumental to pre-eminence in the latter. A national economic interest came to exist, of which the Government made itself the representative head. States became a sort of artificial hothouses for the rearing of urban industries. Production was subjected to systematic regulation with the object of securing the goodness and cheapness of the exported articles, and so maintaining the place of the nation in foreign markets. The industrial control was exercised, in part directly by the state, but largely also through privileged corporations and trading companies. High duties on imports were resorted to, at first perhaps mainly for revenue, but afterwards in the interest of national production. Commercial treaties were a principal object of diplomacy, the end in view being to exclude the competition of other nations in foreign markets, whilst in the home market as little room as possible was given for the introduction of anything but raw materials from abroad. The colonies were prohibited from trading with other European nations than the parent country, to which they supplied either the precious metals or raw produce purchased with home manufactures. It is evident that what is known as the mercantile doctrine was essentially the theoretic counterpart of the practical activities of the time, and that nations and Governments were led to it, not by any form of scientific thought, but by the force of outward circumstance, and the observation of facts which lay on the surface.

And yet, if we regard the question from the highest point of view of philosophic history, we must pronounce the universal enthusiasm of this second modern phase for manufactures and commerce to have been essentially just, as leading the nations into the main avenues of general social development. If the thought of the period, instead of being impelled by contemporary circumstances, could have been guided by sociological prevision, it must have entered with zeal upon the same path which it empirically selected. The organisation of agricultural industry could not at that period make any marked progress, for the direction of its operations was still in the hands of the feudal class, which could not in general really learn the habits of industrial life, or place itself in sufficient harmony with the workers on its domains. The industry of the towns had to precede that of the country, and the latter had to be developed mainly through the indirect action of the former. And it is plain that it was in the life of the manufacturing proletariat, whose labours are necessarily the most continuous and the most social, that a systematic discipline could at a later period be first applied, to be afterwards extended to the rural populations.

That the efforts of Governments for the futherance of manufactures and commerce were really effective towards that end is admitted by Adam Smith, and cannot reasonably be doubted, though free trade doctrinaires have often denied it. Technical skill must have been promoted by their encouragements; whilst new forms of national production were fostered by attracting workmen from other countries, and by lightening the burden of taxation on struggling industries. Communication and transport by land and sea were more rapidly improved with a view to facilitate traffic; and, not the least important effect, the social dignity of the industrial professions was enhanced relatively to that of the classes before exclusively dominant.

It has often been asked to whom the foundation of the mercantile system, in the region whether of thought or of practice, is to be attributed. But the question admits of no absolute answer. That mode of conceiving economic facts arises spontaneously in unscientific minds, and ideas suggested by it are to be found in the Greek and Latin writers. The policy which it dictates was, as we have shown, inspired by the situation of the European nations at the opening of the modern period. Such a policy had been already in some degree practised in the fourteenth and fifteenth centuries, thus preceding any formal exposition or defence of its speculative basis. At the commencement of the sixteenth century it began to exercise a widely extended influence. Charles V. adopted it, and his example contributed much to its predominance. Henry VIII. and Elizabeth conformed their measures to it. The leading states soon entered on a universal competition, in which each power brought into play all its political and financial resources for the purpose of securing to itself manufacturing and commercial preponderance. Through almost the whole of the seventeenth century the prize, so far as commerce was concerned, remained in the possession of Holland, Italy having lost her former ascendency by the opening of the new maritime routes, and by her political misfortunes, and Spain and Germany being depressed by protracted wars and internal dissensions. The admiring envy of Holland felt by English politicians and economists appears in such writers as Raleigh, Mun, Child, and Temple;[1] and how strongly the same spectacle acted on French policy is shown by a well-known letter of Colbert to M. de Pomponne,[2] ambassador to the Dutch States. Cromwell, by the Navigation Act, which destroyed the carrying trade of Holland and founded the English empire of the sea, and Colbert, by his whole economic policy, domestic and international, were the chief practical representatives of the mercantile system. From the latter great statesman the Italian publicist Mengotti gave to that system the name of *Colbertismo ;* but it would be an error to consider the French minister as having absolutely accepted its dogmas. He regarded his measures as temporary only, and spoke of protective duties as crutches by the help of which manufacturers might learn to walk and then throw them away. The policy of exclusions had been previously pursued by Sully, partly with a view to the accumulation of a royal treasure, but

---

[1] Roscher, *Geschichte der N.O. in Deutschland*, p. 227.

[2] Clément, *Histoire de la vie et de l'administration de Colbert* (1846), p. 134.

chiefly from his special enthusiasm for agriculture, and his dislike of the introduction of foreign luxuries as detrimental to the national character. Colbert's tariff of 1664 not merely simplified but considerably reduced the existing duties; the tariff of 1667 indeed increased them, but that was really a political measure directed against the Dutch. It seems certain that France owed in a large measure to his policy the vast development of trade and manufactures which so much impressed the imagination of contemporary Europe, and of which we hear so much from English writers of the time of Petty. But this policy had also undeniably its dark side. Industry was forced by such systematic regulation to follow invariable courses, instead of adapting itself to changing tastes and popular demand. Nor was it free to simplify the processes of production, or to introduce increased division of labour and improved appliances. Spontaneity, initiation, and invention were repressed or discouraged, and thus ulterior sacrificed in a great measure to immediate results. The more enlightened statesmen, and Colbert in particular, endeavoured, it is true, to minimise these disadvantages by procuring, often at great expense, and communicating to the trades through inspectors nominated by the Government, information respecting improved processes employed elsewhere in the several arts; but this, though in some degree a real, was certainly on the whole, and in the long run, an insufficient compensation.

We must not expect from the writers of this stage any exposition of political economy as a whole; the publications which appeared were for the most part evoked by special exigencies, and related to particular questions, usually of a practical kind, which arose out of the great movements of the time. They were in fact of the nature of counsels to the Governments of states, pointing out how best they might develop the productive powers at their disposal and increase the resources of their respective countries. They are conceived (as List claims for them) strictly in the spirit of *national* economy, and cosmopolitanism is essentially foreign

to them. On these monographs the mercantile theory sometimes had little influence, the problems discussed not involving
its tenets. But it must in most cases be taken to be the
scheme of fundamental doctrine (so far as it was ever entitled
to such a description) which in the last resort underlies the
writer's conclusions.

The rise of prices following on the discovery of the American mines was one of the subjects which first attracted the
attention of theorists. This rise brought about a great and
gradually increasing disturbance of existing economic relations,
and so produced much perplexity and anxiety, which were all
the more felt because the cause of the change was not understood. To this was added the loss and inconvenience arising
from the debasement of the currency often resorted to by
sovereigns as well as by republican states. Italy suffered
most from this latter abuse, which was multiplied by her
political divisions. It was this evil which called forth the
work of Count Gasparo Scaruffi (*Discorso sopra le monete e
della vera proporzione fra l'oro e l'argento*, 1582). In this he
put forward the bold idea of a universal money, everywhere
identical in size, shape, composition, and designation. The
project was, of course, premature, and was not adopted even
by the Italian princes to whom the author specially appealed ;
but the reform is one which, doubtless, the future will see
realised. Gian Donato Turbolo, master of the Neapolitan
mint, in his *Discorsi e Relazioni*, 1629, protested against any
tampering with the currency. Another treatise relating to
the subject of money was that of the Florentine Bernardo
Davanzati, otherwise known as the able translator of Tacitus,
Lezioni delle Monete, 1588. It is a slight and somewhat
superficial production, only remarkable as written with con-
ciseness and elegance of style.

A French writer who dealt with the question of money,
but from a different point of view, was Jean Bodin. In his
*Réponse aux paradoxes de M. Malestroit touchant l'enchérisse-
ment de toutes les choses et des monnaies*, 1568, and in his

Discours sur le rehaussement et la diminution des monnaies, 1578, he showed a more rational appreciation than many of his contemporaries of the causes of the revolution in prices, and the relation of the variations in money to the market values of wares in general as well as to the wages of labour. He saw that the amount of money in circulation did not constitute the wealth of the community, and that the prohibition of the export of the precious metals was useless, because rendered inoperative by the necessities of trade. Bodin is no inconsiderable figure in the literary history of the epoch, and did not confine his attention to economic problems; in his *Six livres de la République*, about 1576, he studies the general conditions of the prosperity and stability of states. In harmony with the conditions of his age, he approves of absolute Governments as the most competent to ensure the security and wellbeing of their subjects. He enters into an elaborate defence of individual property against Plato and More, rather perhaps because the scheme of his work required the treatment of that theme than because it was practically urgent in his day, when the excesses of the Anabaptists had produced a strong feeling against communistic doctrines. He is under the general influence of the mercantilist views, and approves of energetic Governmental interference in industrial matters, of high taxes on foreign manufactures and low duties on raw materials and articles of food, and attaches great importance to a dense population. But he is not a blind follower of the system; he wishes for unlimited freedom of trade in many cases; and he is in advance of his more eminent contemporary Montaigne [1] in perceiving that the gain of one nation is not necessarily the loss of another. To the public finances, which he calls the sinews of the state, he devotes much attention, and insists on the duties of the Government in respect to the right adjustment of taxation. In general he deserves the praise of steadily keeping in view the higher aims and

---

[1] "Il ne se faict aucun profit qu'au dommage d'autruy." *Essais*, liv. I, chap. 21.

interests of society in connection with the regulation and development of its material life.

Correct views as to the cause of the general rise of prices are also put forward by the English writer, W. S. (William Stafford), in his *Briefe Conceipte of English Policy*, published in 1581, and dedicated to Queen Elizabeth. It is in the form of a dialogue, and is written with liveliness and spirit. The author seems to have been acquainted with the writings of Bodin. He has just ideas as to the nature of money, and fully understands the evils arising from a debased coinage. He describes in detail the way in which the several interests in the country had been affected by such debasement in previous reigns, as well as by the change in the value of the precious metals. The great popular grievance of his day, the conversion of arable land into pasture, he attributes chiefly to the restrictions on the export of corn, which he desires to see abolished. But in regard to manufactures he is at the same point of view with the later mercantilists, and proposes the exclusion of all foreign wares which might as well be provided at home, and the prohibition of the export of raw materials intended to be worked up abroad.

Out of the question of money, too, arose the first remarkable German production on political economy which had an original national character and addressed the public in the native tongue. Duke George of the Ernestine Saxon line was inclined (1530) to introduce a debasement of the currency. A pamphlet, *Gemeine Stymmen von der Müntze*, was published in opposition to this proceeding, under the auspices of the Albertine branch, whose policy was sounder in the economic sphere no less than in that of ecclesiastical affairs. A reply appeared justifying the Ernestine project. This was followed by a rejoinder from the Albertine side. The Ernestine pamphlet is described by Roscher as ill-written, obscure, inflated, and, as might be expected from the thesis it maintained, sophistical. But it is interesting as containing a statement of the fundamental principles of the mercantile system more than one hundred years before the publication of Mun's book, and forty-six before that of Bodin's *Six livres de la République.* The Albertine tracts, according to Roscher, exhibit such sound views of the conditions and evidences of national wealth, of the nature of money and trade, and of the rights and duties of Governments in relation to economic action, that he regards the unknown author as entitled to a place beside Raleigh and the other English "colonial-theorists" of the end of the sixteenth and beginning of the seventeenth century.

In connection with the same subject of money we meet the great name of Copernicus. His treatise *De monetæ cudendæ ratione,* 1526 (first printed in 1816), was written by order of King Sigismund I., and is an exposition of the principles on which it was proposed to reform the currency of the Prussian provinces of Poland. It advocates unity of the monetary system throughout the entire state, with strict integrity in the quality of the coin, and the charge of a seigniorage sufficient to cover the expenses of mintage.

Antonio Serra is regarded by some as the creator of modern political economy. He was a native of Cosenza in Calabria. His *Breve Trattato delle cause che possono fare abbondare li regni d'oro e d'argento dove non sono miniere,* 1613, was written during his imprisonment, which is believed to have been due to his having taken part in the conspiracy of Campanella for the liberation of Naples from the Spanish yoke and the establishment of a republican government. This work, long overlooked, was brought into notice in the following century by Galiani and others. Its title alone would sufficiently indicate that the author had adopted the principles of the mercantile system, and in fact in this treatise the essential doctrines of that system are expounded in a tolerably formal and consecutive manner. He strongly insists on the superiority of manufactures over agriculture as a source of national wealth, and uses in support of this view the prosperity of Genoa, Florence, and Venice, as contrasted with the depressed condition of Naples. With larger insight than

many of the mercantilists exhibit, he points out the importance, towards the acquisition of wealth, not alone of favourable
external conditions, but of energetic character and industrious
habits in a population, as well as of a stable government and
a good administration of the laws.

The first systematic treatise on our science which proceeded
from a French author was the *Traité de l'Economie Politique*,
published by Montchrétien de Watteville (or Vasteville)[1] in
1615. The use of the title, says Roscher, now for the first
time given to the science, was in itself an important service,
since even Bacon understood by "Economia" only the theory
of domestic management. The general tendencies and aims
of the period are seen in the fact that this treatise, notwithstanding the comprehensive name it bears, does not deal with
agriculture at all, but only with the mechanical arts, navigation,
commerce, and public finance. The author is filled with the
then dominant enthusiasm for foreign trade and colonies.
He advocates the control by princes of the industry of their
subjects, and condemns the too great freedom, which, in his
opinion to their own detriment, the Governments of Spain,
Portugal, and Holland had given to trade. His book may
be regarded as a formal exposition of the principles of the
mercantile system for the use of Frenchmen.

A similar office was performed in England by Thomas Mun.
In his two works, *A Discourse of Trade from England unto
the East Indies*, 2nd ed., 1621, and especially in *England's
Treasure by Foreign Trade*, 1664 (posthumous), we have for
the first time a clear and systematic statement of the theory
of the balance of trade, as well as of the means by which,
according to the author's view, a favourable balance could be
secured for England. The great object of the economic policy
of a state, according to him, should be so to manage its export

---

[1] Montchrétien, having fomented the rebellion in Normandy in 1621,
was slain, with a few followers, by Claude Turgot, lord of Les Tourailles,
who belonged to the elder branch of the noble house from which the
great Turgot was descended.

of manufactures, its direct and carrying trade, and its customs
duties, as to attract to itself money from abroad. He was,
however, opposed to the prohibition of the export of the
precious metals in exchange for foreign wares, but on the
ground, fully according with his general principles, that those
wares might afterwards be re-exported and might then bring
back more treasure than had been originally expended in their
purchase; the first export of money might be, as he said, the
seed-time, of which the ultimate receipt of a larger amount
would be the harvest.[1] He saw, too, that it is inexpedient
to have too much money circulating in a country, as this
enhances the prices of commodities, and so makes them less
saleable to foreigners, but he is favourable to the formation
and maintenance of a state treasure.[2]

One of the most remarkable of the moderate mercantilists
was Sir Josiah Child (*Brief Observations concerning Trade and
the Interest of Money*, 1668, and *A New Discourse of Trade*,
1668 and 1690). He was one of those who held up Holland
as a model for the imitation of his fellow-countrymen. He
is strongly impressed with the importance for national wealth
and wellbeing of a low rate of interest, which he says is to
commerce and agriculture what the soul is to the body, and
which he held to be the "*causa causans* of all the other causes
of the riches of the Dutch people." Instead of regarding
such low rate as dependent on determinate conditions, which
should be allowed to evolve themselves spontaneously, he
thinks it should be created and maintained by public authority.
Child, whilst adhering to the doctrine of the balance of
trade, observes that a people cannot always sell to foreigners

---

[1] On Mun's doctrines, see Smith's *Wealth of Nations*, Bk. iv. chap. i.

[2] Writers of less importance who followed the same direction were
Sir Thomas Culpeper (*A Tract against the High Rate of Usury*, 1623,
and *Useful Remark on High Interest*, 1641), Sir Dudley Digges (*Defence
of Trade*, 1615), G. Malynes (*Consuetudo vel Lex Mercatoria*, 1622),
E. Misselden (*Circle of Commerce*, 1623), Samuel Fortrey (*England's
Interest and Improvement*, 1663 and 1673), and John Pollexfen (*England
and India inconsistent in their Manufactures*, 1697).

without ever buying from them, and denies that the export of the precious metals is necessarily detrimental. He has the ordinary mercantilist partiality for a numerous population. He advocates the reservation by the mother country of the sole right of trade with her colonies, and, under certain limitations, the formation of privileged trading companies. As to the Navigation Act, he takes up a position not unlike that afterwards occupied by Adam Smith, regarding that measure much more favourably from the political than from the economic point of view. It will be seen that he is some-what eclectic in his opinions; but he cannot properly be re-garded, though some have attributed to him that character, as a precursor of the free-trade school of the eighteenth century.

Two other eclectics may be here mentioned, in whom just views are mingled with mercantilist prejudices—Sir William Temple and Charles Davenant. The former in his *Observations upon the United Provinces of the Netherlands*, 1672, and his *Essay on the Trade of Ireland*, 1673, has many excellent remarks on fundamental economic principles, as on the func-tions of labour and of saving in the production of national wealth; but he is infected with the errors of the theory of the balance of trade. He follows the lead of Raleigh and Child in urging his fellow-countrymen to imitate the example of the Dutch in their economic policy—advice which in his case was founded on his observations during a lengthened residence in Holland as ambassador to the States. Davenant in his *Essay on the East-India Trade*, 1696–97, *Essay on the Probable Ways of making the People Gainers in the Balance of Trade*, 1699, &c., also takes up an eclectic position, combining some correct views on wealth and money with mercantilist notions on trade, and recommending Governmental restrictions on colonial commerce as strongly as he advocates freedom of exchange at home.

Whilst the mercantile system represented the prevalent form of economic thought in the seventeenth century, and was alone dominant in the region of practical statesmanship, there was

D

growing up, side by side with it, a body of opinion, different and indeed hostile in character, which was destined ultimately to drive it from the field. The new ideas were first developed in England, though it was in France that in the following century they took hold of the public mind, and became a power in politics. That they should first show themselves here, and afterwards be extended, applied, and propagated throughout Europe by French writers, belongs to the order of things according to which the general negative doctrine in morals and politics, undoubtedly of English origin, found its chief home in France, and was thence diffused in widening circles through the civilised world. In England this movement of economic thought took the shape mainly of individual criticism of the prevalent doctrines, founded on a truer analysis of facts and conceptions ; in France it was penetrated with a powerful social sentiment, furnished the creed of a party, and inspired a protest against institutions and an urgent demand for practical reform.

Regarded from the theoretic side, the characteristic features of the new direction were the following. The view of at least the extreme mercantilists that national wealth depends on the accumulation of the precious metals is proved to be false, and the gifts of nature and the labour of man are shown to be its real sources. The exaggerated estimate of the importance of foreign commerce is reduced, and attention is once more turned to agriculture and the conditions of its successful prosecution. On the side of practical policy, a so-called favourable balance of trade is seen not to be the true object of a nation's or a statesman's efforts, but the procuring for the whole population in the fullest measure the enjoyment of the necessaries and conveniences of life. And—what more than anything else contrasts the new system with the old—the elaborate apparatus of prohibitions, protective duties, bounties, monopolies, and privileged corporations, which the European Governments had created in the supposed interests of manufactures and trade, is denounced or deprecated as more an impediment than a furtherance, and the freedom of industry is insisted on as the one thing needful. This circle of ideas, of course, emerges only gradually, and its earliest representatives in economic literature in general apprehend it imperfectly and advocate it with reserve ; but it rises steadily in importance, being more and more favoured by the highest minds, and finding an increasing body of supporters amongst the intelligent public.

Some occasional traits of an economic scheme in harmony with these new tendencies are to be found in the *De Cive* and *Leviathan* of Hobbes. But the efficacy of that great thinker lay rather in the general philosophic field ; and by systematising, for the first time, the whole negative doctrine, he gave a powerful impulse towards the demolition of the existing social order, which was destined, as we shall see, to have momentous consequences in the economic no less than in the strictly political department of things.

A writer of no such extended range, but of much sagacity and good sense, was Sir William Petty, author of a number of pieces containing germs of a sound economic doctrine. A leading thought in his writings is that "labour is the father and active principle of wealth, lands are the mother." He divides a population into two classes, the productive and the unproductive, according as they are or are not occupied in producing useful material things. The value of any commodity depends, he says, anticipating Ricardo, on the amount of labour necessary for its production. He is desirous of obtaining a universal measure of value, and chooses as his unit the average food of the cheapest kind required for a man's daily sustenance. He understands the nature of the rent of land as the excess of the price of its produce over the cost of production. He disapproves of the attempt to fix by authority a maximum rate of interest, and is generally opposed to Governmental interference with the course of industry. He sees that a country requires for its exchanges a definite quantity of money and may have too much of it, and condemns the prohibition of its exportation. He holds that one

only of the precious metals must be the foundation of the
currency, the other circulating as an ordinary article of merchandise. Petty's name is specially associated with the progress of statistics, with which he was much occupied, and
which he called by the name of political arithmetic. Relying
on the results of such inquiries, he set himself strongly against
the opinion which was maintained by the author of *Britannia
Languens* (1680), Fortrey, Roger Coke, and other writers, that
the prosperity of England was on the decline.

The most thorough-going and emphatic assertion of the free-
trade doctrine against the system of prohibitions, which had
gained strength by the Revolution, was contained in Sir
Dudley North's *Discourses upon Trade*, 1691. He shows
that wealth may exist independently of gold or silver, its
source being human industry, applied either to the cultivation
of the soil or to manufactures. The precious metals, however,
are one element of national wealth, and perform highly important offices. Money may exist in excess, as well as in
defect, in a country; and the quantity of it required for the
purposes of trade will vary with circumstances; its ebb and
flow will regulate themselves spontaneously. It is a mistake
to suppose that stagnation of trade arises from want of money;
it must arise either from a glut of the home market, or from
a disturbance of foreign commerce, or from diminished consumption caused by poverty. The export of money in the
course of traffic, instead of diminishing, increases the national
wealth, trade being only an exchange of superfluities. Nations
are economically related to the world just in the same way as
cities to the state or as families to the city. North emphasises
more than his predecessors the value of the home trade. With
respect to the interest of capital, he maintains that it depends,
like the price of any commodity, on the proportion of demand
and supply, and that a low rate is a result of the relative
increase of capital, and cannot be brought about by arbitrary
regulations, as had been proposed by Child and others. In
arguing the question of free trade, he urges that individuals

often take their private interest as the measure of good and evil, and would for its sake debar others from their equal right of buying and selling, but that every advantage given to one interest or branch of trade over another is injurious to the public.   No trade is unprofitable to the public; if it were, it would be given up; when trades thrive, so does the public, of which they form a part.   Prices must determine themselves, and cannot be fixed by law; and all forcible interference with them does harm instead of good.   No people can become rich by state regulations,—only by peace, industry, freedom, and unimpeded economic activity.   It will be seen how closely North's view of things approaches to that embodied some eighty years later in Adam Smith's great work.[1]

Locke is represented by Roscher as, along with Petty and North, making up the "triumvirate" of eminent British economists of this period who laid the foundations of a new and more rational doctrine than that of the mercantilists. But this view of his claims seems capable of being accepted only with considerable deductions.   His specially economic writings are *Considerations of the lowering of Interest and raising the value of Money*, 1691, and *Further Considerations*, 1695.   Though Leibnitz declared with respect to these treatises that nothing more solid or intelligent could be said on their subject, it is difficult absolutely to adopt that verdict.   Locke's spirit of sober observation and patient analysis led him indeed to some just conclusions; and he is entitled to the credit of having energetically resisted the debasement of the currency, which was then recommended by some who were held to be eminent practical authorities.   But he falls into errors which show that he had not by any means completely emancipated himself from the ideas of the mercantile system.   He attaches far too much importance to money as such.   He says expressly that riches consist in a plenty of gold and silver, that is, as he

[1] Yet M. Eugène Daire asserts (*Œuvres de Turgot*, i. 322) that "Hume et Tucker sont les deux premiers écrivains qui se soient élevés, en Angleterre, au-dessus des théories du système mercantile."

explains, in having more in proportion of those metals than
the rest of the world or than our neighbours. " In a country
not furnished with mines, there are but two ways of growing
rich, either conquest or commerce." Hence he accepts the
doctrine of the balance of trade. He shows that the rate of
interest can no more be fixed by law than the rent of houses
or the hire of ships, and opposes Child's demand for legislative interference with it. But he erroneously attributed the
fall of the rate which had taken place generally in Europe to
the increase of the quantity of gold and silver by the discovery
of the American mines. He sets too absolute a value on a
numerous population, in this point agreeing with Petty. On
wages he observes that the rate must be such as to cover the
indispensable wants of the labourer ; when the price of subsistence rises, wages must rise in a like ratio, or the working
population must come on the poor-rates. The fall of the rent
of land he regards as a sure sign of the decline of national
wealth. " Taxes, however contrived, and out of whose hands
soever immediately taken, do, in a country where their great
fund is in land, for the most part terminate upon land." In
this last proposition we see a foreshadowing of the *impôt
unique* of the physiocrats. Whatever may have been Locke's
direct economic services, his principal importance, like that of
Hobbes, lies in his general philosophic and political principles,
which powerfully affected French and indeed European thought,
exciting a spirit of opposition to arbitrary power, and laying the
foundation of the doctrine developed in the *Contrat Social*.[1]

[1] Minor English writers who followed the new economic direction
were Lewis Roberts, *Treasure of Traffick*, 1641 ; Rice Vaughan, *Discourse
of Coin and Coinage*, 1675 ; Nicholas Barbon, *Discourse concerning Coin-
ing the new money lighter*, 1696, in which some of Locke's errors were
pointed out ; and the author of an anonymous book entitled *Considerations on the East India Trade*, 1701. Practical questions much debated
at this period were those connected with banking, on which a lengthened
controversy took place, S. Lamb, W. Potter, F. Cradocke, M. Lewis,
M. Godfrey, R. Murray, H. Chamberlen, and W. Paterson, founder of
the Bank of England (1694), producing many pamphlets on the subject ;
and the management of the poor, which was treated by Locke, Sir
Matthew Hale, R. Haines, T. Firmin, and others.

CHAPTER V.

THIRD MODERN PHASE. SYSTEM OF NATURAL LIBERTY.

THE changes introduced during the third phase in the internal organisation of the industrial world were (1) the more complete separation of banking from general commerce, and the wider extension of its operations, especially through the system of public credit; and (2) the great development of the use of machinery in production. The latter did not become very prominent during the first half of the eighteenth century. Whilst tending to promote the dignity of the working classes by relieving them from degrading and exhausting physical labour, it widened the gulf between them and the capitalist employers. It thus became plain that for the definitive constitution of industry a moral reform was the necessary preliminary condition.

With respect to the political relations of industry, a remarkable inversion now showed itself. The systematic encouragements which the European Governments had extended to it in the preceding phase had been prompted by their desire to use it as an instrument for achieving the military superiority which was the great end of their policy. Now, on the contrary, the military spirit subordinated itself to the industrial, and the armies and the diplomacy of governments were placed at the service of commerce. The wars which filled a large part of the eighteenth century were essentially Commercial wars, arising out of the effort to sustain or extend the colonial establishments founded in the previous phase, or to deprive rival nations of the industrial advantages connected with the possession of such establishments. This change of attitude, notwithstanding its deplorable tendency to foster international enmities and jealousies, marked a real and important progress by pointing to industrial activity as the one permanent practical destination of modern societies.

But, whilst by this sort of action furthering the ascendency of the new forces, the ruling powers, both in England and France, betrayed the alarm they felt at the subversive tendencies which appeared inherent in the modern movement by taking up in their domestic policy an attitude of resistance. Reaction became triumphant in France during the latter half of the reign of Louis XIV. under the disastrous influence of Madame de Maintenon. In England, after the transaction of 1688, by which the Government was consolidated on the double basis of aristocratic power and official orthodoxy, the state policy became not so much retrograde as stationary, industrial conquest being put forward to satisfy the middle class and wean it from the pursuit of a social renovation. In both countries there was for some time a noticeable check in the intellectual development, and Roscher and others have observed that, in economic studies particularly, the first three decades of the eighteenth century were a period of general stagnation, eclecticism for the most part taking the place of originality. The movement was, however, soon to be resumed, but with an altered and more formidable character. The negative doctrine, which had risen and taken a definite form in England, was diffused and popularised in France, where it became evident, even before the decisive explosion, that the only possible issue lay in a radical social transformation. The partial schools of Voltaire and Rousseau in different ways led up to a violent crisis, whilst taking little thought of the conditions of a system which could replace the old; but the more complete and organic school, of which Diderot is the best representative, looked through freedom to a thorough reorganisation. Its constructive aim is shown by the design of the *Encyclopédie*,—a project, however, which could have only a temporary success, because no real synthesis was forth-coming, and this joint production of minds often divergent could possess no more than an external unity. It was with this great school that the physiocrats were specially connected ; and, in common with its other members, whilst pushing towards an entire change of the existing system, they yet would gladly have avoided political demolition through the exercise of a royal dictatorship, or contemplated it only as the necessary condition of a new and better order of things. But, though marked off by such tendencies from the purely revo-lutionary sects, their method and fundamental ideas were negative, resting, as they did, essentially on the basis of the *ius naturæ*. We shall follow in detail these French develop-ments in their special relation to economic science, and after-wards notice the corresponding movements in other European countries which showed themselves before the appearance of Adam Smith, or were at least unaffected by his influence.

BEFORE ADAM SMITH.

France.

The more liberal, as well as more rational, principles put forward by the English thinkers of the new type began, early in the eighteenth century, to find an echo in France, where the clearer and more vigorous intellects were prepared for their reception by a sense of the great evils which exaggerated mercantilism, serving as instrument of political ambition, had produced in that country. The impoverished condition of the agricultural population, the oppressive weight and unequal imposition of taxation, and the unsound state of the public finances had produced a general feeling of disquiet, and led several distinguished writers to protest strongly against the policy of Colbert and to demand a complete reform.

The most important amongst them was Pierre Boisguillebert, whose whole life was devoted to these controversies. In his statistical writings (*Détail de la France sous le règne présent,*

1697; *Factum de la France*, 1707), he brings out in gloomy colours the dark side of the age of Louis XIV., and in his theoretic works (*Traité de la nature et du commerce des grains; Dissertations sur la nature des richesses de l'argent et des tributs;* and *Essai sur la rareté de l'argent*) he appears as an earnest, even passionate, antagonist of the mercantile school. He insists again and again on the fact that national wealth does not consist in gold and silver, but in useful things, foremost among which are the products of agriculture. He even goes so far as to speak of "argent criminel," which from being the slave of trade, as it ought to be, had become its tyrant. He sets the "genuinely French Sully" far above the "Italianising Colbert," and condemns all arbitrary regulations affecting either foreign or internal commerce, especially as regards the corn trade. National wealth does not depend on Governments, whose interference does more harm than good; the natural laws of the economic order of things cannot be violated or neglected with impunity; the interests of the several classes of society in a system of freedom are identical, and those of individuals coincide with that of the state. A similar solidarity exists between different nations; in their economic dealings they are related to the world as individual towns to a nation, and not merely plenty, but peace and harmony, will result from their unfettered intercourse. Men he divides into two classes—those who do nothing and enjoy everything, and those who labour from morning to night often without earning a bare subsistence; the latter he would favour in every way. Here we catch the breath of popular sympathy which fills the social atmosphere of the eighteenth century. He dwells with special emphasis on the claims of agriculture, which had in France fallen into unmerited neglect, and with a view to its improvement calls for a reform in taxation. He would replace indirect taxes by taxes on income, and would restore the payment of taxes in kind, with the object of securing equality of burden and eliminating every element of the arbitrary. He has some interesting views of a general character : thus he approximates to a correct conception of agricultural rent, and he points to the order in which human wants follow each other,—those of necessity, convenience, comfort, superfluity, and ostentation succeeding in the order named, and ceasing in the inverse order to be felt as wealth decreases. The depreciating tone in which Voltaire speaks of Boisguillebert (*Siècle de Louis XIV.*, chap. 30) is certainly not justified ; he had a great economic talent, and his writings contain important germs of truth. But he appears to have exerted little influence, theoretical or practical, in his own time.

The same general line of thought was followed by Marshal Vauban (1633–1707) in his economic tracts, especially that bearing the title of *Projet d'une dixme Royale,* 1707, which was suppressed by the authorities, and lost for him the favour of his sovereign, but has added lustre to his name in the judgment of posterity. He is deeply impressed with the deplorable condition of the working classes of France in his day. He urges that the aim of the Government should be the welfare of all orders of the community ; that all are entitled to like favour and furtherance ; that the often despised and wronged lower class is the basis of the social organisation ; that labour is the foundation of all wealth, and agriculture the most important species of labour ; that the most essential condition of successful industry is freedom ; and that all unnecessary or excessive restrictions on manufactures and commerce should be swept away. He protests in particular against the inequalities of taxation, and the exemptions and privileges enjoyed by the higher ranks. With the exception of some duties on consumption he would abolish all the existing taxes, and substitute for them a single tax on income and land, impartially applied to all classes, which he describes under the name of "Dixme Royale," that is to say, a tenth in kind of all agricultural produce, and a tenth of money income chargeable on manufacturers and traders.[1]

---

[1] An English translation of the *Dixme Royale* was published in 1708.

The liberal and humane spirit of Fénelon led him to aspire after freedom of commerce with foreign nations, and to preach the doctrine that the true superiority of one state over another lies in the number indeed, but also in the morality, intelligence, and industrious habits of its population. The *Télémaque*, in which these views were presented in an attractive form, was welcomed and read amongst all ranks and classes, and was thus an effective organ for the propagation of opinion.

After these writers there is a marked blank in the field of French economic thought, broken only by the *Réflexions Politiques sur les Finances et le Commerce* (1738) of Dutot, a pupil of Law, and the semi-mercantilist *Essais Politiques sur le Commerce* (1731) of Mélon, till we come to the great name of Montesquieu. The *Esprit des Lois*, so far as it deals with economic subjects, is written upon the whole from a point of view adverse to the mercantile system, especially in his treatment of money, though in his observations on colonies and elsewhere he falls in with the ideas of that system. His immortal service, however, was not rendered by any special research, but by his enforcement of the doctrine of natural laws regulating social no less than physical phenomena. There is no other thinker of importance on economic subjects in France till the appearance of the physiocrats, which marks an epoch in the history of the science.

The heads of the physiocratic school were François Quesnay (1694–1774) and Jean Claude Marie Vincent, sieur de Gournay (1712–1759). The principles of the school had been put forward in 1755 by Richard Cantillon, a French merchant of Irish extraction (*Essai sur la nature du Commerce en général*), whose biography Jevons has elucidated,[1] and whom he regards as the true founder of political economy;

---

[1] "Richard Cantillon and the Nationality of Political Economy," in *Contemporary Review*, Jan. 1881. Cantillon is quoted in the *Wealth of Nations*, bk. i. chap. 8.

but it was in the hands of Quesnay and Gournay[1] that they
acquired a systematic form, and became the creed of a united
group of thinkers and practical men, bent on carrying them
into action. The members of the group called themselves
"les économistes," but it is more convenient, because unam-
biguous, to designate them by the name "physiocrates,"
invented by Dupont de Nemours, who was one of their
number. In this name, intended to express the fundamental
idea of the school, much more is implied than the subjection
of the phenomena of the social, and in particular the economic,
world to fixed relations of co-existence and succession. This
is the positive doctrine which lies at the bottom of all true
science. But the law of nature referred to in the title of the
sect was something quite different. The theological dogma
which represented all the movements of the universe as
directed by divine wisdom and benevolence to the production
of the greatest possible sum of happiness had been trans-
formed in the hands of the metaphysicians into the conception
of a *jus naturæ*, a harmonious and beneficial code established
by the favourite entity of these thinkers, Nature, antecedent
to human institutions, and furnishing the model to which
they should be made to conform. This idea, which Buckle
apparently supposes to have been an invention of Hutcheson's,
had come down through Roman juridical theory from the
speculations of Greece.[2] It was taken in hand by the modern
negative school from Hobbes to Rousseau, and used as a powerful weapon of assault upon the existing order of society, with
which the "natural" order was perpetually contrasted as offering the perfect type from which fact had deplorably diverged.
The theory received different applications according to the
diversity of minds or circumstances. By some it was directed
against the artificial manners of the times, by others against

---

[1] Gournay strongly recommended to his friends Cantillon's book as
"ouvrage excellent qu'on negligeait." *Mémoires de Morellet*, i. 38.
[2] See Cliffe Leslie's *Essays in Political and Moral Philosophy*, p.
151.

contemporary political institutions; it was specially employed by the physiocrats in criticising the economic practice of European Governments.

The general political doctrine is as follows. Society is composed of a number of individuals all having the same natural rights. If all do not possess (as some members of the negative school maintained) equal capacities, each can at least best understand his own interest, and is led by nature to follow it. The social union is really a contract between these individuals, the object of which is the limitation of the natural freedom of each, just so far as it is inconsistent with the rights of the others. Government, though necessary, is a necessary evil; and the governing power appointed by consent should be limited to the amount of interference absolutely required to secure the fulfilment of the contract. In the economic sphere, this implies the right of the individual to such natural enjoyments as he can acquire by his labour. That labour, therefore, should be undisturbed and unfettered; and its fruits should be guaranteed to the possessor; in other words, property should be sacred. Each citizen must be allowed to make the most of his labour; and therefore freedom of exchange should be ensured, and competition in the market should be unrestricted, no monopolies or privileges being permitted to exist.

The physiocrats then proceed with the economic analysis as follows. Only those labours are truly "productive" which add to the quantity of raw materials available for the purposes of man; and the real annual addition to the wealth of the community consists of the excess of the mass of agricultural products (including, of course, minerals) over their cost of production. On the amount of this "produit net" depends the wellbeing of the community, and the possibility of its advance in civilisation. The manufacturer merely gives a new form to the materials extracted from the earth; the higher value of the object, after it has passed through his hands, only represents the quantity of provisions and other materials used and consumed in its elaboration. Commerce does nothing more than transfer the wealth already existing from one hand to another; what the trading classes gain thereby is acquired at the cost of the nation, and it is desirable that its amount should be as small as possible. The occupations of the manufacturer and merchant, as well as the liberal professions, and every kind of personal service, are " useful " indeed, but they are " sterile," drawing their income, not from any fund which they themselves create, but from the superfluous earnings of the agriculturist. Perfect freedom of trade not only rests, as we have already seen, on the foundation of natural right, but is also recommended by the consideration that it makes the " produit net," on which all wealth and general progress depend, as large as possible. " Laissez faire, laissez passer " should therefore be the motto of Governments. The revenue of the state, which must be derived altogether from this net product, ought to be raised in the most direct and simplest way,—namely, by a single impost of the nature of a land tax.

The special doctrine relating to the exclusive productiveness of agriculture arose out of a confusion between "value " on the one hand and " matter and energy" on the other. Smith and others have shown that the attempt to fix the character of " sterility " on manufactures and commerce was founded in error. And the proposal of a single *impôt territorial* falls to the ground with the doctrine on which it was based. But such influence as the school exerted depended little, if at all, on these peculiar tenets, which indeed some of its members did not hold. The effective result of its teaching was mainly destructive. It continued in a more systematic form the efforts in favour of the freedom of industry already begun in England and France. The essential historical office of the physiocrats was to discredit radically the methods followed by the European Governments in their dealings with industry. For such criticism as theirs there was, indeed, ample room : the policy of Colbert, which could be only temporarily useful,

had been abusively extended and intensified; Governmental
action had intruded itself into the minutest details of business,
and every process of manufacture and transaction of trade was
hampered by legislative restrictions. It was to be expected
that the reformers should, in the spirit of the negative philosophy, exaggerate the vices of established systems; and there
can be no doubt that they condemned too absolutely the
economic action of the state, both in principle and in its
historic manifestations, and pushed the "laissez faire" doctrine
beyond its just limits. But this was a necessary incident of
their connection with the revolutionary movement, of which
they really formed one wing. In the course of that movement,
the primitive social contract, the sovereignty of the people,
and other dogmas now seen to be untenable, were habitually
invoked in the region of politics proper, and had a transitory
utility as ready and effective instruments of warfare. And so
also in the economic sphere the doctrines of natural rights of
buying and selling, of the sufficiency of enlightened selfishness
as a guide in mutual dealings, of the certainty that each
member of the society will understand and follow his true
interests, and of the coincidence of those interests with the
public welfare, though they will not bear a dispassionate
examination, were temporarily useful as convenient and serviceable weapons for the overthrow of the established order.
The tendency of the school was undoubtedly to consecrate the
spirit of individualism, and the state of non-government. But
this tendency, which may with justice be severely condemned
in economists of the present time, was then excusable because
inevitable. And, whilst it now impedes the work of reconstruction which is for us the order of the day, it then aided
the process of social demolition, which was the necessary,
though deplorable, condition of a new organisation.

These conclusions as to the revolutionary tendencies of the
school are not at all affected by the fact that the form of
government preferred by Quesnay and some of his chief followers was what they called a legal despotism, which should

embrace within itself both the legislative and the executive function. The reason for this preference was that an enlightened central power could more promptly and efficaciously introduce the policy they advocated than an assembly representing divergent opinions, and fettered by constitutional checks and limitations. Turgot, as we know, used the absolute power of the crown to carry into effect some of his measures for the liberation of industry, though he ultimately failed because unsustained by the requisite force of character in Louis XVI. But what the physiocratic idea with respect to the normal method of government was appears from Quesnay's advice to the dauphin, that when he became king he should " do nothing, but let the laws rule," the laws having been of course first brought into conformity with the *jus naturæ*. The partiality of the school for agriculture was in harmony with the sentiment in favour of " nature " and primitive simplicity which then showed itself in so many forms in France, especially in combination with the revolutionary spirit, and of which Rousseau was the most eloquent exponent. It was also associated in these writers with a just indignation at the wretched state in which the rural labourers of France had been left by the scandalous neglect of the superior orders of society—a state of which the terrible picture drawn by La Bruyère is an indestructible record. The members of the physiocratic group were undoubtedly men of thorough uprightness, and inspired with a sincere desire for the public good, especially for the material and moral elevation of the working classes. Quesnay was physician to Louis XV., and resided in the palace at Versailles; but in the midst of that corrupt court he maintained his integrity, and spoke with manly frankness what he believed to be the truth. And never did any statesman devote himself with greater singleness of purpose or more earnest endeavour to the service of his country than Turgot, who was the principal practical representative of the school.

The publications in which Quesnay expounded his system were the following:—Two articles, on " Fermiers " and on

"Grains," in the *Encyclopédie* of Diderot and D'Alembert (1756, 1757); a discourse on the law of nature in the *Physiocratie* of Dupont de Nemours (1768); *Maximes générales de gouvernement économique d'un royaume agricole* (1758), and the simultaneously published *Tableau Économique avec son explication, ou Extrait des Économies Royales de Sully* (with the celebrated motto "pauvres paysans, pauvre royaume; pauvre royaume, pauvre roi"); *Dialogue sur le commerce et les travaux des artisans;* and other minor pieces. The *Tableau Économique*, though on account of its dryness and abstract form it met with little general favour, may be considered the principal manifesto of the school. It was regarded by the followers of Quesnay as entitled to a place amongst the foremost products of human wisdom, and is named by the elder Mirabeau, in a passage quoted by Adam Smith,[1] as one of the three great inventions which have contributed most to the stability of political societies, the other two being those of writing and of money. Its object was to exhibit by means of certain formulas the way in which the products of agriculture, which is the only source of wealth, would in a state of perfect liberty be distributed among the several classes of the community (namely, the productive classes of the proprietors and cultivators of land, and the unproductive class composed of manufacturers and merchants), and to represent by other formulas the modes of distribution which take place under systems of Governmental restraint and regulation, with the evil results arising to the whole society from different degrees of such violations of the natural order. It follows from Quesnay's theoretic views that the one thing deserving the solicitude of the practical economist and the statesman is the increase of the net product; and he infers also what Smith afterwards affirmed on not quite the same ground, that the interest of the landowner is "strictly and inseparably connected with the general interest of the society."[2]

---

[1] *Wealth of Nations,* bk. iv. chap. 9. [2] Ibid. bk. i., chap. 11.

M. de Gournay, as we have seen, was regarded as one of
the founders of the school, and appears to have exercised some
influence even upon the formation of Quesnay's own opinions.
With the exception of translations of Culpeper and Child,[1]
Gournay wrote nothing but memoirs addressed to ministers,
which have not seen the light ; but we have a full statement
of his views in the *Éloge* dedicated to his memory by his
illustrious friend Turgot.   Whilst Quesnay had spent his
youth amidst rural scenes, and had been early familiar with
the labours of the field, Gournay had been bred as a merchant,
and had passed from the counting-house to the office of intendant of commerce.   They thus approached the study of political
economy from different sides, and this diversity of their ante-
cedents may in part explain the amount of divergence which
existed between their views.   Gournay softened the rigour
of Quesnay's system, and brought it nearer to the truth, by
rejecting what Smith calls its "capital error" —the doctrine,
namely, of the unproductiveness of manufactures and commerce.   He directed his efforts to the assertion and vindica-
tion of the principle of industrial liberty, and it was by him
that this principle was formulated in the phrase, since so often
heard for good and for evil, "Laissez faire et laissez passer."
One of the earliest and most complete adherents of the physiocratic school, as well as an ardent and unwearied propagator
of its doctrines, was Victor Mirabeau, whose sincere and independent, though somewhat perverse and whimsical, character
is familiar to English readers through Carlyle's essay on his
more celebrated son.   He had expressed some physiocratic
views earlier than Quesnay, but owned the latter for his spiritual
father, and adopted most of his opinions, the principal difference being that he was favourable to the *petite* as opposed
to the *grande culture*, which latter was preferred by his
chief as giving, not indeed the largest gross, but the largest

---

[1] Gournay's inspiration was, without doubt, largely English. "Il
avait lu," says Morellet, "de bons livres Anglais d'Économie politique,
tels que Petty, Davenant, Gee, Child, &c."—*Mémoires*, i. 38.

net product. Mirabeau's principal writings were *Ami des Hommes, ou traité sur la population* (1756, 1760), *Théorie de l'impôt* (1760), *Les Économiques* (1769), and *Philosophie rurale, ou Économie générale et politique de l'Agriculture* (1763). The last of these was the earliest complete exposition of the physiocratic system. Another earnest and persevering apostle of the system was Dupont de Nemours (1739–1817), known by his treatises *De l'exportation et de l'importation des grains* (1764), *De l'origine et des progrès d'une science nouvelle* (1767), *Du commerce de la Compagnie des Indes* (1767), and especially by his more comprehensive work *Physiocratie, ou Constitution naturelle du gouvernement le plus avantageux au genre humain* (1768). The title of this work gave, as has been already mentioned, a name to the school. Another formal exposition of the system, to which Adam Smith refers as the "most distinct and best connected account" of it, was produced by Mercier-Larivière, under the title *L'Ordre naturel et essentiel des sociétés politiques* (1767), a title which is interesting as embodying the idea of the *jus naturæ*. Both he and Dupont de Nemours professed to study human communities, not only in relation to their economic, but also to their political and general social aspects; but, notwithstanding these larger pretensions, their views were commonly restricted in the main to the economic sphere; at least material considerations decidedly preponderated in their inquiries, as was naively indicated by Larivière when he said, "Property, security, liberty— these comprise the whole social order; the right of property is a tree of which all the institutions of society are branches."

The most eminent member of the group was without doubt Anne Robert Jacques Turgot (1727–1781). This is not the place to speak of his noble practical activity, first as intendant of Limoges, and afterwards for a brief period as finance minister, or of the circumstances which led to his removal from office, and the consequent failure of his efforts for the salvation of France. His economic views are explained in the introductions to his edicts and ordinances, in letters and occasional papers, but especially in his *Réflexions sur la forma-tion et la distribution des richesses* (1766). This is a con-densed but eminently clear and attractive exposition of the fundamental principles of political economy, as they were con-ceived by the physiocrats. It embodies, indeed, the erroneous no less than the sound doctrines of that school; but several subjects, especially the various forms of land-economy, the different employments of capital, and the legitimacy of interest, are handled in a generally just as well as striking manner; and the mode of presentation of the ideas, and the luminous arrangement of the whole, are Turgot's own. The treatise, which contains a surprising amount of matter in pro-portion to its length, must always retain a place among the classics of the science.

The physiocratic school never obtained much direct popular influence, even in its native country, though it strongly attracted many of the more gifted and earnest minds. Its members, writing on dry subjects in an austere and often heavy style, did not find acceptance with a public which demanded before all things charm of manner in those who addressed it. When Morellet, one of their number, entered the lists with Galiani, it was seen how *esprit* and eloquence could triumph over science, solid indeed, but clumsy in its movements.[1] The physiocratic tenets, which were in fact partially erroneous, were regarded by many as chimerical, and were ridiculed in the contemporary literature, as, for example, the *impôt unique* by Voltaire in his *L'homme aux quarante écus*, which was directed in particular against Mercier-Larivière. It was justly objected to the group that they were

[1] On Galiani's *Dialogues*, see page 72. Soon after the appearance of this book Turgot wrote to Mlle. Lespinasse—"Je crois possible de lui faire une très bonne réponse ; mais cela demande bien de l'art. Les économistes sont trop confiants pour combattre contre un si adroit ferrailleur. Pour l'abbé Morellet, il ne faut pas qu'il y pense." Morellet's work was prohibited by the Controller-General Terray ; though printed in 1770, some months after Galiani's, it was not published till 1774.

too absolute in their view of things; they supposed, as Smith remarks in speaking of Quesnay, that the body-politic could thrive only under one precise régime,—that, namely, which they recommended,—and thought their doctrines universally and immediately applicable in practice.[1] They did not, as theorists, sufficiently take into account national diversities,[2] or different stages in social development; nor did they, as politicians, adequately estimate the impediments which ignorance, prejudice, and interested opposition present to enlightened statesmanship. It is possible that Turgot himself, as Grimm suggests, owed his failure in part to the too unbending rigour of his policy and the absence of any attempt at conciliation. Be this as it may, his defeat helped to impair the credit of his principles, which were represented as having been tried and found wanting.

The physiocratic system, after guiding in some degree the policy of the Constituent Assembly, and awakening a few echoes here and there in foreign countries, soon ceased to exist as a living power; but the good elements it comprised were not lost to mankind, being incorporated into the sounder and more complete construction of Adam Smith.

ITALY.

In Italy, as in the other European nations, there was little activity in the economic field during the first half of the eighteenth century. It was then, however, that a really remarkable man appeared, the archdeacon Salustio Antonio Bandini (1677–1760), author of the *Discorso sulla Maremma Sienese*, written in 1737, but not published till 1775. The

---

[1] Hume, in a letter to Morellet, 1769, calls them "the set of men the most chimerical and arrogant that now exist." He seems intentionally to ignore Morellet's close connection with them.

[2] Turgot said, "Quiconque n'oublie pas qu'il y a des états politiques séparés les uns des autres et constitués diversement, ne traitera jamais bien aucune question d'Économie politique."—*Letter to Mlle. Lespinasse,* 1770.

object of the work was to raise the Maremma from the wretched condition into which it had fallen through the decay of agriculture. This decay he showed to be, at least in part, the result of the wretched fiscal system which was in force; and his book led to important reforms in Tuscany, where his name is held in high honour. Not only by Pecchio and other Italian writers, but by Roscher also, he is alleged to have anticipated some leading doctrines of the physiocrats, but this claim is disputed. There was a remarkable renascence of economic studies in Italy during the latter half of the century, partly due to French influence, and partly, it would appear, to improved government in the northern states.

The movement at first followed the lines of the mercantile school. Thus, in Antonio Broggia's *Trattati dei tributi e delle monete e del governo politico della società* (1743), and Girolamo Belloni's *Dissertazione sopra il commercio* (1750), which seems to have had a success and reputation much above its merits, mercantilist tendencies decidedly preponderate. But the most distinguished writer who represented that economic doctrine in Italy in the last century was Antonio Genovesi, a Neapolitan (1712–1769). He felt deeply the depressed intellectual and moral state of his fellow-countrymen, and aspired after a revival of philosophy and reform of education as the first condition of progress and wellbeing. With the object of protecting him from the theological persecutions which threatened him on account of his advanced opinions, Bartolomeo Intieri, of whom we shall hear again in relation to Galiani, founded in 1755, expressly for Genovesi, a chair of commerce and mechanics, one of the conditions of foundation being that it should never be filled by a monk. This was the first professorship of economics established in Europe; the second was founded at Stockholm in 1758, and the third in Lombardy ten years later, for Beccaria. The fruit of the labours of Genovesi in this chair was his *Lezioni di commercio, ossia di economia civile* (1769), which contained the first systematic treatment of the whole subject which had appeared in Italy.

As the model for Italian imitation he held up England, a country for which, says Pecchio, he had a predilection almost amounting to fanaticism. He does not rise above the false economic system which England then pursued; but he rejects some of the grosser errors of the school to which he belonged; he advocates the freedom of the corn trade, and deprecates regulation of the interest on loans. In the spirit of his age, he denounces the relics of mediæval institutions, such as entails and tenures in mortmain, as impediments to the national prosperity. Ferdinando Galiani was another distinguished disciple of the mercantile school. Before he had completed his twenty-first year he published a work on money (*Della moneta libri cinque*, 1750), the principles of which are supposed to have been dictated by two experienced practical men, the Marquis Rinuccini and Bartolomeo Intieri, whose name we have already met. But his reputation was made by a book written in French and published in Paris, where he was secretary of embassy, in 1770, namely, his *Dialogues sur le commerce des blés*. This work, by its light and pleasing style, and the vivacious wit with which it abounded, delighted Voltaire, who spoke of it as a book in the production of which Plato and Molière might have been combined![1] The author, says Pecchio, treated his arid subject as Fontenelle did the vortices of Descartes, or Algarotti the Newtonian system of the world. The question at issue was that of the freedom of the corn trade, then much agitated, and, in particular, the policy of the royal edict of 1764, which permitted the exportation of grain so long as the price had not arrived at a certain height. The general principle he maintains is that the best system in regard to this trade is to have no system, —countries differently circumstanced requiring, according to him, different modes of treatment. This seems a lame and impotent conclusion from the side of science; yet doubtless

---

[1] So also Grimm : "C'est Platon avec la verve et les gestes d'Arlequin." Diderot called the book "modèle de dialogues qui restera à côté des lettres de Pascal."

the physiocrats, with whom his controversy lay, prescribed
on this, as on other subjects, rules too rigid for the safe
guidance of statesmen, and Galiani may have rendered a
real service by protesting against their absolute solutions of
practical problems. He fell, however, into some of the most
serious errors of the mercantilists,—holding, as indeed did also
Voltaire and even Verri, that one country cannot gain without another losing, and in his earlier treatise going so far as to
defend the action of Governments in debasing the currency.

Amongst the Italian economists who were most under the
influence of the modern spirit, and in closest harmony with the
general movement which was impelling the Western nations
towards a new social order, Cesare Beccaria (1738–1794) holds
a foremost place. He is best known by his celebrated treatise
Dei delitti e delle pene, by which Voltaire said he had made
himself a benefactor of all Europe, and which, we are ·told,
has been translated into twenty-two languages. The Empress
Catherine having invited him to fix his residence at St.
Petersburg, the Austrian Government of Lombardy, in order
to keep him at home, established expressly for him a chair of
political economy; and in his *Elementi di economia pubblica*
(1769–1771; not published, however, till 1804) are embodied
his teachings as professor. The work is unfinished: he had
divided the whole subject under the heads of agriculture,
manufactures, commerce, taxation, government; but he has
treated adequately only the first two heads, and the last two
not at all, having been called to take part in the councils of the
state. He was in some degree under the influence of physiocratic ideas, and holds that agriculture is the only strictly
productive form of industry, whilst manufactures and artisans
are a sterile class. He was strongly opposed to monopolies
and privileges, and to corporations in arts and trades; in
general he warmly advocated internal industrial freedom,
though in regard to foreign commerce a protectionist. In the
special case of the corn trade he was not, any more than
Galiani, a partisan of absolute liberty. His exposition of

economic principles is concise and sententious, and he often
states correctly the most important considerations relating to
his subject without adding the developments which would
be desirable to assist comprehension and strengthen conviction. Thus on fixed capital (*capitali fondatori*), as distinct
from circulating (*annui*), in its application to agriculture, he
presents in a condensed form essentially the same explanations as Turgot about the same time gave ; and on the division
of labour and the circumstances which cause different rates of
wages in different employments, he in substance comes near
to Smith, but without the fulness of illustration which is so
attractive a feature of the *Wealth of Nations.* Pietro Verri
(1728–1797), an intimate and life-long friend of Beccaria, was
for twenty-five years one of the principal directors of the
administration of Lombardy, in which capacity he originated
many economic and other reforms. In his *Riflessioni sulle
leggi vincolanti, principalmente nel commercio de' grani* (written
in 1769, printed in 1796), he considers the question of the
regulation of the corn trade both historically and in the light
of theoretic principles, and arrives at the conclusion that
liberty is the best remedy against famine and against excessive
fluctuations of price. He is generally opposed to Governmental interference with internal commerce, as well as to
trade corporations, and the attempts to limit prices or fix the
rate of interest, but is in favour of the protection of national
industry by a judiciously framed tariff. These views are
explained in his *Meditazioni sull' economia politica* (1771), an
elementary treatise on the science, which was received with
favour, and translated into several foreign languages. A
primary principle with him is what he calls the augmentation of reproduction—that is, in Smith's language, of "the
annual produce of the land and labour" of a nation; and
by its tendency to promote or to restrict this augmentation,
he tests every enactment and institution. Accordingly,
unlike Beccaria, he prefers the *petite* to the *grande culture*,
as giving a larger total produce. In dealing with taxation,

he rejects the physiocratic proposal of a single *impôt terri-*
torial.[1] Giovanni R. Carli (1720–1795), also an official pro-
moter of the reforms in the government of Austrian Lombardy,
besides learned and sound treatises on money, was author of
Ragionamenti sopra i bilanci economici delle nazioni, in which
he shows the falsity of the notion that a state gains or loses in
foreign commerce according to the so-called balance of trade.
In his letter to Pompeo Neri *Sul libero commercio de' grani*
(1771), he takes up a position similar to that of Galiani,
regarding the question of the freedom of the corn trade as not
so much a scientific as an administrative one, to be dealt with
differently under different local or other conditions. Rejecting the physiocratic doctrine of the exclusive productiveness
of agriculture, he illustrates in an interesting way the necessity of various economic classes in a society, and the reflex
agency of manufactures in stimulating the cultivation of the
soil. Giambattista Vasco (1733–1796) wrote discourses on
several questions proposed by academies and sovereigns. In
these he condemns trade corporations and the attempts by
Governments to fix the price of bread and to limit the interest
on loans. In advocating the system of a peasant proprietary,
he suggests that the law should determine the minimum and
maximum portions of land which a citizen should be permitted to possess. He also, with a view to prevent the undue
accumulation of property, proposes the abolition of the right
of bequest, and the equal division of the inheritance amongst
the children of the deceased. Gaetano Filangieri (1752–1788),
one of the Italian writers of the last century whose names are
most widely known throughout Europe, devoted to economic

---

[1] J. S. Mill, in his *Principles*, bk. i. chap. 1, takes credit to his father
for having first illustrated and made prominent in relation to production what he strangely calls "a fundamental principle of Political
Economy," namely, that "all that man does or can do with matter" is
to "move one thing to or from another." But this is clearly put forward
by Verri in his *Meditazioni*, sect. 3: "Accostare e separare sono gli
unici elementi che l'ingegno umano ritrova analizzando l'idea della
riproduzione."

questions the second book of his *Scienza della legislazione* (5 vols., 1780–1785). Filled with reforming ardour and a passionate patriotism, he employed his vehement eloquence in denouncing all the abuses of his time. Apparently without any knowledge of Adam Smith, he insists on unlimited freedom of trade, calls for the abolition of the mediæval institutions which impeded production and national wellbeing, and condemns the colonial system then followed by England, Spain, and Holland. He prophecies, as Raynal, Turgot, and Genovesi had done before him, that all America would one day be independent, a prediction which probably helped to elicit Benjamin Franklin's tribute of admiration for his work. Rather a propagator than a discoverer, he sometimes adopted from others erroneous opinions, as, for example, when he approves the *impôt unique* of the physiocrats. On the whole, however, he represents the most advanced political and social tendencies of his age; whilst strongly contrasted with Beccaria in temperament and style, he was a worthy labourer in the same cause of national and universal progress. Ludovico Ricci (1742–1799) was author of an able report *Sulla riforma degli istituti pii della città di Modena* (1787). He treated the subject of poor relief and charitable institutions in so general a way that the work possesses a universal and permanent interest. He dwells on the evils of indiscriminate relief as tending to increase the misery it seeks to remove, and as lowering the moral character of a population. He exposes especially the abuses connected with lying-in and foundling hospitals. There is much in him which is akin to the views of Malthus; like him he is opposed to any state provision for the destitute, who ought, he thinks, to be left to voluntary private beneficence. Ferdinando Paoletti (1717–1801) was an excellent and public-spirited priest, who did much for the diffusion of intelligence amongst the agricultural population of Tuscany, and for the lightening of the taxes which pressed upon them. He corresponded with Mirabeau ("Friend of Men"), and appears to have accepted the physiocratic doc-

trines, at least in their general substance. He was author of
Pensieri sopra l'agricoltura (1769), and of *I veri mezzi di
render felici le società* (1772); in the latter he advocates the
freedom of the corn trade. The tract *Il Colbertismo* (1791)
by Count Francesco Mengotti is a vigorous protest against the
extreme policy of prohibition and protection, which may still
be read with interest. Mengotti also wrote (1791) a treatise
Del commercio de' Romani, directed mainly against the exaggerations of Huet in his *Histoire du commerce et de la
navigation des anciens* (1716), and useful as marking the broad
difference between the ancient and modern civilisations.

Here lastly may be mentioned another Italian thinker who,
eminently original and even eccentric, cannot easily be classed
among his contemporaries, though some Continental writers
of our own century have exhibited similar modes of thought.
This was Giammaria Ortes (1713–1790). He is opposed to
the liberalist tendencies of his time, but does not espouse the
doctrines of the mercantile system, rejecting the theory of the
balance of trade, and demanding commercial freedom. It is
in the Middle Ages that he finds his social and economic
type. He advocates the maintenance of church property, is
averse to the ascendency of the money power, and has the
mediæval dislike for interest on loans. He entertains the
singular idea that the wealth of communities is always and
everywhere in a fixed ratio to their population, the latter being
determined by the former. Poverty, therefore, necessarily
waits on wealth, and the rich, in becoming so, only gain what
the poor lose. Those who are interested in the improvement of the condition of the people labour in vain, so long
as they direct their efforts to the increase of the sum
of the national wealth, which it is beyond their power
to alter, instead of to the distribution of that wealth, which
it is possible to modify. The true remedy for poverty lies
in mitigating the gain-pursuing propensities in the rich and
in men of business. Ortes studied in a separate work the
subject of population; he formulates its increase as "geo-

metrical," but recognises that, as a limit is set to such increase amongst the lower animals by mutual destruction, so is it in the human species by "reason"—the "prudential restraint" of which Malthus afterwards made so much. He regards the institution of celibacy as no less necessary and advantageous than that of marriage. He enunciates what has since been known as the "law of diminishing returns to agricultural industry." He was careless as to the diffusion of his writings; and hence they remained almost unknown till they were included in the Custodi collection of Italian economists, when they attracted much attention by the combined sagacity and waywardness which marked their author's intellectual character.

SPAIN.

The same breath of a new era which was in the air elsewhere in Europe made itself felt also in Spain.

In the earlier part of the eighteenth century Geronimo Ustariz had written his *Teorica y Practica del Comercio y Marina* (1724; published, 1740; Eng. transl. by John Kippax, 1751; French by Forbonnais, 1753), in which he carries mercantile principles to their utmost extreme.

The reforming spirit of the latter half of the century was best represented in that country by Pedro Rodriguez, Count of Campomanes (1723–1802). He pursued with ardour the same studies and in some degree the same policy as his illustrious contemporary Turgot, without, however, having arrived at so advanced a point of view. He was author of *Respuesta fiscal sobre abolir la tasa y establecer el comercio de granos* (1764), *Discurso sobre el fomento de industria popular* (1774), and *Discurso sobre la educacion de los artesanos y su fomento* (1775). By means of these writings, justly eulogised by Robertson,[1] as well as by his personal efforts as minister, he sought to establish the freedom of the corn trade, to remove the hindrances to industry arising from mediæval survivals,

---

[1] *History of America*, note 193.

to give a large development to manufactures, and to liberate agriculture from the odious burdens to which it was subject. He saw that, notwithstanding the enlightened administration of Charles III., Spain still suffered from the evil results of the blind confidence reposed by her people in her gold mines, and enforced the lesson that the real sources of the wealth and power of his country must be sought, not in America, but in her own industry.

In both Italy and Spain, as is well observed by Comte,[1] the impulse towards social change took principally the direction of economic reform, because the pressure exercised by Governments prevented so large a measure of free speculation in the fields of philosophy and general politics as was possible in France. In Italy, it may be added, the traditions of the great industrial past of the northern cities of that country also tended to fix attention chiefly on the economic side of public policy and legislation.

GERMANY.

We have seen that in Italy and England political economy had its beginnings in the study of practical questions relating chiefly to money or to foreign commerce. In Germany it arose (as Roscher has shown) out of the so-called cameralistic sciences. Soon after the close of the Middle Ages there existed in most German countries a council, known as the Kammer (Lat. *camera*), which was occupied with the management of the public domain and the guardianship of regal rights. The Emperor Maximilian found this institution existing in Burgundy, and established, in imitation of it, aulic councils at Innspruck and Vienna in 1498 and 1501. Not only finance and taxation, but questions also of economic police, came to be entrusted to these bodies. A special preparation became necessary for their members, and chairs of cameralistic science

---

[1] *Philosophie Positive*, vol. v. p. 759.

were founded in universities for the teaching of the appropriate body of doctrine. One side of the instruction thus given borrowed its materials from the sciences of external nature, dealing, as it did, with forestry, mining, general technology, and the like; the other related to the conditions of national prosperity as depending on human relations and institutions; and out of the latter, German political economy was at first developed.

In no country had mercantilist views a stronger hold than in Germany, though in none, in the period we are now considering, did the system of the balance of trade receive a less extensive practical application. All the leading German economists of the seventeenth century — Bornitz, Besold, Klock, Becher, Horneck, Seckendorf, and Schröder—stand on the common basis of the mercantile doctrine. And the same may be said of the writers of the first half of the eighteenth century in general, and notably of Justi (d. 1771), who was the author of the first systematic German treatise on political economy, a work which, from its currency as a text book, had much effect on the formation of opinion. Only in Zincke (1692–1769) do we find occasional expressions of a circle of ideas at variance with the dominant system, and pointing in the direction of industrial freedom. But these writers, except from the national point of view, are unimportant, not having exercised any influence on the general movement of European thought.

The principles of the physiocratic system met with a certain amount of favour in Germany. Karl Friedrich, Margrave of Baden, wrote for the use of his sons an *Abrégé des principes d'Économie Politique*, 1772, which is in harmony with the doctrines of that system. It possesses, however, little scientific value. Schlettwein (1731–1802) and Mauvillon (1743–1794) were followers of the same school. Theodor Schmalz (1764–1831), who is commonly named as "the last of the physiocrats," may be here mentioned, though somewhat out of the historic order. He compares Colbertism with the

Ptolemaic system, physiocratism with the Copernican. Adam Smith he represents as the Tycho Brahe of political economy, —a man of eminent powers, who could not resist the force of truth in the physiocrats, but partly could not divest himself of rooted prejudices, and partly was ambitious of the fame of a discoverer and a reconciler of divergent systems. Though Smith was now "the fashion," Schmalz could not doubt that Quesnay's doctrine was alone true, and would ere long be triumphant everywhere.

Just before the appearance of Smith, as in England Steuart, and in Italy Genovesi, so in Austria Sonnenfels (1733–1817), the first distinguished economist of that country, sought to present the mercantile system in a modified and more enlightened form ; and his work (*Grundsätze der Polizei, Handlung, und Finanz,* 1765 ; 8th ed., 1822), exercised even during a considerable part of the present century much influence on opinion and on policy in Austria.

But the greatest German economist of the eighteenth century was, in Roscher's opinion, Justus Möser (1720–1794), the author of *Patriotische Phantasieen* (1774), a series of fragments, which, Goethe nevertheless declares, form "ein wahrhaftes Ganzes." The poet was much influenced by Möser in his youth, and has eulogised in the *Dichtung und Wahrheit* (Bk. xiii.) his spirit, intellect, and character, and his thorough insight into all that goes on in the social world. Whilst others occupied themselves with larger and more prominent public affairs and transactions, Möser observed and reproduced the common daily life of his nation, and the thousand "little things" which compose the texture of popular existence. He has been compared to Franklin for the homeliness, verve, and freshness of his writings. In opinions he is akin to the Italian Ortes. He is opposed to the whole spirit of the "Aufklärung," and to the liberal and rationalistic direction of which Smith's work became afterwards the expression. He is not merely conservative but reactionary, manifesting a preference for mediæval institutions such as the trade guilds,

F

and, like Carlyle in our own time, seeing advantages even in
serfdom, when compared with the sort of freedom enjoyed
by the modern drudge. He has a marked antipathy for the
growth of the money power and of manufactures on the large
scale, and for the highly developed division of labour. He is
opposed to absolute private property in land, and would gladly
see revived such a system of restrictions as in the interest
of the state, the commune, and the family were imposed on
mediæval ownership. In his wayward and caustic style, he
often criticises effectively the doctrinaire narrowness of his
contemporaries, throws out many striking ideas, and in particular sheds real light on the economic phenomena and general
social conditions of the Middle Ages.

ADAM SMITH, WITH HIS IMMEDIATE PREDECESSORS AND HIS FOLLOWERS.

England.

The stagnation in economic inquiry which showed itself in
England in the early part of the eighteenth century was not
broken by any notable manifestation before 1735, when Bishop
Berkeley put forward in his *Querist*, with much force and
point, views opposed to those of the mercantile school on
the nature of national wealth and the functions of money,
though not without an admixture of grave error. But soon
a more decisive advance was made. Whilst in France the
physiocrats were working after their own fashion towards the
construction of a definitive system of political economy, a
Scottish thinker of the first order was elucidating, in a series
of short but pregnant essays, some of the fundamental conceptions of the science. What had been written on these
questions in the English language before his time had remained
almost altogether within the limits of the directly practical
sphere. With Locke, indeed, the general system of the modern
critical philosophy had come into relation with economic
inquiry, but only in a partial and indeterminate way. But

in Hume the most advanced form of this philosophy was represented, and his appearance in the field of economics decisively marks the tendency of the latter order of speculation to place itself in connection with the largest and deepest thought on human nature and general human history. Most of the essays here referred to first appeared in 1752, in a volume entitled *Political Discourses*, and the number was completed in the collection of *Essays and Treatises on Several Subjects*, published in the following year. The most important of them are those on Commerce, on Money, on Interest, and on the Balance of Trade. Yet these should not be separated from the rest, for, notwithstanding the unconnected form of these little treatises, there runs through them a profound unity of thought, so that they indeed compose in a certain sense an economic system. They exhibit in full measure Hume's wonderful acuteness and subtlety, which indeed sometimes dispose him to paradox, in combination with the breadth, the absence of prejudice, and the social sympathies which so eminently distinguish him; and they offer, besides, the charm of his easy and natural style and his rare power of lucid exposition.

In the essay on money he refutes the mercantilist error, which tended to confound it with wealth. "Men and commodities," he says, "are the real strength of any community." "In the national stock of labour consists all real power and riches." Money is only the oil which makes the movements of the mechanism of commerce more smooth and easy. He shows that, from the domestic as distinguished from the international point of view, the absolute quantity of money, supposed as of fixed amount, in a country is of no consequence, whilst an excessive quantity, larger, that is, than is required for the interchange of commodities, may be injurious as raising prices and driving foreigners from the home markets. He goes so far, in one or two places, as to assert that the value of money is chiefly fictitious or conventional, a position which cannot be defended; but it must not be pressed against him, as he builds nothing on it. He has some very ingenious observations (since, however, questioned by J. S. Mill) on the effects of the increase of money in a country in stimulating industry during the interval which takes place before the additional amount is sufficiently diffused to alter the whole scale of prices. He shows that the fear of the money of an industrious community being lost to it by passing into foreign countries is groundless, and that, under a system of freedom, the distribution of the precious metals which is adapted to the requirements of trade will spontaneously establish itself. " In short, a Government has great reason to preserve with care its people and its manufactures ; its money it may safely trust to the course of human affairs without fear or jealousy."

A very important service was rendered by his treatment of the rate of interest. He exposes the erroneous idea often entertained that it depends on the quantity of money in a country, and shows that the reduction of it must in general be the result of " the increase of industry and frugality, of arts and commerce," so that it may serve as a barometer, its lowness being an almost infallible sign of the flourishing condition of a people. It may be observed in passing that in the essay devoted to this subject he brings out a principle of human nature which economists too often overlook, " the constant and insatiable desire of the mind for exercise and employment," and the consequent action of *ennui* in prompting to exertion.

With respect to commerce, he points to its natural foundation in what has since been called "the territorial division of labour," and proves that the prosperity of one nation, instead of being a hindrance, is a help to that of its neighbours. " Not only as a man, but as a British subject," he says, " I pray for the flourishing commerce of Germany, Spain, Italy, and even France itself." He condemns the "numberless bars, obstructions, and imposts which all nations of Europe, and none more than England, have put upon trade." Yet on the question of protection to national industry he is not quite at

the free-trade point of view, for he approves of a tax on
German linen as encouraging home manufactures, and of a
tax on brandy as increasing the sale of rum and supporting
our southern colonies. Indeed it has been justly observed
that there are in him several traces of a refined mercantilism,
and that he represents a state of opinion in which the transition from the old to the new views is not yet completely
effected.

We cannot do more than refer to the essay on taxes, in
which, amongst other things, he repudiates the *impôt unique*
of the physiocrats, and to that on public credit, in which he
criticises the "new paradox that public encumbrances are
of themselves advantageous, independent of the necessity of
contracting them," and objects, perhaps too absolutely, to the
modern expedient of raising the money required for national
enterprises by way of loan, and so shifting our burdens upon
the shoulders of posterity.

The characteristics of Hume, which are most important in
the history of economic investigation, are (1) his practice of
bringing economic facts into connection with all the weighty
interests of social and political life, and (2) his tendency to
introduce the historical spirit into the study of those facts.
He admirably illustrates the mutual action of the several
branches of industry, and the influences of progress in the
arts of production and in commerce on general civilisation,
exhibits the striking contrasts of the ancient and modern
system of life (see especially the essay *On the Populousness
of Ancient Nations*), and considers almost every phenomenon
which comes under discussion in its relations to the contemporary stage of social development. It cannot be doubted
that Hume exercised a most important influence on Adam
Smith, who in the *Wealth of Nations* calls him "by far the
most illustrious philosopher and historian of the present age,"
and who esteemed his character so highly that, after a friend-
ship of many years had been terminated by Hume's decease,
he declared him to have "approached as nearly to the ideal

of a perfectly wise and virtuous man as perhaps the nature of human frailty will permit."

Josiah Tucker, dean of Gloucester (d. 1799), holds a distinguished place among the immediate predecessors of Smith. Most of his numerous productions had direct reference to contemporary questions, and, though marked by much sagacity and penetration, are deficient in permanent interest. In some of these he urged the impolicy of restrictions on the trade of Ireland, advocated a union of that country with England, and recommended the recognition of the independence of the United States of America. The most important of his general economic views are those relating to international commerce. He is an ardent supporter of free-trade doctrines, which he bases on the principles that there is between nations no necessary antagonism, but rather a harmony, of interests, and that their several local advantages and different aptitudes naturally prompt them to exchange. He had not, however, got quite clear of mercantilism, and favoured bounties on exported manufactures and the encouragement of population by a tax on celibacy. Dupont, and after him Blanqui, represent Tucker as a follower of the physiocrats, but there seems to be no ground for this opinion except his agreement with them on the subject of the freedom of trade. Turgot translated into French (1755), under the title of *Questions Importantes sur le Commerce*, a tract by Tucker on *The Expediency of a Law for the Naturalisation of Foreign Protestants*.

In 1767 was published Sir James Steuart's *Inquiry into the Principles of Political Economy*. This was one of the most unfortunate of books. It was the most complete and systematic survey of the science from the point of view of moderate mercantilism which had appeared in England. Steuart was a man of no ordinary abilities, and had prepared himself for his task by long and serious study. But the time for the mercantile doctrines was past, and the system of natural liberty was in possession of an intellectual ascendency which foreshadowed its political triumph. Nine years later the

Wealth of Nations was given to the world, a work as superior
to Steuart's in attractiveness of style as in scientific soundness.
Thus the latter was predestined to fail, and in fact never
exercised any considerable theoretic or practical influence.
Smith never quotes or mentions it; being acquainted with
Steuart, whose conversation he said was better than his book,
he probably wished to keep clear of controversy with him.[1]
The German economists have examined Steuart's treatise
more carefully than English writers have commonly done;
and they recognise its high merits, especially in relation to the
theory of value and the subject of population. They have
also pointed out that, in the spirit of the best recent research,
he has dwelt on the special characters which distinguish the
economies proper to different nations and different grades in
social progress.

Coming now to the great name of Adam Smith (1723–1790),
it is of the highest importance that we should rightly understand his position and justly estimate his claims. It is plainly
contrary to fact to represent him, as some have done, as the
creator of political economy. The subject of social wealth
had always in some degree, and increasingly in recent times,
engaged the attention of philosophic minds. The study had
even indisputably assumed a systematic character, and, from
being an assemblage of fragmentary disquisitions on particular
questions of national interest, had taken the form, notably
in Turgot's *Réflexions*, of an organised body of doctrine. The
truth is, that Smith took up the science when it was already
considerably advanced; and it was this very circumstance
which enabled him, by the production of a classical treatise,
to render most of his predecessors obsolete. But, whilst all
the economic labours of the preceding centuries prepared the
way for him, they did not anticipate his work. His appear-

---

[1] Smith says, in a letter to Pulteney (1772)—" I have the same opinion
of Sir James Steuart's book that you have. Without once mentioning
it, I flatter myself that any false principle in it will meet with a clear
and distinct confutation in mine."

ance at an earlier stage, or without those previous labours, would be inconceivable; but he built, on the foundation which had been laid by others, much of his own that was precious and enduring.

Even those who do not fall into the error of making Smith the creator of the science, often separate him too broadly from Quesnay and his followers, and represent the history of modern Economics as consisting of the successive rise and reign of three doctrines—the mercantile, the physiocratic, and the Smithian. The last two are, it is true, at variance in some even important respects. But it is evident, and Smith himself felt, that their agreements were much more fundamental than their differences; and, if we regard them as historical forces, they must be considered as working towards identical ends. They both urged society towards the abolition of the previously prevailing industrial policy of European Governments; and their arguments against that policy rested essentially on the same grounds. Whilst Smith's criticism was more searching and complete, he also analysed more correctly than the physiocrats some classes of economic phenomena,—in particular dispelling the illusions into which they had fallen with respect to the unproductive nature of manufactures and commerce. Their school disappeared from the scientific field, not merely because it met with a political check in the person of Turgot, but because, as we have already said, the *Wealth of Nations* absorbed into itself all that was valuable in their teaching, whilst it continued more effectually the impulse they had given to the necessary work of demolition.

The history of economic opinion in modern times, down to the third decade of our own century, is, in fact, strictly bipartite. The first stage is filled with the mercantile system, which, as we have shown, was rather a practical policy than a speculative doctrine, and which came into existence as the spontaneous growth of social conditions acting on minds not trained to scientific habits. The second stage is occupied with the gradual rise and ultimate ascendency of another system founded on the idea of the right of the individual to an unimpeded sphere for the exercise of his economic activity. With the latter, which is best designated as the "system of natural liberty," we ought to associate the memory of the physiocrats as well as that of Smith, without, however, maintaining their services to have been equal to his.

The teaching of political economy was in the Scottish universities associated with that of moral philosophy. Smith, as we are told, conceived the entire subject he had to treat in his public lectures as divisible into four heads, the first of which was natural theology, the second ethics, the third jurisprudence ; whilst in the fourth "he examined those political regulations which are founded upon expediency, and which are calculated to increase the riches, the power, and the prosperity of a state." The last two branches of inquiry are regarded as forming but a single body of doctrine in the well-known passage of the *Theory of Moral Sentiments* in which the author promises to give in another discourse "an account of the general principles of law and government, and of the different revolutions they have undergone in the different ages and periods of society, not only in what concerns justice, but in what concerns police, revenue, and arms, and whatever else is the subject of law." This shows how little it was Smith's habit to separate (except provisionally), in his conceptions or his researches, the economic phenomena of society from all the rest. The words above quoted have, indeed, been not unjustly described as containing " an anticipation, wonderful for his period, of general Sociology, both statical and dynamical, an anticipation which becomes still more remarkable when we learn from his literary executors that he had formed the plan of a connected history of the liberal sciences and elegant arts, which must have added to the branches of social study already enumerated a view of the intellectual progress of society." Though these large designs were never carried out in their integrity, as indeed at that period they could not have been adequately realised, it has resulted from them that, though economic phenomena form the special subject of the *Wealth of Nations*, Smith yet incorporated into that work much that relates to the other social aspects, incurring thereby the censure of some of his followers, who insist with pedantic narrowness on the strict isolation of the economic domain.

There has been much discussion on the question—What is the scientific method followed by Smith in his great work? By some it is considered to have been purely deductive, a view which Buckle has perhaps carried to the greatest extreme. He asserts that in Scotland the inductive method was unknown, that the inductive philosophy exercised no influence on Scottish thinkers; and, though Smith spent some of the most important years of his youth in England, where the inductive method was supreme, and though he was widely read in general philosophical literature, he yet thinks he adopted the deductive method because it was habitually followed in Scotland,—and this though Buckle maintains that it is the only appropriate, or even possible, method in political economy, which surely would have been a sufficient reason for choosing it. That the inductive spirit exercised no influence on Scottish philosophers is certainly not true; as will be presently shown, Montesquieu, whose method is essentially inductive, was in Smith's time studied with quite peculiar care and regarded with special veneration by Smith's fellow-countrymen. As to Smith himself, what may justly be said of him is that the deductive bent was certainly not the predominant character of his mind, nor did his great excellence lie in the "dialectic skill" which Buckle ascribes to him. What strikes us most in his book is his wide and keen observation of social facts, and his perpetual tendency to dwell on these and elicit their significance, instead of drawing conclusions from abstract principles by elaborate chains of reasoning. It is this habit of his mind which gives us, in reading him, so strong and abiding a sense of being in contact with the realities of life.

That Smith does, however, largely employ the deductive

method is certain ; and that method is quite legitimate when
the premises from which the deduction sets out are known
universal facts of human nature and properties of external
objects. Whether this mode of proceeding will carry us far
may indeed well be doubted ; but its soundness cannot be
disputed. But there is another vicious species of deduction
which, as Cliffe Leslie has shown, seriously tainted the
philosophy of Smith,—in which the premises are not facts
ascertained by observation, but the same *a priori* assumptions,
half theological half metaphysical, respecting a supposed
harmonious and beneficent natural order of things which
we found in the physiocrats, and which, as we saw, were
embodied in the name of that sect. In his view, Nature has
made provision for social wellbeing by the principle of the
human constitution which prompts every man to better his
condition : the individual aims only at his private gain, but
in doing so is "led by an invisible hand" to promote the
public good, which was no part of his intention ; human
institutions, by interfering with the action of this principle
in the name of the public interest, defeat their own end ; but,
when all systems of preference or restraint are taken away,
"the obvious and simple system of natural liberty establishes
itself of its own accord." This theory is, of course, not
explicitly presented by Smith as a foundation of his economic doctrines, but it is really the secret substratum on which
they rest. Yet, whilst such latent postulates warped his
view of things, they did not entirely determine his method.
His native bent towards the study of things as they are preserved him from extravagances into which many of his followers have fallen. But besides this, as Leslie has pointed
out, the influence of Montesquieu tended to counterbalance
the theoretic prepossessions produced by the doctrine of the
jus naturæ. That great thinker, though he could not, at his
period, understand the historical method which is truly appropriate to sociological inquiry, yet founded his conclusions
on induction. It is true, as Comte has remarked, that his

accumulation of facts, borrowed from the most different states of civilisation, and not subjected to philosophic criticism, necessarily remained on the whole sterile, or at least could not essentially advance the study of society much beyond the point at which he found it. His merit, as we have before mentioned, lay in the recognition of the subjection of all social phenomena to natural laws, not in the discovery of those laws. But this limitation was overlooked by the philosophers of the time of Smith, who were much attracted by the system he followed of tracing social facts to the special circumstances, physical or moral, of the communities in which they were observed. Leslie has shown that Lord Kaimes, Dalrymple, and Millar—contemporaries of Smith, and the last his pupil—were influenced by Montesquieu; and he might have added the more eminent name of Ferguson, whose respect and admiration for the great Frenchman are expressed in striking terms in his *History of Civil Society.*[1] We are even informed that Smith himself in his later years was occupied in preparing a commentary on the *Esprit des Lois.*[2]

[1] "When I recollect what the President Montesquieu has written, I am at a loss to tell why I should treat of human affairs; but I too am instigated by my reflections and my sentiments; and I may utter them more to the comprehension of ordinary capacities, because I am more on the level of ordinary men. . . . The reader should be referred to what has been already delivered on the subject by this profound politician and amiable moralist " (Part I. sect. 10). Hume speaks of Montesquieu as an "illustrious writer," who "has established . . . a system of political knowledge, which abounds in ingenious and brilliant thoughts and is not wanting in solidity " (*Principles of Morals*, sect. 3, and note).

[2] The following paragraph appeared in the *Moniteur Universel* of March 11, 1790 :—"On prétend que le célèbre M. Smith, connu si avantageusement par son traité des causes de la richesse des nations, prépare et va mettre à l'impression un examen critique de l'Esprit des Lois ; c'est le résultat de plusieurs années de méditation, et l'on sait assez ce qu'on a droit d'attendre d'une tête comme celle de M. Smith. Ce livre fera époque dans l'histoire de la politique et de la philosophie ; tel est du moins le jugement qu'en portent des gens instruits qui en connaissent des fragments dont ils ne parlent qu'avec un enthousiasme du plus heureux augure."

He was thus affected by two different and incongruous systems of thought,—one setting out from an imaginary code of nature intended for the benefit of man, and leading to an optimistic view of the economic constitution founded on enlightened self-interest ; the other following inductive processes, and seeking to explain the several states in which human societies are found existing, as results of circumstances or institutions which have been in actual operation.   And we find accordingly in his great work a combination of these two modes of treatment—inductive inquiry on the one hand, and, on the other, *a priori* speculation founded on the " Nature " hypothesis. The latter vicious proceeding has in some of his followers been greatly aggravated, while the countervailing spirit of inductive investigation has fallen into the background, and indeed the necessity or utility of any such investigation in the economic field has been sometimes altogether denied.

Some have represented Smith's work as of so loose a texture and so defective in arrangement that it may be justly described as consisting of a series of monographs.   But this is certainly an exaggeration.   The book, it is true, is not framed on a rigid mould, nor is there any parade of systematic divisions and subdivisions ; and this doubtless recommended it to men of the world and of business, for whose instruction it was, at least primarily, intended.   But, as a body of exposition, it has the real and pervading unity which results from a mode of thinking homogeneous throughout and the general absence of such contradictions as would arise from an imperfect digestion of the subject.

Smith sets out from the thought that the annual labour of a nation is the source from which it derives its supply of the necessaries and conveniences of life.   He does not of course contemplate labour as the only factor in production ; but it has been supposed that by emphasising it at the outset he at once strikes the note of difference between himself on the one hand and both the mercantilists and the physiocrats on the other.   The improvement in the productiveness of labour

depends largely on its division; and he proceeds accordingly
to give his unrivalled exposition of that principle, of the
grounds on which it rests, and of its greater applicability to
manufactures than to agriculture, in consequence of which the
latter relatively lags behind in the course of economic development.[1] The origin of the division of labour he finds in the
propensity of human nature "to truck, barter, or exchange
one thing for another." He shows that a certain accumulation
of capital is a condition precedent of this division, and that
the degree to which it can be carried is dependent on the
extent of the market. When the division of labour has been
established, each member of the society must have recourse
to the others for the supply of most of his wants; a medium
of exchange is thus found to be necessary, and money comes
into use. The exchange of goods against each other or against
money gives rise to the notion of value. This word has two
meanings—that of utility, and that of purchasing power; the
one may be called value in use, the other value in exchange.
Merely mentioning the former, Smith goes on to study the
latter. What, he asks, is the measure of value? what regulates the amount of one thing which will be given for another?
"Labour," Smith answers, "is the real measure of the ex-
changeable value of all commodities." "Equal quantities
of labour, at all times and places, are of equal value to the
labourer."[2] "Labour alone, therefore, never varying in its
own value, is alone the ultimate and real standard by which
the value of all commodities can at all times and places be
estimated and compared. It is their real price; money is
their nominal price only." Money, however, is in men's
actual transactions the measure of value, as well as the vehicle

[1] Smith takes no account in this place of the *evils* which may arise
from a highly developed division of labour. But see Bk. v. chap. i.

[2] This sentence, which on close examination will be found to have no
definite intelligible sense, affords a good example of the way in which
metaphysical modes of thought obscure economic ideas. What is a
"quantity of labour," the kind of labour being undetermined? And
what is meant by the phrase "of equal value"?

of exchange; and the precious metals are best suited for this
function, as varying little in their own value for periods of
moderate length; for distant times, corn is a better standard
of comparison. In relation to the earliest social stage, we
need consider nothing but the amount of labour employed in
the production of an article as determining its exchange value;
but in more advanced periods price is complex, and consists
in the most general case of three elements—wages, profit, and
rent. Wages are the reward of labour. Profit arises as soon
as stock, being accumulated in the hands of one person, is
employed by him in setting others to work, and supplying
them with materials and subsistence, in order to make a gain
by what they produce. Rent arises as soon as the land of a
country has all become private property; " the landlords, like
all other men, love to reap where they never sowed, and demand a rent even for its natural produce." In every improved
society, then, these three elements enter more or less into the
price of the far greater part of commodities. There is in every
society or neighbourhood an ordinary or average rate of wages
and profit in every different employment of labour and stock,
regulated by principles to be explained hereafter, as also an
ordinary or average rate of rent. These may be called the
natural rates at the time when and the place where they prevail; and the natural price of a commodity is what is sufficient
to pay for the rent of the land,[1] the wages of the labour, and
the profit of the stock necessary for bringing the commodity
to market. The market price may rise above or fall below
the amount so fixed, being determined by the proportion
between the quantity brought to market and the demand of
those who are willing to pay the natural price. Towards the
natural price as a centre the market price, regulated by competition, constantly gravitates. Some commodities, however,
are subject to a monopoly of production, whether from the
peculiarities of a locality or from legal privilege : their price

---

[1] Smith's expressions on this point are lax, as will be seen when we
come to examine the (so-called) Ricardian Theory of Rent.

is always the highest that can be got; the natural price of
other commodities is the lowest which can be taken for any
length of time together. The three component parts or factors
of price vary with the circumstances of the society. The rate
of wages is determined by a " dispute " or struggle of opposite
interests between the employer and the workman. A minimum
rate is fixed by the condition that they must be at least sufficient to enable a man and his wife to maintain themselves
and, in general, bring up a family. The excess above this
will depend on the circumstances of the country, and the consequent demand for labour,—wages being high when national
wealth is increasing, low when it is declining. The same
circumstances determine the variation of profits, but in an
opposite direction; the increase of stock, which raises wages,
tending to lower profit through the mutual competition of
capitalists. " The whole of the advantages and disadvantages
of the different employments of labour and stock must, in the
same neighbourhood, be either perfectly equal or continually
tending to equality;" if one had greatly the advantage over
the others, people would crowd into it, and the level would
soon be restored. Yet pecuniary wages and profits are very
different in different employments,—either from certain circumstances affecting the employments, which recommend or
disparage them in men's notions, or from national policy,
"which nowhere leaves things at perfect liberty." Here
follows Smith's admirable exposition of the causes which produce the inequalities in wages and profits just referred to, a
passage affording ample evidence of his habits of nice observation of the less obvious traits in human nature, and also of
the operation both of these and of social institutions on economic facts. The rent of land comes next to be considered,
as the last of the three elements of price. Rent is a monopoly price, equal, not to what the landlord could afford to take,
but to what the farmer can afford to give. " Such parts only
of the produce of land can commonly be brought to market,
of which the ordinary price is sufficient to replace the stock

which must be employed in bringing them thither, together with the ordinary profits. If the ordinary price is more than this, the surplus part will naturally go to the rent of the land. If it is not more, though the commodity may be brought to market, it can afford no rent to the landlord. Whether the price is or is not more depends on the demand." "Rent, therefore, enters into the price of commodities in a different way from wages and profits. High or low wages and profit are the causes of high or low price; high or low rent is the effect of it."

Rent, wages, and profits, as they are the elements of price, are also the constituents of income; and the three great orders of every civilised society, from whose revenues that of every other order is ultimately derived, are the landlords, the labourers, and the capitalists. The relation of the interests of these three classes to those of society at large is different. The interest of the landlord always coincides with the general interest: whatever promotes or obstructs the one has the same effect on the other. So also does that of the labourer: when the wealth of the nation is progressive, his wages are high; they are low when it is stationary or retrogressive. "The interest of the third order has not the same connection with the general interest of the society as that of the other two; . . . it is always in some respects different from and opposite to that of the public."

The subject of the second book is "the nature, accumulation, and improvement of stock." A man's whole stock consists of two portions—that which is reserved for his immediate consumption, and that which is employed so as to yield a revenue to its owner. This latter, which is his "capital," is divisible into the two classes of "fixed" and "circulating." The first is such as yields a profit without passing into other hands. The second consists of such goods, raised, manufactured, or purchased, as are sold for a profit and replaced by other goods; this sort of capital is therefore constantly going from and returning to the hands of its owner. The whole capital of a society falls under the same two heads. Its fixed capital consists chiefly of (1) machines, (2) buildings which are the means of procuring a revenue, (3) agricultural improvements, and (4) the acquired and useful abilities of all members of the society (since sometimes known as "personal capital "). Its circulating capital is also composed of four parts—(1) money, (2) provisions in the hands of the dealers, (3) materials, and (4) completed work in the hands of the manufacturer or merchant. Next comes the distinction of the gross national revenue from the net,—the first being the whole produce of the land and labour of a country, the second what remains after deducting the expense of maintaining the fixed capital of the country and that part of its circulating capital which consists of money. Money, "the great wheel of circulation," is altogether different from the goods which are circulated by means of it ; it is a costly instrument by means of which all that each individual receives is distributed to him ; and the expenditure required, first to provide it, and afterwards to maintain it, is a deduction from the net revenue of the society. In development of this consideration, Smith goes on to explain the gain to the community arising from the substitution of paper money for that composed of the precious metals ; and here occurs the remarkable illustration in which the use of gold and silver money is compared to a highway on the ground, that of paper money to a waggon-way through the air. In proceeding to consider the accumulation of capital, he is led to the distinction between productive and unproductive labour, —the former being that which is fixed or realised in a particular object or vendible article, the latter that which is not so realised. The former is exemplified in the labour of the manufacturing workman, the latter in that of the menial servant. A broad line of demarcation is thus drawn between the labour which results in commodities or increased value of commodities, and that which does no more than render services : the former is productive, the latter unproductive. " Productive " is by no means equivalent to "useful :" the labours of the magistrate, the soldier, the churchman, lawyer, and physician are, in Smith's sense, unproductive. Productive labourers alone are employed out of capital; unproductive labourers, as well as those who do not labour at all, are all maintained by revenue. In advancing industrial communities, the portion of annual produce set apart as capital bears an increasing proportion to that which is immediately destined to constitute a revenue, either as rent or as profit. Parsimony is the source of the increase of capital; by augmenting the fund devoted to the maintenance of productive hands, it puts in motion an additional quantity of industry, which adds to the value of the annual produce. What is annually saved is as regularly consumed as what is spent, but by a different set of persons, by productive labourers instead of idlers or unproductive labourers; and the former reproduce with a profit the value of their consumption. The prodigal, encroaching on his capital, diminishes, as far as in him lies, the amount of productive labour, and so the wealth of the country; nor is this result affected by his expenditure being on home-made, as distinct from foreign, commodities. Every prodigal, therefore, is a public enemy; every frugal man a public benefactor. The only mode of increasing the annual produce of the land and labour is to increase either the number of productive labourers or the productive powers of those labourers. Either process will in general require additional capital, the former to maintain the new labourers, the latter to provide improved machinery or to enable the employer to introduce a more complete division of labour. In what are commonly called loans of money, it is not really the money, but the money's worth, that the borrower wants; and the lender really assigns to him the right to a certain portion of the annual produce of the land and labour of the country. As the general capital of a country increases, so also does the particular portion of it from which the possessors wish to derive a revenue without being at the trouble of employing it themselves; and, as the quantity of stock thus available for loans is augmented, the

interest diminishes, not merely " from the general causes which
make the market price of things commonly diminish as their
quantity increases," but because, with the increase of capital,
" it becomes gradually more and more difficult to find within
the country a profitable method of employing any new capital,"
—whence arises a competition between different capitals, and
a lowering of profits, which must diminish the price which
can be paid for the use of capital, or in other words the rate
of interest.   It was formerly wrongly supposed, and even Locke
and Montesquieu did not escape this error, that the fall in the
value of the precious metals consequent on the discovery of
the American mines was the real cause of the permanent lowering of the rate of interest in Europe.   But this view, already
refuted by Hume, is easily seen to be erroneous.   " In some
countries the interest of money has been prohibited by law.
But, as something can everywhere be made by the use of
money, something ought everywhere to be paid for the use of
it," and will in fact be paid for it; and the prohibition will
only heighten the evil of usury by increasing the risk to the
lender.   The legal rate should be a very little above the lowest
market rate ; sober people will then be preferred as borrowers
to prodigals and projectors, who at a higher legal rate would
have an advantage over them, being alone willing to offer that
higher rate.[1]

As to the different employments of capital, the quantity of
productive labour put in motion by an equal amount varies
extremely according as that amount is employed—(1) in the
improvement of lands, mines, or fisheries, (2) in manufactures,
(3) in wholesale or (4) retail trade.   In agriculture " Nature
labours along with man," and not only the capital of the
farmer is reproduced with his profits, but also the rent of the
landlord.   It is therefore the employment of a given capital
which is most advantageous to society.   Next in order come
manufactures ; then wholesale trade—first the home trade,

---

[1] See p. 110, on Bentham.

secondly the foreign trade of consumption, last the carrying trade. All these employments of capital, however, are not only advantageous, but necessary, and will introduce themselves in the due degree, if they are left to the spontaneous action of individual enterprise.

These first two books contain Smith's general economic scheme; and we have stated it as fully as was consistent with the necessary brevity, because from this formulation of doctrine the English classical school set out, and round it the discussions of more recent times in different countries have in a great measure revolved. Some of the criticisms of his successors and their modifications of his doctrines will come under our notice as we proceed.

The critical philosophers of the eighteenth century were often destitute of the historical spirit, which was no part of the endowment needed for their principal social office. But some of the most eminent of them, especially in Scotland, showed a marked capacity and predilection for historical studies. Smith was amongst the latter; Knies and others justly remark on the masterly sketches of this kind which occur in the *Wealth of Nations*. The longest and most elaborate of these occupies the third book; it is an account of the course followed by the nations of modern Europe in the successive development of the several forms of industry. It affords a curious example of the effect of doctrinal prepossessions in obscuring the results of historical inquiry. Whilst he correctly describes the European movement of industry, and explains it as arising out of adequate social causes, he yet, in accordance with the absolute principles which tainted his philosophy, protests against it as involving an entire inversion of the "natural order of things." First agriculture, then manufactures, lastly foreign commerce; any other order than this he considers "unnatural and retrograde." Hume, a more purely positive thinker, simply sees the facts, accepts them, and classes them under a general law. "It is a violent method," he says, "and in most cases impracticable, to oblige the labourer to toil in

order to raise from the land more than what subsists himself
and family. Furnish him with manufactures and commodities,
and he will do it of himself." "If we consult history, we
shall find that, in most nations, foreign trade has preceded any
refinement in home manufactures, and given birth to domestic
luxury."

The fourth book is principally devoted to the elaborate
and exhaustive polemic against the mercantile system which
finally drove it from the field of science, and has exercised a
powerful influence on economic legislation.   When protection
is now advocated, it is commonly on different grounds from
those which were in current use before the time of Smith.
He believed that to look for the restoration of freedom of
foreign trade in Great Britain would have been "as absurd
as to expect that an Oceana or Utopia should be established
in it;" yet, mainly in consequence of his labours, that object
has been completely attained; and it has lately been said
with justice that free trade might have been more generally
accepted by other nations if the patient reasoning of Smith
had not been replaced by dogmatism. His teaching on the
subject is not altogether unqualified; but, on the whole,
with respect to exchanges of every kind, where economic
motives alone enter, his voice is in favour of freedom.   He
has regard, however, to political as well as economic interests,
and on the ground that "defence is of much more importance
than opulence," pronounces the Navigation Act to have been
"perhaps the wisest of all the commercial regulations of
England." Whilst objecting to the prevention of the export
of wool, he proposes a tax on that export as somewhat less
injurious to the interest of growers than the prohibition,
whilst it would "afford a sufficient advantage" to the domestic
over the foreign manufacturer. This is, perhaps, his most
marked deviation from the rigour of principle; it was doubtless a concession to popular opinion with a view to an attain-
able practical improvement. The wisdom of retaliation in
order to procure the repeal of high duties or prohibitions

imposed by foreign Governments depends, he says, altogether
on the likelihood of its success in effecting the object aimed
at, but he does not conceal his contempt for the practice of
such expedients. The restoration of freedom in any manufacture, when it has grown to considerable dimensions by
means of high duties, should, he thinks, from motives of
humanity, be brought about only by degrees and with cir-
cumspection,—though the amount of evil which would be
caused by the immediate abolition of the duties is, in his
opinion, commonly exaggerated. The case in which J. S.
Mill would tolerate protection—that, namely, in which an industry well adapted to a country is kept down by the acquired
ascendency of foreign producers—is referred to by Smith ;
but he is opposed to the admission of this exception for
reasons which do not appear to be conclusive.[1] He is perhaps
scarcely consistent in approving the concession of temporary monopolies to joint-stock companies undertaking risky
enterprises " of which the public is afterwards to reap the
benefit."[2]

He is less absolute in his doctrine of Governmental non-
interference when he comes to consider in his fifth book
the " expenses of the sovereign or the commonwealth." He
recognises as coming within the functions of the state the
erection and maintenance of those public institutions and
public works which, though advantageous to the society,
could not repay, and therefore must not be thrown upon,

---

[1] It must, however, always be borne in mind that the adoption by a state
of this sort of protection is liable to three practical dangers :—(1) of encouragement being procured through political influences for industries
which could never have an independent healthy life in the country ; (2) of
such encouragement being continued beyond the term during which it
might be usefully given ; (3) of a retaliatory spirit of exclusion being
provoked in other communities.

[2] Professor Bastable calls the author's attention to the interesting
fact that the proposal of an export duty on wool and the justification
of a temporary monopoly to joint-stock companies both appear for the
first time in the edition of 1784.

individuals or small groups of individuals. He remarks in a
just historical spirit that the performance of these functions
requires very different degrees of expense in the different
periods of society. Besides the institutions and works intended for public defence and the administration of justice,
and those required for facilitating the commerce of the society,
he considers those necessary for promoting the instruction of
the people. He thinks the public at large may with propriety
not only facilitate and encourage, but even impose upon
almost the whole body of the people, the acquisition in youth
of the most essential elements of education. He suggests
as the mode of enforcing this obligation the requirement
of submission to a test examination " before any one could
obtain the freedom in any corporation, or be allowed to set
up a trade in any village or town corporate." Similarly, he
is of opinion that some probation, even in the higher and
more difficult sciences, might be enforced as a condition of
exercising any liberal profession, or becoming a candidate for
any honourable office. The expense of the institutions for
religious instruction as well as for general education, he holds,
may without injustice be defrayed out of the funds of the whole
society, though he would apparently prefer that it should be
met by the voluntary contributions of those who think they
have occasion for such education or instruction. There is
much that is sound, as well as interesting and suggestive, in
this fifth book, in which he shows a political instinct and a
breadth of view by which he is favourably contrasted with the
Manchester school. But, if we may say so without disrespect
to so great a man, there are traces in it of what is now
called Philistinism—a low view of the ends of art and poetry
—which arose perhaps in part from personal defect, though
it was common enough in even the higher minds in his
century. There are also indications of a certain deadness to
the lofty aims and perennial importance of religion, which
was no doubt chiefly due to the influences of an age when
the critical spirit was doing an indispensable work, in the

performance of which the transitory was apt to be confounded with the permanent.

For the sake of considering as a whole Smith's view of the functions of government, we have postponed noticing his treatment of the physiocratic system, which occupies a part of his fourth book. He had formed the acquaintance of Quesnay, Turgot, and other members of their group during his sojourn in France in 1765, and would, as he told Dugald Stewart, had the patriarch of the school lived long enough, have dedicated to him the *Wealth of Nations*. He declares that, with all its imperfections, the system of Quesnay is "perhaps the nearest approximation to the truth that had yet appeared on the subject of political economy." Yet he seems not to be adequately conscious of the degree of coincidence between his own doctrines and those of the physiocrats. Dupont de Nemours complained that he did not do Quesnay the justice of recognising him as his spiritual father. It is, however, alleged, on the other side, that already in 1753 Smith had been teaching as professor a body of economic doctrine the same in its broad features with that contained in his great work. This is indeed said by Stewart; and, though he gives no evidence of it, it is possibly quite true; if so, Smith's doctrinal descent must be traced rather from Hume than from the French school. The principal error of this school, that, namely, of representing agricultural labour as alone productive, he refutes in the fourth book, though in a manner which has not always been considered effective. Traces of the influence of their mistaken view appear to remain in his own work, as, for example, his assertion that in agriculture nature labours along with man, whilst in manufactures nature does nothing, man does all; and his distinction between productive and unproductive labour, which was doubtless suggested by their use of those epithets, and which is scarcely consistent with his recognition of what is now called "personal capital." To the same source M'Culloch and others refer the origin of Smith's view, which they represent as an obvious error, that "individual advantage is not always a true test of the public advantageousness of different employments." But that view is really quite correct, as Professor Nicholson has clearly shown.[1] That the form taken by the use of capital, profits being given, is not indifferent to the working class as a whole even Ricardo admitted; and Cairnes, as we shall see, built on this consideration some of the most far-reaching conclusions in his *Leading Principles.*

On Smith's theory of taxation in his fifth book it is not necessary for us to dwell. The well-known canons which he lays down as prescribing the essentials of a good system have been generally accepted. They have lately been severely criticised by Professor Walker—of whose objections, however, there is only one which appears to be well founded. Smith seems to favour the view that the contribution of the individual to public expenses may be regarded as payment for the services rendered to him by the state, and ought to be proportional to the extent of those services. If he held this opinion, which some of his expressions imply, he was certainly so far wrong in principle.

We shall not be held to anticipate unduly if we remark here on the way in which opinion, revolted by the aberrations of some of Smith's successors, has tended to turn from the disciples to the master. A strong sense of his comparative freedom from the vicious tendencies of Ricardo and his followers has recently prompted the suggestion that we ought now to recur to Smith, and take up once more from him the line of the economical succession. But notwithstanding his indisputable superiority, and whilst fully recognising the great services rendered by his immortal work, we must not forget that, as has been already said, that work was, on the whole, a product, though an exceptionally eminent one, of the negative philosophy of the last century, resting largely in its ultimate foundation on metaphysical bases. The mind of Smith was mainly occupied with the work of criticism so urgent in his

[1] In the *Introductory Essay* to his edition of the *Wealth of Nations.*

time ; his principal task was to discredit and overthrow the
economic system then prevalent, and to demonstrate the
radical unfitness of the existing European Governments to
direct the industrial movement. This office of his fell in
with, and formed a part of, the general work of demolition
carried on by the thinkers who gave to the eighteenth century
its characteristic tone.   It is to his honour that, besides this
destructive operation, he contributed valuable elements to the
preparation of an organic system of thought and of life.   In his
special domain he has not merely extinguished many errors
and prejudices, and cleared the ground for truth, but has left
us a permanent possession in the judicious analyses of economic
facts and ideas, the wise practical suggestions, and the luminous
indications of all kinds with which his work abounds.   Belonging to the best philosophical school of his period, that
with which the names of Hume and Diderot are associated,
he tended strongly towards the positive point of view.   But
it was not possible for him to attain it ; and the final and
fully normal treatment of the economic life of societies must
be constituted on other and more lasting foundations than
those which underlie his imposing construction.

It has been well said that of philosophic doctrines the saying
" By their fruits ye shall know them " is eminently true.   And
it cannot be doubted that the germs of the vicious methods
and false or exaggerated theories of Smith's successors are to
be found in his own work, though his good sense and practical
bent prevented his following out his principles to their extreme
consequences.   The objections of Hildebrand and others to
the entire historical development of doctrine which the Germans
designate as " Smithianismus " are regarded by those critics
as applicable, not merely to his school as a whole, but, though
in a less degree, to himself.   The following are the most
important of these objections.   It is said—(1.) Smith's conception of the social economy is essentially individualistic.
In this he falls in with the general character of the negative
philosophy of his age.   That philosophy, in its most typical

forms, even denied the natural existence of the disinterested
affections, and explained the altruistic feelings as secondary
results of self-love. Smith, however, like Hume, rejected
these extreme views ; and hence it has been held that in the
Wealth of Nations he consciously, though tacitly, abstracted
from the benevolent principles in human nature, and as a
logical artifice supposed an " economic man " actuated by purely
selfish motives. However this may be, he certainly places
himself habitually at the point of view of the individual, whom
he treats as a purely egoistic force, working uniformly in the
direction of private gain, without regard to the good of others
or of the community at large. (2.) He justifies this personal
attitude by its consequences, presenting the optimistic view
that the good of the community is best attained through
the free-play of individual cupidities, provided only that the
law prevents the interference of one member of the society
with the self-seeking action of another. He assumes with
the negative school at large—though he has passages which
are not in harmony with these propositions—that every one
knows his true interest and will pursue it, and that the
economic advantage of the individual coincides with that of
the society. To this last conclusion he is secretly led, as we
have seen, by *a priori* theological ideas, and also by metaphysical conceptions of a supposed system of nature, natural
right, and natural liberty. (3.) By this reduction of every
question to one of individual gain, he is led to a too exclusive
consideration of exchange value as distinct from wealth in
the proper sense. This, whilst lending a mechanical facility
in arriving at conclusions, gives a superficial character to
economic investigation, divorcing it from the physical and
biological sciences, excluding the question of real social
utility, leaving no room for a criticism of production, and
leading to a denial, like J. S. Mill's, of any economic doctrine
dealing with consumption—in other words, with the use of
wealth. (4.) In condemning the existing industrial policy,
he tends too much towards a glorification of non-government

and a repudiation of all social intervention for the regulation of economic life. (5.) He does not keep in view the moral destination of our race, nor regard wealth as a means to the higher ends of life, and thus incurs, not altogether unjustly, the charge of materialism, in the wider sense of that word. Lastly, (6.) his whole system is too absolute in its character; it does not sufficiently recognise the fact that, in the language of Hildebrand, man, as a member of society, is a child of civilisation and a product of history, and that account ought to be taken of the different stages of social development as implying altered economic conditions and calling for altered economic action, or even involving a modification of the actor. Perhaps in all the respects here enumerated, certainly in some of them, and notably in the last, Smith is less open to criticism than most of the later English economists; but it must, we think, be admitted that to the general principles which lie at the basis of his scheme the ultimate growth of these several vicious tendencies is traceable.

Great expectations had been entertained respecting Smith's work by competent judges before its publication, as is shown by the language of Ferguson on the subject in his *History of Civil Society*.[1] That its merits received prompt recognition is proved by the fact of six editions having been called for within the fifteen years after its appearance.[2] From the year

[1] " The public will probably soon be furnished with a theory of national œconomy, equal to what has ever appeared on any subject of science whatever " (Part III. sect. 4).

[2] Five editions of the *Wealth of Nations* appeared during the life of the author :—the second in 1779, the third in 1784, the fourth in 1786, and the fifth in 1789. After the third edition Smith made no change in the text. The principal editions containing matter added by other economists are those by William Playfair, with notes, 1805 ; by David Buchanan, with notes, 1814 ; by J. R. M'Culloch, with life of the author, introductory discourse, notes, and supplemental dissertations, 1828 (also, with numerous additions, 1839 ; since reprinted several times with further additions) ; by the author of *England and America* (Edward Gibbon Wakefield), with a commentary, which, however, is not continued beyond the second book, 1835-9 ; by James E. Thorold Rogers, Professor of

1783 it was more and more quoted in Parliament. Pitt was greatly impressed by its reasonings ; Smith is reported to have said that that Minister understood the book as well as himself. Pulteney said in 1797 that Smith would persuade the then living generation and would govern the next.[1]

Smith's earliest critics were Bentham and Lauderdale, who, though in general agreement with him, differed on special points. Jeremy Bentham was author of a short treatise entitled *A Manual of Political Economy* and various economic monographs, the most celebrated of which was his *Defence of Usury* (1787). This contained (Letter xiii.) an elaborate criticism of a passage in the *Wealth of Nations*, already cited, in which Smith had approved of a legal maximum rate of interest fixed but a very little above the lowest market rate, as tending to throw the capital of the country into the hands of sober persons, as opposed to "prodigals and projectors." Smith is said to have admitted that Bentham had made out his case. He certainly argues it with great ability ;[2] and the true doctrine no doubt is that, in a developed industrial society, it is expedient to let the rate be fixed by contract between the lender and the borrower, the law interfering only in case of fraud.

Bentham's main significance does not belong to the economic field. But, on the one hand, what is known as Benthamism was undoubtedly, as Comte has said,[3] a derivative from political economy, and in particular from the system of natural

political economy at Oxford, with biographical preface and a careful verification of all Smith's quotations and references, 1869 (2d ed., 1880) ; and by J. S. Nicholson, professor at Edinburgh, with notes referring to sources of further information on the various topics handled in the text, 1884. There is a careful *Abridgment* by W. P. Emerton (2d ed., 1881), founded on the earlier *Analysis* of Jeremiah Joyce (3d ed., 1821).

[1] *Parl. Hist.*, vol. xxxiii. p. 778.

[2] It must be remembered, however, that the same doctrine had been supported with no less ability as early as 1769 by Turgot in his *Mémoire sur les prêts d'argent*.

[3] *Lettres d' A. Comte à J. S. Mill*, p. 4.

liberty; and, on the other, it promoted the temporary ascendency of that system by extending to the whole of social and moral theory the use of the principle of individual interest and the method of deduction from that interest. This alliance between political economy and the scheme of Bentham is seen in the personal group of thinkers which formed itself round him,—thinkers most inaptly characterised by J. S. Mill as " profound," but certainly possessed of much acuteness and logical power, and tending, though vaguely, towards a positive sociology, which, from their want of genuinely scientific culture and their absolute modes of thought, they were incapable of founding.

Lord Lauderdale, in his *Inquiry into the Nature and Origin of Public Wealth* (1804), a book still worth reading, pointed out certain real weaknesses in Smith's account of value and the measure of value, and of the productivity of labour, and threw additional light on several subjects, such as the true mode of estimating the national income, and the reaction of the distribution of wealth on its production.

Smith stood just at the beginning of a great industrial revolution. The world of production and commerce in which he lived was still, as Cliffe Leslie has said, a " very early " and comparatively narrow one; " the only steam-engine he refers to is Newcomen's," and the cotton trade is mentioned by him only once, and that incidentally. " Between the years 1760 and 1770," says Mr. Marshall, " Roebuck began to smelt iron by coal, Brindley connected the rising seats of manufactures with the sea by canals, Wedgwood discovered the art of making earthenware cheaply and well, Hargreaves invented the spinning-jenny, Arkwright utilised Wyatt's and High's inventions for spinning by rollers and applied water-power to move them, and Watt invented the condensing steam-engine. Crompton's mule and Cartwright's power-loom came shortly after." Out of this rapid evolution followed a vast expansion of industry, but also many deplorable results, which, had Smith been able to foresee them, might have made him a less enthusiastic believer in the benefits to be wrought by the mere liberation of effort, and a less vehement denouncer of old institutions which in their day had given a partial protection to labour. Alongside of these evils of the new industrial system, Socialism appeared as the alike inevitable and indispensable expression of the protest of the working classes and the aspiration after a better order of things ; and what we now call " the social question," that inexorable problem of modern life, rose into the place which it has ever since maintained. This question was first effectually brought before the English mind by Thomas Robert Malthus (1766–1834), not, however, under the impulse of revolutionary sympathies, but in the interests of a conservative policy.

The first edition of the work which achieved this result appeared anonymously in 1798 under the title—*An Essay on the Principle of Population, as it affects the future improvement of Society, with remarks on the speculations of Mr. Godwin, M. Condorcet, and other writers.* This book arose out of certain private controversies of its author with his father, Daniel Malthus, who had been a friend of Rousseau, and was an ardent believer in the doctrine of human progress as preached by Condorcet and other French thinkers and by their English disciples. The most distinguished of the latter was William Godwin, whose *Enquiry concerning Political Justice* had been published in 1793. The views put forward in that work had been restated by its author in the *Enquirer* (1797), and it was on the essay in this volume entitled " Avarice and Profusion " that the discussion between the father and the son arose, " the general question of the future improvement of society " being thus raised between them— the elder Malthus defending the doctrines of Godwin, and the younger assailing them. The latter " sat down with an intention of merely stating his thoughts on paper in a clearer manner than he thought he could do in conversation," and the *Essay* on population was the result.

The social scheme of Godwin was founded on the idea that

the evils of society arise from the vices of human institutions. There is more than enough of wealth available for all, but it is not equally shared : one has too much, another has little or nothing. Let this wealth, as well as the labour of producing it, be equally divided ; then every one will by moderate exertion obtain sufficient for plain living ; there will be abundant leisure, which will be spent in intellectual and moral self-improvement ; reason will determine human actions; government and every kind of force will be unnecessary ; and, in time, by the peaceful influence of truth, perfection and happiness will be established on earth. To these glowing anticipations Malthus opposes the facts of the necessity of food and the tendency of mankind to increase up to the limit of the available supply of it. In a state of universal physical wellbeing, this tendency, which in real life is held in check by the difficulty of procuring a subsistence, would operate without restraint. Scarcity would follow the increase of numbers ; the leisure would soon cease to exist ; the old struggle for life would recommence ; and inequality would reign once more. If Godwin's ideal system, therefore, could be established, the single force of the principle of population, Malthus maintained, would suffice to break it down.

It will be seen that the essay was written with a polemical object ; it was an occasional pamphlet directed against the utopias of the day, not at all a systematic treatise on population suggested by a purely scientific interest. As a polemic, it was decidedly successful ; it was no difficult task to dispose of the scheme of equality propounded by Godwin. Already, in 1761, Dr. Robert Wallace had published a work (which was used by Malthus in the composition of his essay) entitled *Various Prospects of Mankind, Nature, and Providence*, in which, after speaking of a community of goods as a remedy for the ills of society, he confessed that he saw one fatal objection to such a social organisation, namely, " the excessive population that would ensue." With Condorcet's extravagances, too, Malthus easily dealt. That eminent man, amidst

H

the tempest of the French Revolution, had written, whilst in hiding from his enemies, his *Esquisse d'un tableau historique de l'esprit humain.* The general conception of this book makes its appearance an epoch in the history of the rise of sociology. In it, if we except some partial sketches by Turgot,[1] is for the first time explained the idea of a theory of social dynamics founded on history; and its author is on this ground recognised by Comte as his principal immediate predecessor. But in the execution of his great project Condorcet failed. His negative metaphysics prevent his justly appreciating the past, and he indulges, at the close of his work, in vague hypotheses respecting the perfectibility of our race, and in irrational expectations of an indefinite extension of the duration of human life. Malthus seems to have little sense of the nobleness of Condorcet's attitude, and no appreciation of the grandeur of his leading idea. But of his chimerical hopes he is able to make short work; his good sense, if somewhat limited and prosaic, is at least effectual in detecting and exposing utopias.

The project of a formal and detailed treatise on population was an after-thought of Malthus. The essay in which he had studied a hypothetic future led him to examine the effects of the principle he had put forward on the past and present state of society; and he undertook an historical examination of these effects, and sought to draw such inferences in relation to the actual state of things as experience seemed to warrant. The consequence of this was such a change in the nature and composition of the essay as made it, in his own language, "a new work." The book, so altered, appeared in 1803 under the title, *An Essay on the Principle of Population, or a View of its Past and Present Effects on Human Happiness; with an Enquiry into our prospects respecting the future removal or mitigation of the evils which it occasions.*

---

[1] In his discourse at the Sorbonne (1750), *Sur les progrès successifs de l'esprit humain.*

In the original form of the essay he had spoken of no checks to population but those which came under the head either of vice or of misery. He now introduces the new element of the preventive check supplied by what he calls "moral restraint," and is thus enabled to "soften some of the harshest conclusions" at which he had before arrived. The treatise passed through six editions [1] in his lifetime, and in all of them he introduced various additions and corrections.   That of 1817 is the last he fully revised, and presents the text substantially as it has since been reprinted.

Notwithstanding the great development which he gave to his work, and the almost unprecedented amount of discussion to which it gave rise, it remains a matter of some difficulty to discover what solid contribution he has made to our knowledge, nor is it easy to ascertain precisely what practical precepts, not already familiar, he founded on his theoretic principles. This twofold vagueness is well brought out in his celebrated correspondence with Senior, in the course of which it seems to be made apparent that his doctrine is new not so much in its essence as in the phraseology in which it is couched. He himself tells us that when, after the publication of the original essay, the main argument of which he had deduced from Hume, Wallace, Smith, and Price, he began to inquire more closely into the subject, he found that "much more had been done" upon it "than he had been aware of." It had "been treated in such a manner by some of the French economists, occasionally by Montesquieu, and, among our own writers, by Dr. Franklin, Sir James Steuart, Mr. Arthur Young, and Mr. Townsend, as to create a natural surprise that it had not excited more of the public attention."   "Much, however," he thought, "remained yet to be done. The comparison between the increase of population and food had not, perhaps, been stated with sufficient force and precision," a nd "few inquiries had been made into the various modes by

---

[1] Their dates are 1798, 1803, 1806, 1807, 1817, 1826.

which the level" between population and the means of
subsistence "is effected." The first desideratum here mentioned—the want, namely, of an accurate statement of the
relation between the increase of population and food—Malthus
doubtless supposed to have been supplied by the celebrated
proposition that "population increases in a geometrical, food
in an arithmetical ratio." This proposition, however, has been
conclusively shown to be erroneous, there being no such difference of law between the increase of man and that of the
organic beings which form his food. J. S. Mill is indignant
with those who criticise Malthus's formula, which he ground-
lessly describes as a mere "passing remark," because, as he
thinks, though erroneous, it sufficiently suggests what is true ;
but it is surely important to detect unreal science, and to
test strictly the foundations of beliefs. When the formula
which we have cited is not used, other somewhat nebulous
expressions are frequently employed, as, for example, that
"population has a tendency to increase faster than food," a
sentence in which both are treated as if they were spontaneous
growths, and which, on account of the ambiguity of the word
"tendency," is admittedly consistent with the fact asserted
by Senior, that food tends to increase faster than population.
It must always have been perfectly well known that population will probably (though not necessarily) increase with every
augmentation of the supply of subsistence, and may, in some
instances, inconveniently press upon, or even for a certain time
exceed, the number properly corresponding to that supply.
Nor could it ever have been doubted that war, disease, poverty
—the last two often the consequences of vice—are causes
which keep population down. In fact, the way in which
abundance, increase of numbers, want, increase of deaths,
succeed each other in the natural economy, when reason does
not intervene, had been fully explained by the Rev. Joseph
Townsend in his *Dissertation on the Poor Laws* (1786),
which was known to Malthus. Again, it is surely plain
enough that the apprehension by individuals of the evils of

poverty, or a sense of duty to their possible offspring, may retard the increase of population, and has in all civilised communities operated to a certain extent in that way. It is only when such obvious truths are clothed in the technical terminology of "positive" and "preventive checks" that they appear novel and profound; and yet they appear to contain the whole message of Malthus to mankind. The laborious apparatus of historical and statistical facts respecting the several countries of the globe, adduced in the altered form of the essay, though it contains a good deal that is curious and interesting, establishes no general result which was not previously well known, and is accordingly ignored by James Mill and others, who rest the theory on facts patent to universal observation. Indeed, as we have seen, the entire historical inquiry was an after-thought of Malthus, who, before entering on it, had already announced his fundamental principle.

It would seem, then, that what has been ambitiously called Malthus's theory of population, instead of being a great discovery, as some have represented it, or a poisonous novelty, as others have considered it, is no more than a formal enunciation of obvious, though sometimes neglected, facts. The pretentious language often applied to it by economists is objectionable, as being apt to make us forget that the whole subject with which it deals is as yet very imperfectly understood—the causes which modify the force of the sexual instinct, and those which lead to variations in fecundity, still awaiting a complete investigation.[1]

It is the law of diminishing returns from land (of which more will be said hereafter), involving as it does—though only hypothetically—the prospect of a continuously increasing difficulty in obtaining the necessary sustenance for all the members of a society, that gives the principal importance to population as an economic factor. It is, in fact, the conflu-

[1] On this subject see the speculations of Mr. Herbert Spencer in his *Principles of Biology*, Part VI. chaps. xii. xiii.

ence of the Malthusian ideas with the theories of Ricardo, especially with the corollaries which the latter, as we shall see, deduced from the doctrine of rent (though these were not accepted by Malthus), that has led to the introduction of population as an element in the discussion of so many economic questions in recent times.

Malthus had undoubtedly the great merit of having called public attention in a striking and impressive way to a subject which had neither theoretically nor practically been sufficiently considered. But he and his followers appear to have greatly exaggerated both the magnitude and the urgency of the dangers to which they pointed.[1] In their conceptions a single social imperfection assumed such portentous dimensions that it seemed to overcloud the whole heaven and threaten the world with ruin. This doubtless arose from his having at first omitted altogether from his view of the question the great counteracting agency of moral restraint. Because a force exists, capable, if unchecked, of producing certain results, it does not follow that those results are imminent or even possible in the sphere of experience. A body thrown from the hand would, under the single impulse of projection, move for ever in a straight line; but it would not be reasonable to take special action for the prevention of this result, ignoring the fact that it will be sufficiently counteracted by the other forces which will come into play. And such other forces exist in the case we are considering. If the inherent energy of the principle of population (supposed everywhere the same) is measured by the rate at which numbers increase under the most favourable circumstances, surely the force of less favourable circumstances, acting through prudential or altruistic motives, is measured by the great difference between this maximum rate and those which are observed to prevail in most European countries. Under a rational system of insti-

---

[1] Malthus himself said :—"It is probable that, having found the bow bent too much one way, I was induced to bend it too much the other in order to make it straight."

tutions, the adaptation of numbers to the means available for their support is effected by the felt or anticipated pressure of circumstances and the fear of social degradation, within a tolerable degree of approximation to what is desirable. To bring the result nearer to the just standard, a higher measure of popular enlightenment and more serious habits of moral reflection ought indeed to be encouraged. But it is the duty of the individual to his actual or possible offspring, and not any vague notions as to the pressure of the national population on subsistence, that will be adequate to influence conduct.

The only obligation on which Malthus insists is that of abstinence from marriage so long as the necessary provision for a family has not been acquired or cannot be reasonably anticipated. The idea of post-nuptial continence, which has since been put forward by J. S. Mill and others, is foreign to his view. He even suggests that an allowance might be made from the public funds for every child in a family beyond the number of six, on the ground that, when a man marries, he cannot tell how many children he shall have, and that the relief from an unlooked-for distress afforded by such a grant would not operate as an encouragement to marriage. The duty of economic prudence in entering on the married state is plain; but in the case of working men the idea of a secured provision must not be unduly pressed, and it must also be remembered that the proper age for marriage in any class depends on the duration of life in that class. Too early marriages, however, are certainly not unfrequent, and they are attended with other than material evils, so that possibly even legal measures might with advantage be resorted to for preventing them in all ranks by somewhat postponing the age of full civil competence. On the other hand, however, the Malthusians often speak too lightly of involuntary celibacy, not recognising sufficiently that it is a deplorable necessity. They do not adequately estimate the value of domestic life as a school of the civic virtues, and the social importance (even apart from personal happiness) of the mutual affective education arising from the relations of the sexes in a well-constituted union.

Malthus further infers from his principles that states should not artificially stimulate population, and in particular that poor-laws should not be established, and, where they exist, should be abolished. The first part of this proposition cannot be accepted as applying to every social phase, for it is evident that in a case like that of ancient Rome, where continuous conquest was the chief occupation of the national activity, or in other periods when protracted wars threatened the independence or security of nations, statesmen might wisely take special action of the kind deprecated by Malthus. In relation to modern industrial communities he is doubtless in general right, though the promotion of immigration in new states is similar in principle to the encouragement of population. The question of poor-laws involves other considerations. The English system of his day was, indeed, a vicious one, though acting in some degree as a corrective of other evils in our social institutions; and efforts for its amendment tended to the public good. But the proposal of abolition is one from which statesmen have recoiled, and which general opinion has never adopted. It is difficult to believe that the present system will be permanent; it is too mechanical and undiscriminating; on some sides too lax, it is often unduly rigorous in the treatment of the worthy poor who are the victims of misfortune; and, in its ordinary modes of dealing with the young, it is open to grave objection. But it would certainly be rash to abolish it; it is one of several institutions which will more wisely be retained until the whole subject of the life of the working classes has been more thoroughly, and also more sympathetically, studied. The position of Malthus with respect to the relief of destitution is subject to this general criticism, that, first proving too much, he then shrinks from the consequences of his own logic. It follows from his arguments, and is indeed explicitly stated in a celebrated passage of his original essay, that he who has brought children into the world without

adequate provision for them should be left to the punishment
of Nature, that " it is a miserable ambition to wish to snatch
the rod from her hand," and to defeat the action of her laws,
which are the laws of God, and which " have doomed him
and his family to suffer." Though his theory leads him to
this conclusion, he could not, as a Christian clergyman, maintain the doctrine that, seeing our brother in need, we ought
to shut up our bowels of compassion from him ; and thus he
is involved in the radical inconsequence of admitting the law-
fulness, if not the duty, of relieving distress in cases where he
yet must regard the act as doing mischief to society.   Buckle,
who was imposed on by more than one of the exaggerations
of the economists, accepts the logical inference which Malthus
evaded.   He alleges that the only ground on which we are
justified in relieving destitution is the essentially self-regard-
ing one, that by remaining deaf to the appeal of the sufferer we
should probably blunt the edge of our own finer sensibilities.

It can scarcely be doubted that the favour which was at
once accorded to the views of Malthus in certain circles was
due in part to an impression, very welcome to the higher ranks
of society, that they tended to relieve the rich and powerful
of responsibility for the condition of the working classes, by
showing that the latter had chiefly themselves to blame, and
not either the negligence of their superiors or the institutions
of the country.   The application of his doctrines, too, made
by some of his successors had the effect of discouraging all
active effort for social improvement.   Thus Chalmers "reviews
seriatim and gravely sets aside all the schemes usually proposed for the amelioration of the economic condition of the
people" on the ground that an increase of comfort will lead
to an increase of numbers, and so the last state of things will
be worse than the first.

Malthus has in more recent times derived a certain degree
of reflected lustre from the rise and wide acceptance of the
Darwinian hypothesis.   Its author himself, in tracing its
filiation, points to the phrase "struggle for existence" used by

Malthus in relation to the social competition.   Darwin believes
that man has advanced to his present high condition through
such a struggle, consequent on his rapid multiplication.   He
regards, it is true, the agency of this cause for the improvement of our race as largely superseded by moral influences in
the more advanced social stages.   Yet he considers it, even
in these stages, of so much importance towards that end,
that notwithstanding the individual suffering arising from
the struggle for life, he deprecates any great reduction in
the natural, by which he seems to mean the ordinary, rate of
increase.

There has been of late exhibited in some quarters a tendency to apply the doctrine of the "survival of the fittest"
to human society in such a way as to intensify the harsher
features of Malthus's exposition by encouraging the idea that
whatever cannot sustain itself is fated, and must be allowed,
to disappear.   But what is repellent in this conception is
removed by a wider view of the influence of Humanity, as
a disposing power, alike on vital and on social conditions.   As
in the general animal domain the supremacy of man introduces
a new force consciously controlling and ultimately determining
the destinies of the subordinate species, so human providence
in the social sphere can intervene for the protection of the
weak, modifying by its deliberate action what would otherwise
be a mere contest of comparative strengths inspired by selfish
instincts.[1]

David Ricardo (1772–1823) is essentially of the school of
Smith, whose doctrines he in the main accepts, whilst he
seeks to develop them, and to correct them in certain par-

[1] The *Essay on Population* and the *Inquiry into the Nature and Progress of Rent* (1815), to be hereafter mentioned, are by far the most important contributions of Malthus to the science.   He was also author of
Principles of Political Economy (1820), *Definitions in Political Economy*
(1827), and other minor pieces.   On these less important writings of
Malthus, and on his personal history, see *Malthus and his Work* (1885),
by James Bonar, who has also edited (1888) his *Letters to Ricardo.*

ticulars.   But his mode of treatment is very different from Smith's.   The latter aims at keeping close to the realities of life as he finds them,—at representing the conditions and relations of men and things as they are ; and, as Hume remarked on first reading his great work, his principles are everywhere exemplified and illustrated with curious facts. Quite unlike this is the way in which Ricardo proceeds.   He moves in a world of abstractions.   He sets out from more or less arbitrary assumptions, reasons deductively from these, and announces his conclusions as true, without allowing for the partial unreality of the conditions assumed or confronting his results with experience.   When he seeks to illustrate his doctrines, it is from hypothetical cases,—his favourite device being that of imagining two contracting savages, and considering how they would be likely to act.   He does not explain— probably he had not systematically examined, perhaps was not competent to examine—the appropriate method of political economy; and the theoretic defence of his mode of proceeding was left to be elaborated by J. S. Mill and Cairnes. But his example had a great effect in determining the practice of his successors.   There was something highly attractive to the ambitious theorist in the sweeping march of logic which seemed in Ricardo's hands to emulate the certainty and comprehensiveness of mathematical proof, and in the portable and pregnant formulæ which were so convenient in argument, and gave a prompt, if often a more apparent than real, solution of difficult problems.   Whatever there was of false or narrow in the fundamental positions of Smith had been in a great degree corrected by his practical sense and strong instinct for reality, but was brought out in its full dimensions and even exaggerated in the abstract theorems of Ricardo and his followers.

The dangers inherent in his method were aggravated by the extreme looseness of his phraseology.   Senior pronounces him "the most incorrect writer who ever attained philosophical eminence."   His most ardent admirers find him fluctuating and uncertain in the use of words, and generally trace his errors to a confusion between the ordinary employment of a term and some special application of it which he has himself devised.

The most complete exposition of his system is to be found in his *Principles of Political Economy and Taxation* (1817). This work is not a complete treatise on the science, but a rather loosely connected series of disquisitions on value and price, rent, wages and profits, taxes, trade, money and banking. Yet, though the connection of the parts is loose, the same fundamental ideas recur continually, and determine the character of the entire scheme.

The principal problem to which he addresses himself in this work is that of distribution,—that is to say, the proportions of the whole produce of the country which will be allotted to the proprietor of land, to the capitalist, and to the labourer. And it is important to observe that it is especially the variations in their respective portions which take place in the progress of society that he professes to study,—one of the most unhistorical of writers thus indicating a sense of the necessity of a doctrine of economic dynamics—a doctrine which, from his point of view, it was impossible to supply.

The principle which he puts first in order, and which is indeed the key to the whole, is this—that the exchange value of any commodity the supply of which can be increased at will is regulated, under a *régime* of free competition, by the labour necessary for its production. Similar propositions are to be found in the *Wealth of Nations*, not to speak of earlier English writings. Smith had said that, "in the early and rude state of society which precedes both the accumulation of stock and the appropriation of land, the proportion between the quantities of labour necessary for acquiring different objects seems to be the only circumstance which can afford any rule for exchanging them with one another." But he wavers in his conception, and presents as the measure of value sometimes the quantity of labour necessary for the production of the object, sometimes the quantity of labour which the object would command in the market, which would be identical only for a given time and place. The theorem requires correction for a developed social system by the introduction of the consideration of capital, and takes the form in which it is elsewhere quoted from Malthus by Ricardo, that the real price of a commodity "depends on the greater or less quantity of capital and labour which must be employed to produce it." (The expression "quantity of capital" is lax, the element of time being omitted, but the meaning is obvious.) Ricardo, however, constantly takes no notice of capital, mentioning labour alone in his statement of this principle, and seeks to justify his practice by treating capital as "accumulated labour;" but this artificial way of viewing the facts obscures the nature of the co-operation of capital in production, and by keeping the necessity of this co-operation out of sight has encouraged some socialistic errors. Ricardo does not sufficiently distinguish between the cause or determinant and the measure of value; nor does he carry back the principle of cost of production as regulator of value to its foundation in the effect of that cost on the limitation of supply. It is the "natural price" of a commodity that is fixed by the theorem we have stated; the market price will be subject to accidental and temporary variations from this standard, depending on changes in demand and supply; but the price will, permanently and in the long run, depend on cost of production defined as above. On this basis Ricardo goes on to explain the laws according to which the produce of the land and the labour of the country is distributed amongst the several classes which take part in production.

The theory of rent, with which he begins, though commonly associated with his name, and though it certainly forms the most vital part of his general economic scheme, was not really his, nor did he lay claim to it. He distinctly states in the preface to the *Principles*, that "in 1815 Mr Malthus, in his *Inquiry into the Nature and Progress of Rent*, and a fellow of University College, Oxford, in his *Essay on the Application of*

Capital to Land, presented to the world, nearly at the same moment, the true doctrine of rent." The second writer here referred to was Sir Edward West, afterwards a judge of the supreme court of Bombay. Still earlier than the time of Malthus and West, as M'Culloch has pointed out, this doctrine had been clearly conceived and fully stated by Dr. James Anderson in his *Enquiry into the Nature of Corn-Laws*, published at Edinburgh in 1777.[1] That this tract was unknown to Malthus and West we have every reason to believe; but the theory is certainly as distinctly enunciated and as satisfactorily supported in it as in their treatises; and the whole way in which it is put forward by Anderson strikingly resembles the form in which it is presented by Ricardo.

The essence of the theory is that rent, being the price paid by the cultivator to the owner of land for the use of its productive powers, is equal to the excess of the price of the produce of the land over the cost of production on that land. With the increase of population, and therefore of demand for food, inferior soils will be taken into cultivation; and the price of the entire supply necessary for the community will be regulated by the cost of production of that portion of the supply which is produced at the greatest expense. But for the land which will barely repay the cost of cultivation no rent will be paid. Hence the rent of any quality of land will be equal to the difference between the cost of production on that land and the cost of production of that produce which is raised at the greatest expense.

The doctrine is perhaps most easily apprehended by means of the supposition here made of the coexistence in a country of a series of soils of different degrees of fertility which are successively taken into cultivation as population increases. But it would be an error to believe, though Ricardo sometimes seems to imply it, that such difference is a necessary

[1] Anderson's account of the origin of rent is reprinted in the *Select Collection of Scarce and Valuable Economical Tracts*, edited for Lord Overstone by J. R. M'Culloch, 1859.

condition of the existence of rent. If all the land of a country were of equal fertility, still if it were appropriated, and if the price of the produce were more than an equivalent for the labour and capital applied to its production, rent would be paid. This imaginary case, however, after using it to clear our conceptions, we may for the future leave out of account.

The price of produce being, as we have said, regulated by the cost of production of that which pays no rent, it is evident that " corn is not high because a rent is paid, but a rent is paid because corn is high," and that " no reduction would take place in the price of corn although landlords should forego the whole of their rent." Rent is, in fact, no determining element of price; it is paid, indeed, out of the price, but the price would be the same if no rent were paid, and the whole price were retained by the cultivator.

It has often been doubted whether or not Adam Smith held this theory of rent. Sometimes he uses language which seems to imply it, and states propositions which, if developed, would infallibly lead to it. Thus he says, in a passage already quoted, " Such parts only of the produce of land can commonly be brought to market of which the ordinary price is sufficient to replace the stock which must be employed in bringing them thither, together with its ordinary profits. If the ordinary price is more than this, the surplus part of it will naturally go to the rent of land. If it is not more, though the commodity can be brought to market, it can afford no rent to the landlord. Whether the price is or is not more depends on the demand." Again, in Smith's application of these considerations to mines, "the whole principle of rent," Ricardo tells us, "is admirably and perspicuously explained." But he had formed the opinion that there is in fact no land which does not afford a rent to the landlord; and, strangely, he seems not to have seen that this appearance might arise from the aggregation into an economic whole of parcels of land which can and others which cannot pay rent. The truth, indeed, is, that the fact, if it were a fact, that all the land in a country pays rent would be irrelevant as an argument against the Andersonian theory, for it is the same thing in substance if there be any capital employed on land already cultivated which yields a return no more than equal to ordinary profits. Such last-employed capital cannot afford rent at the existing rate of profit, unless the price of produce should rise.

The belief which some have entertained that Smith, notwithstanding some vague or inaccurate expressions, really held the Andersonian doctrine, can scarcely be maintained when we remember that Hume, writing to him after having read for the first time the *Wealth of Nations*, whilst expressing general agreement with his opinions, said (apparently with reference to Bk. I. chap. vii.), "I cannot think that the rent of farms makes any part of the price of the produce, but that the price is determined altogether by the quantity and the demand." It is further noteworthy that a statement of the theory of rent is given in the same volume, published in 1777, which contains Anderson's polemic against Smith's objections to a bounty on the exportation of corn; this volume can hardly have escaped Smith's notice, yet neither by its contents nor by Hume's letter was he led to modify what he had said in his first edition on the subject of rent.

It must be remembered that not merely the unequal fertilities of different soils will determine differences of rent; the more or less advantageous situation of a farm in relation to markets, and therefore to roads and railways, will have a similar effect. Comparative lowness of the cost of transit will enable the produce to be brought to market at a smaller expense, and will thus increase the surplus which constitutes rent. This consideration is indicated by Ricardo, though he does not give it prominence, but dwells mainly on the comparative productiveness of soils.

Rent is defined by Ricardo as the price paid for the use of "the original and indestructible powers of the soil." He thus differentiates rent, as he uses the term, from what is popularly designated by the word; and, when it is to be taken in his sense, it is often qualified as the "true" or "economic" rent. Part of what is paid to the landlord is often really profit on his expenditure in preparing the farm for cultivation by the tenant. But it is to be borne in mind that wherever such improvements are "amalgamated with the land," and "add permanently to its productive powers," the return for them follows the laws, not of profit, but of rent. Hence it becomes difficult, if not impossible, in practice to discriminate with any degree of accuracy the amount received by the landlord "for the use of the original powers of the soil" from the amount received by him as remuneration for his improvements or those made by his predecessors. These have raised the farm, as an instrument for producing food, from one class of productiveness to a higher, and the case is the same as if nature had originally placed the land in question in that higher class.

Smith had treated it as the peculiar privilege of agriculture, as compared with other forms of production, that in it "nature labours along with man," and therefore, whilst the workmen in manufactures occasion the reproduction merely of the capital which employs them with its owner's profits, the agricultural labourer occasions the reproduction, not only of the employer's capital with profits, but also of the rent of the landlord. This last he viewed as the free gift of nature which remained "after deducting or compensating everything which can be regarded as the work of man." Ricardo justly observes in reply that "there is not a manufacture which can be mentioned in which nature does not give her assistance to man." He then goes on to quote from Buchanan the remark that "the notion of agriculture yielding a produce and a rent in consequence, because nature concurs with industry in the process of cultivation, is a mere fancy. It is not from the produce, but from the price at which the produce is sold, that the rent is derived; and this price is got, not because nature assists in the production, but because it is the price which suits the consump-

I

tion to the supply."[1]　There is no gain to the society at large
from the rise of rent; it is advantageous to the landlords
alone, and their interests are thus permanently in opposition
to those of all other classes.　The rise of rent may be retarded,
or prevented, or even temporarily changed to a fall, by agricultural improvements, such as the introduction of new manures
or of machines or of a better organisation of labour (though
there is not so much room for this last as in other branches
of production), or the opening of new sources of supply in
foreign countries; but the tendency to a rise is constant so
long as the population increases.

The great importance of the theory of rent in Ricardo's
system arises from the fact that he makes the general economic condition of the society to depend altogether on the
position in which agricultural exploitation stands.　This will
be seen from the following statement of his theory of wages
and profits.　The produce of every expenditure of labour and
capital being divided between the labourer and the capitalist,
in proportion as one obtains more the other will necessarily obtain less.　The productiveness of labour being given,
nothing can diminish profit but a rise of wages, or increase
it but a fall of wages.　Now the price of labour, being the
same as its cost of production, is determined by the price of
the commodities necessary for the support of the labourer.
The price of such manufactured articles as he requires has a
constant tendency to fall, principally by reason of the progressive application of the division of labour to their production.　But the cost of his maintenance essentially depends,
not on the price of those articles, but on that of his food;
and, as the production of food will in the progress of society

---

[1] Senior, however, has pointed out that Smith is partly right; whilst
it is true that rent is demanded because the productive powers of nature
are limited, and increased population requires a less remunerative expenditure in order to obtain the necessary supply; on the other hand,
it is the power which most land possesses of producing the subsistence
of more persons than are required for its cultivation that supplies the
fund out of which rent can be paid.

and of population require the sacrifice of more and more labour, its price will rise ; money wages will consequently rise, and with the rise of wages profits will fall. Thus it is to the necessary gradual descent to inferior soils, or less productive expenditure on the same soil, that the decrease in the rate of profit which has historically taken place is to be attributed (Smith ascribed this decrease to the competition of capitalists, though in one place, Book I. chap. ix.,[1] he had a glimpse of the Ricardian view). This gravitation of profits towards a minimum is happily checked at times by improvements of the machinery employed in the production of necessaries, and especially by such discoveries in agriculture and other causes as reduce the cost of the prime necessary of the labourer; but here again the tendency is constant. Whilst the capitalist thus loses, the labourer does not gain; his increased money wages only enable him to pay the increased price of his necessaries, of which he will have no greater and probably a less share than he had before. In fact, the labourer can never for any considerable time earn more than what is required to enable the class to subsist in such a degree of comfort as custom has made indispensable to them, and to perpetuate their race without either increase or diminution. That is the " natural " price of labour ; and if the market rate temporarily rises above it population will be stimulated, and the rate of wages will again fall. Thus whilst rent has a constant tendency to rise and profit to fall, the rise or fall of wages will depend on the rate of increase of the working classes. For the improvement of their condition Ricardo thus has to fall back on the Malthusian remedy, of the effective application of which he does not, however, seem to have much expectation. The securities against a

---

[1] " As the colony increases, the profits of stock gradually diminish. When the most fertile and best situated lands have been all occupied, less profit can be made by the cultivation of what is inferior both in soil and situation, and less interest can be afforded for the stock which is so employed." The view in question had been anticipated by West.

superabundant population to which he points are the gradual abolition of the poor-laws—for their amendment would not content him—and the development amongst the working classes of a taste for greater comforts and enjoyments.

It will be seen that the socialists have somewhat exaggerated in announcing, as Ricardo's "iron law" of wages, their absolute identity with the amount necessary to sustain the existence of the labourer and enable him to continue the race. He recognises the influence of a "standard of living" as limiting the increase of the numbers of the working classes, and so keeping their wages above the lowest point. But he also holds that, in long-settled countries, in the ordinary course of human affairs, and in the absence of special efforts restricting the growth of population, the condition of the labourer will decline as surely, and from the same causes, as that of the landlord will be improved.

If we are asked whether this doctrine of rent, and the consequences which Ricardo deduced from it, are true, we must answer that they are hypothetically true in the most advanced industrial communities, and there only (though they have been rashly applied to the cases of India and Ireland), but that even in those communities neither safe inference nor sound action can be built upon them. As we shall see hereafter, the value of most of the theorems of the classical economics is a good deal attenuated by the habitual assumptions that we are dealing with "economic men," actuated by one principle only; that custom, as against competition, has no existence; that there is no such thing as combination; that there is equality of contract between the parties to each transaction, and that there is a definite universal rate of profit and wages in a community; this last postulate implying (1) that the capital embarked in any undertaking will pass at once to another in which larger profits are for the time to be made; (2) that a labourer, whatever his local ties of feeling, family, habit, or other engagements, will transfer himself immediately to any place where, or employment in which, for the time, larger wages are to be earned than those he had previously obtained;[1] and (3) that both capitalists and labourers have a perfect knowledge of the condition and prospects of industry throughout the country, both in their own and other occupations. But in Ricardo's speculations on rent and its consequences there is still more of abstraction. The influence of emigration, which has assumed vast dimensions since his time, is left out of account, and the amount of land at the disposal of a community is supposed limited to its own territory, whilst contemporary Europe is in fact largely fed by the western States of America. He did not adequately appreciate the degree in which the augmented productiveness of labour, whether from increased intelligence, improved organisation, introduction of machinery, or more rapid and cheaper communication, steadily keeps down the cost of production. To these influences must be added those of legal reforms in tenure, and fairer conditions in contracts, which operate in the same direction. As a result of all these causes, the pressure anticipated by Ricardo is not felt, and the cry is of the landlords over falling rents, not of the consumer over rising prices. The entire conditions are in fact so altered that Professor Nicholson, no enemy to the "orthodox" economics, when recently conducting an inquiry into the present state of the agricultural question,[2] pronounced the so-called Ricardian theory of rent "too abstract to be of practical utility."

A particular economic subject on which Ricardo has thrown a useful light is the nature of the advantages derived from foreign commerce, and the conditions under which such commerce can go on. Whilst preceding writers had represented those benefits as consisting in affording a vent for surplus produce, or enabling a portion of the national capital to replace itself with a profit, he pointed out that they consist

---

[1] Adam Smith says :—" It appears evidently from experience that man is, of all sorts of luggage, the most difficult to be transported" (*Wealth of Nations*, Bk. I. chap. viii.).

[2] *Tenant's Gain not Landlord's Loss* (1883), p. 83.

"simply and solely in this, that it enables each nation to obtain, with a given amount of labour and capital, a greater quantity of all commodities taken together." This is no doubt the point of view at which we should habitually place ourselves; though the other forms of expression employed by his predecessors, including Adam Smith, are sometimes useful as representing real considerations affecting national production, and need not be absolutely disused. Ricardo proceeds to show that what determines the purchase of any commodity from a foreign country is not the circumstance that it can be produced there with less labour and capital than at home. If we have a greater positive advantage in the production of some other article than in that of the commodity in question, even though we have an advantage in producing the latter, it may be our interest to devote ourselves to the production of that in which we have the greatest advantage, and to import that in producing which we should have a less, though a real, advantage. It is, in short, not absolute cost of production, but comparative cost, which determines the interchange. This remark is just and interesting, though an undue importance seems to be attributed to it by J. S. Mill and Cairnes, the latter of whom magniloquently describes it as "sounding the depths" of the problem of international dealings,—though, as we shall see hereafter, he modifies it by the introduction of certain considerations respecting the conditions of domestic production.

For the nation as a whole, according to Ricardo, it is not the gross produce of the land and labour, as Smith seems to assert, that is of importance, but the net income—the excess, that is, of this produce over the cost of production, or, in other words, the amount of its rent and its profits; for the wages of labour, not essentially exceeding the maintenance of the labourers, are by him considered only as a part of the "necessary expenses of production." Hence it follows, as he himself in a characteristic and often-quoted passage says, that, " provided the net real income of the nation be the same, it is of no importance whether it consists of ten or twelve millions of inhabitants. If five millions of men could produce as much food and clothing as was necessary for ten millions, food and clothing for five millions would be the net revenue. Would it be of any advantage to the country that to produce this same net revenue seven millions of men should be required,—that is to say, that seven millions should be employed to produce food and clothing sufficient for twelve millions? The food and clothing of five millions would be still the net revenue. The employing a greater number of men would enable us neither to add a man to our army and navy nor to contribute one guinea more in taxes." Industry is here viewed, just as by the mercantilists, in relation to the military and political power of the state, not to the maintenance and improvement of human beings, as its end and aim. The labourer, as Held has remarked, is regarded not as a member of society, but as a means to the ends of society, on whose sustenance a part of the gross income must be expended, as another part must be spent on the sustenance of horses. We may well ask, as Sismondi did in a personal interview with Ricardo, "What! is wealth then everything? are men absolutely nothing?"

On the whole what seems to us true of Ricardo is this, that, whilst he had remarkable powers, they were not the powers best fitted for sociological research. Nature intended him rather for a mathematician of the second order than for a social philosopher. Nor had he the due previous preparation for social studies; for we must decline to accept Bagehot's idea that, though "in no high sense an educated man," he had a specially apt training for such studies in his practice as an eminently successful dealer in stocks. The same writer justly notices the "anxious penetration with which he follows out rarefied minutiæ." But he wanted breadth of survey, a comprehensive view of human nature and human life, and the strong social sympathies which, as the greatest minds have recognised, are a most valuable aid in this department of study.

On a subject like that of money, where a few elementary propositions—into which no moral ingredient enters—have alone to be kept in view, he was well adapted to succeed; but in the larger social field he is at fault. He had great deductive readiness and skill (though his logical accuracy, as Mr. Sidgwick remarks, has been a good deal exaggerated). But in human affairs phenomena are so complex, and principles so constantly limit or even compensate one another, that rapidity and daring in deduction may be the greatest of dangers, if they are divorced from a wide and balanced appreciation of facts. Dialectic ability is, no doubt, a valuable gift, but the first condition for success in social investigation is to see things as they are.

A sort of Ricardo-mythus for some time existed in economic circles. It cannot be doubted that the exaggerated estimate of his merits arose in part from a sense of the support his system gave to the manufacturers and other capitalists in their growing antagonism to the old aristocracy of landowners. The same tendency, as well as his affinity to their too abstract and unhistorical modes of thought, and their eudæmonistic doctrines, recommended him to the Benthamite group, and to the so-called Philosophical Radicals generally. Brougham said he seemed to have dropped from the skies—a singular avatar, it must be owned. His real services in connection with questions of currency and banking naturally created a prepossession in favour of his more general views. But, apart from those special subjects, it does not appear that, either in the form of solid theoretic teaching or of valuable practical guidance, he has really done much for the world, whilst he admittedly misled opinion on several important questions. De Quincey's presentation of him as a great revealer of truth is now seen to be an extravagance. J. S. Mill and others speak of his "superior lights" as compared with those of Adam Smith; but his work, as a contribution to our knowledge of human society, will not bear a moment's comparison with the *Wealth of Nations.*

It is interesting to observe that Malthus, though the combination of his doctrine of population with the principles of Ricardo composed the creed for some time professed by all the "orthodox" economists, did not himself accept the Ricardian scheme. He prophesied that "the main part of the structure would not stand." "The theory," he says, "takes a partial view of the subject, like the system of the French economists; and, like that system, after having drawn into its vortex a great number of very clever men, it will be unable to support itself against the testimony of obvious facts, and the weight of those theories which, though less simple and captivating, are more just, on account of their embracing more of the causes which are in actual operation in all economical results."

We saw that the foundations of Smith's doctrine in general philosophy were unsound, and the ethical character of his scheme in consequence injuriously affected; but his method, consisting in a judicious combination of induction and deduction, we found (so far as the statical study of economic laws is concerned) little open to objection. Mainly through the influence of Ricardo, economic method was perverted. The science was led into the mistaken course of turning its back on observation, and seeking to evolve the laws of phenomena out of a few hasty generalisations by a play of logic. The principal vices which have been in recent times not unjustly attributed to the members of the "orthodox" school were all encouraged by his example, namely,—(1) the viciously abstract character of the conceptions with which they deal, (2) the abusive preponderance of deduction in their processes of research, and (3) the too absolute way in which their conclusions are conceived and enunciated.

The works of Ricardo have been collected in one volume, with a biographical notice, by J. R. M'Culloch (1846).[1]

[1] A sketch of Ricardo's personal history, and an account of his writings on monetary questions, which could not conveniently be introduced here, will be found under his name in the *Encyclopædia Britannica*, 9th edition.

After Malthus and Ricardo, the first of whom had fixed public attention irresistibly on certain aspects of society, and the second had led economic research into new, if questionable, paths, came a number of minor writers who were mainly their expositors and commentators, and whom, accordingly, the Germans, with allusion to Greek mythical history, designate as the Epigoni. By them the doctrines of Smith and his earliest successors were thrown into more systematic shape, limited and guarded so as to be less open to criticism, couched in a more accurate terminology, modified in subordinate particulars, or applied to the solution of the practical questions of their day.

James Mill's *Elements* (1821) deserves special notice, as exhibiting the system of Ricardo with thorough-going rigour, and with a compactness of presentation, and a skill in the disposition of materials, which give to it in some degree the character of a work of art. The *a priori* political economy is here reduced to its simplest expression. J. R. M'Culloch (1779–1864), author of a number of laborious statistical and other compilations, criticised current economic legislation in the *Edinburgh Review* from the point of view of the Ricardian doctrine, taking up substantially the same theoretic position as was occupied at a somewhat later period by the Manchester school. He is altogether without originality, and never exhibits any philosophic elevation or breadth. His confident dogmatism is often repellent; he admitted in his later years that he had been too fond of novel opinions, and defended them with more heat and pertinacity than they deserved. It is noticeable that, though often spoken of in his own time both by those who agreed with his views, and those, like Sismondi, who differed from them, as one of the lights of the reigning school, his name is now tacitly dropped in the writings of the members of that school. Whatever may have been his partial usefulness in vindicating the policy of free trade, it is at least plain that for the needs of our social future he has nothing to offer. Nassau William Senior (1790–1864),

who was professor of political economy in the university of
Oxford, published, besides a number of separate lectures, a
treatise on the science, which first appeared as an article in
the *Encyclopædia Metropolitana*. He is a writer of a high
order of merit. He made considerable contributions to the
elucidation of economic principles, specially studying exact-
ness in nomenclature and strict accuracy in deduction. His
explanations on cost of production and the way in which it
affects price, on rent, on the difference between rate of wages
and price of labour, on the relation between profit and wages
(with special reference to Ricardo's theorem on this subject,
which he corrects by the substitution of proportional for
absolute amount), and on the distribution of the precious
metals between different countries, are particularly valuable.
His new term "abstinence," invented to express the conduct
for which interest is the remuneration, was useful, though
not quite appropriate, because negative in meaning. It is on
the theory of wages that Senior is least satisfactory. He
makes the average rate in a country (which, we must maintain, is not a real quantity, though the rate in a given employment and neighbourhood is) to be expressed by the fraction
of which the numerator is the amount of the wages fund (an
unascertainable and indeed, except as actual total of wages
paid, imaginary sum) and the denominator the number of the
working population; and from this he proceeds to draw the
most important and far-reaching consequences, though the
equation on which he founds his inferences conveys at most
only an arithmetical fact, which would be true of every case
of a division amongst individuals, and contains no economic
element whatever. The phrase "wages fund" originated in
some expressions of Adam Smith[1] used only for the purpose
of illustration, and never intended to be rigorously interpreted;

---

[1] Thus, in *Wealth of Nations*, Bk. I. chap. viii., we have the phrases—
"the funds which are destined to the payment of wages," "the funds
destined for employing industry," "the funds destined for the maintenance of servants."

and we shall see that the doctrine has been repudiated by several members of what is regarded as the orthodox school of political economy. As regards method, Senior makes the science a purely deductive one, in which there is no room for any other "facts" than the four fundamental propositions from which he undertakes to deduce all economic truth. And he does not regard himself as arriving at hypothetic conclusions; his postulates and his inferences are alike conceived as corresponding to actual phenomena.[1] Colonel Robert Torrens (1780–1864) was a prolific writer, partly on economic theory, but principally on its applications to financial and commercial policy. Almost the whole of the programme which was carried out in legislation by Sir Robert Peel had been laid down in principle in the writings of Torrens. He gave substantially the same theory of foreign trade which was afterwards stated by J. S. Mill in one of his *Essays on Unsettled Questions*.[2] He was an early and earnest advocate of the repeal of the corn laws, but was not in favour of a general system of absolute free trade, maintaining that it is expedient to impose retaliatory duties to countervail similar duties imposed by foreign countries, and that a lowering of import duties on the productions of countries retaining their hostile tariffs would occasion an abstraction of the precious metals, and a decline in prices, profits, and wages. His principal writings of a general character were—*The Economist* [*i.e.*, Physiocrat] *Refuted*, 1808; *Essay on the Production of Wealth*, 1821; *Essay on the External Corn-trade* (eulogised by Ricardo), 3d ed., 1826; *The Budget, a Series of Letters on Financial, Commercial, and Colonial Policy*, 1841–3. Harriet Martineau (1802–1876) popularised the doctrines of Malthus and Ricardo in her *Illustrations of Political Economy* (1832–

---

[1] See the last of his *Four Introductory Lectures on Political Economy*, 1852.

[2] Mill, however, tells us in his *Preface* to those Essays that his own views on that subject had been entertained and committed to writing before the publication by Torrens of similar opinions.

34), a series of tales, in which there is much excellent description, but the effect of the narrative is often marred by the somewhat ponderous disquisitions here and there thrown in, usually in the form of dialogue.

Other writers who ought to be named in any history of the science are Charles Babbage, *On the Economy of Machinery and Manufactures* (1832), chiefly descriptive, but also in part theoretic; William Thomas Thornton, *Overpopulation and its Remedy* (1846), *A Plea for Peasant Proprietors* (1848), *On Labour* (1869; 2d ed., 1870); Herman Merivale, *Lectures on Colonisation and Colonies* (1841–2; new ed., 1861); T. C. Banfield, *The Organisation of Industry Explained* (1844; 2d ed., 1848); and Edward Gibbon Wakefield, *A View of the Art of Colonisation* (1849). Thomas Chalmers, well known in other fields of thought, was author of *The Christian and Civic Economy of Large Towns* (1821–36), and *On Political Economy in Connection with the Moral State and Moral Prospects of Society* (1832); he strongly opposed any system of legal charity, and, whilst justly insisting on the primary importance of morality, industry, and thrift as conditions of popular wellbeing, carried the Malthusian doctrines to excess. Nor was Ireland without a share in the economic movement of the period.[1] Whately, having been second Drummond professor of political economy at Oxford (in succession to Senior), and delivered in that capacity his *Introductory Lectures* (1831), founded in 1832, when he went to Ireland as archbishop of Dublin, a similar professorship in Trinity College, Dublin. It was first held by Mountifort Longfield, afterwards Judge of the Landed Estates Court, Ireland (d. 1884). He published

---

[1] Samuel Crumpe, M.D., had published at Dublin in 1793 an *Essay on the Best Means of Providing Employment for the People*, which obtained a prize offered by the Royal Irish Academy for the best dissertation on that subject. This is a meritorious work, and contains a good statement of some of the leading principles of Adam Smith. John Hely Hutchinson's *Commercial Restraints of Ireland* (1779) is important for the economic history of that country.

lectures on the science generally (1834), on *Poor Laws* (1834), and on *Commerce and Absenteeism* (1835), which were marked by independence of thought and sagacious observation. He was laudably free from many of the exaggerations of his contemporaries; he said, in 1835, "in political economy we must not abstract too much," and protested against the assumption commonly made that "men are guided in all their conduct by a prudent regard to their own interest." James A. Lawson (afterwards Mr. Justice Lawson, d. 1887) also published some lectures (1844), delivered from the same chair, which may still be read with interest and profit; his discussion of the question of population is especially good; he also asserted against Senior that the science is *avide de faits*, and that it must reason about the world and mankind as they really are.

The most systematic and thorough-going of the earlier critics of the Ricardian system was Richard Jones (1790–1855), professor at Haileybury. Jones has received scant justice at the hands of his successors. J. S. Mill, whilst using his work, gave his merits but faint recognition. Even Roscher says that he did not thoroughly understand Ricardo, without giving any proof of that assertion, whilst he is silent as to the fact that much of what has been preached by the German historical school is found distinctly indicated in Jones's writings. He has been sometimes represented as having rejected the Andersonian doctrine of rent; but such a statement is incorrect. Attributing the doctrine to Malthus, he says that that economist "showed satisfactorily that when land is cultivated by capitalists living on the profits of their stock, and able to move it at pleasure to other employments, the expense of tilling the worst quality of land cultivated determines the average price of raw produce, while the difference of quality of the superior lands measures the rents yielded by them." What he really denied was the application of the doctrine to all cases where rent is paid; he pointed out in his *Essay on the Distribution of Wealth and on the Sources of Taxation*, 1831, that, besides "farmers' rents," which, under the supposed conditions, conform to the above law, there are "peasant rents," paid everywhere through the most extended periods of history, and still paid over by far the largest part of the earth's surface, which are not so regulated. Peasant rents he divided under the heads of (1) serf, (2) métayer, (3) ryot, and (4) cottier rents, a classification afterwards adopted in substance by J. S. Mill ; and he showed that the contracts fixing their amount were, at least in the first three classes, determined rather by custom than by competition. Passing to the superstructure of theory erected by Ricardo on the doctrine of rent which he had so unduly extended, Jones denied most of the conclusions he had deduced, especially the following :— that the increase of farmers' rents is always contemporary with a decrease in the productive powers of agriculture, and comes with loss and distress in its train ; that the interests of landlords are always and necessarily opposed to the interests of the state and of every other class of society; that the diminution of the rate of profits is exclusively dependent on the returns to the capital last employed on the land ; and that wages can rise only at the expense of profits.

The method followed by Jones is inductive; his conclusions are founded on a wide observation of contemporary facts, aided by the study of history. "If," he said, "we wish to make ourselves acquainted with the economy and arrangements by which the different nations of the earth produce and distribute their revenues, I really know but of one way to attain our object, and that is, to look and see. We must get comprehensive views of facts, that we may arrive at principles that are truly comprehensive. If we take a different method, if we snatch at general principles, and content ourselves with confined observations, two things will happen to us. First, what we call general principles will often be found to have no generality—we shall set out with declaring propositions to be universally true which, at every step of our further progress, we shall be obliged to confess are frequently false ; and, secondly, we shall miss a great mass of useful knowledge which those who advance to principles by a comprehensive examination of facts necessarily meet with on their road." The world he professed to study was not an imaginary world, inhabited by abstract "economic men," but the real world with the different forms which the ownership and cultivation of land, and, in general, the conditions of production and distribution, assume at different times and places. His recognition of such different systems of life in communities occupying different stages in the progress of civilisation led to his proposal of what he called a "political economy of nations." This was a protest against the practice of taking the exceptional state of facts which exists, and is indeed only partially realised, in a small corner of our planet as representing the uniform type of human societies, and ignoring the effects of the early history and special development of each community as influencing its economic phenomena.

It is sometimes attempted to elude the necessity for a wider range of study by alleging a universal tendency in the social world to assume this now exceptional shape as its normal and ultimate constitution. Even if this tendency were real (which is only partially true, for the existing order amongst ourselves cannot be regarded as entirely definitive), it could not be admitted that the facts witnessed in our civilisation and those exhibited in less advanced communities are so approximate as to be capable of being represented by the same formulæ. As Whewell, in editing Jones's *Remains*, 1859, well observed, it is true in the physical world that "all things tend to assume a form determined by the force of gravity; the hills tend to become plains, the waterfalls to eat away their beds and disappear, the rivers to form lakes in the valleys, the glaciers to pour down in cataracts." But are we to treat these results as achieved, because forces are in operation which may ultimately bring them about? All human questions are largely questions of time; and the economic phenomena which really belong to the several stages of the human movement must be studied as they are, unless we are content to fall into grievous error both in our theoretic treatment of them and in the solution of the practical problems they present.

Jones is remarkable for his freedom from exaggeration and one-sided statement ; thus, whilst holding Malthus in, perhaps, undue esteem, he declines to accept the proposition that an increase of the means of subsistence is necessarily followed by an increase of population; and he maintains what is undoubtedly true, that with the growth of population, in all well-governed and prosperous states, the command over food, instead of diminishing, increases.

Much of what he has left us—a large part of which is unfortunately fragmentary—is akin to the labours of Cliffe Leslie at a later period. The latter, however, had the advantage of acquaintance with the sociology of Comte, which gave him a firmer grasp of method, as well as a wider view of the general movement of society ; and, whilst the voice of Jones was but little heard amidst the general applause accorded to Ricardo in the economic world of his time, Leslie wrote when disillusion had set in, and the current was beginning to turn in England against the *a priori* economics.

Comte somewhere speaks of the "transient predilection" for political economy which had shown itself generally in western Europe. This phase of feeling was specially noticeable in England from the third to the fifth decade of the present century. "Up to the year 1818," said a writer in the *Westminster Review*, "the science was scarcely known or talked of beyond a small circle of philosophers ; and legislation, so far from being in conformity with its principles, was daily receding from them more and more." Mill has told us what a change took place within a few years. "Political economy," he says, "had asserted itself with great vigour in public affairs by the petition of the merchants of London for free trade, drawn up in 1820 by Mr. Tooke and presented by Mr. Alexander Baring,[1] and by the noble exertions of Ricardo

---

[1] Afterwards Lord Ashburton. For this Petition, see M'Culloch's

during the few years of his parliamentary life. His writings, following up the impulse given by the bullion controversy, and followed up in their turn by the expositions and comments of my father and M'Culloch (whose writings in the *Edinburgh Review* during those years were most valuable), had drawn general attention to the subject, making at least partial converts in the Cabinet itself; and Huskisson, supported by Canning, had commenced that gradual demolition of the protective system which one of their colleagues virtually completed in 1846, though the last vestiges were only swept away by Mr. Gladstone in 1860." Whilst the science was thus attracting and fixing the attention of active minds, its unsettled condition was freely admitted. The differences of opinion among its professors were a frequent subject of complaint. But it was confidently expected that these discrepancies would soon disappear, and Colonel Torrens predicted that in twenty years there would scarcely "exist a doubt respecting any of its more fundamental principles." " The prosperity," says Mr. Sidgwick, "that followed on the abolition of the corn laws gave practical men a most impressive and satisfying proof of the soundness of the abstract reasoning by which the expediency of free trade had been inferred," and when, in 1848, "a masterly expositor of thought had published a skilful statement of the chief results of the controversies of the preceding generation," with the due "explanations and qualifications " of the reigning opinions, it was for some years generally believed that political economy had " emerged from the state of polemical discussion," at least on its leading doctrines, and that at length a sound construction had been erected on permanent bases.

This expositor was John Stuart Mill (1806–73). He exercised, without doubt, a greater influence in the field of English economics than any other writer since Ricardo. His systematic treatise has been, either directly or through

Literature of Political Economy, p. 57, or Senior's *Lectures on the Transmission of the Precious Metals*, &c., 2d ed., p. 78.

manuals founded on it, especially that of Fawcett, the source
from which most of our contemporaries in these countries
have derived their knowledge of the science. But there are
other and deeper reasons, as we shall see, which make him, in
this as in other departments of knowledge, a specially interesting and significant figure.

In 1844 he published five *Essays on some Unsettled Questions of Political Economy*, which had been written as early
as 1829 and 1830, but had, with the exception of the fifth,
remained in manuscript. In these essays is contained any
dogmatic contribution which he can be regarded as having
made to the science. The subject of the first is the laws
of interchange between nations. He shows that, when two
countries trade together in two commodities, the prices of the
commodities exchanged on both sides (which, as Ricardo had
proved, are not determined by cost of production) will adjust
themselves, through the play of reciprocal demand, in such a
way that the quantities required by each country of the article
which it imports from its neighbour shall be exactly sufficient
to pay for one another. This is the law which appears, with
some added developments, in his systematic treatise under
the name of the "equation of international demand." He
then discusses the division of the gains. The most important
practical conclusion (not, however, by any means an undis-
puted one) at which he arrives in this essay is, that the
relaxation of duties on foreign commodities, not operating as
protection but maintained solely for revenue, should be made
contingent on the adoption of some corresponding degree of
freedom of trade with England by the nation from which the
commodities are imported. In the second essay, on the influence of consumption on production, the most interesting
results arrived at are the propositions—(1) that absenteeism
is a local, not a national, evil, and (2) that, whilst there
cannot be permanent excess of production, there may be a
temporary excess, not only of any one article, but of commodities generally,—this last, however, not arising from over-

production, but from a want of commercial confidence. The third essay relates to the use of the words "productive" and "unproductive" as applied to labour, to consumption, and to expenditure. The fourth deals with profits and interest, especially explaining and so justifying Ricardo's theorem that "profits depend on wages, rising as wages fall and falling as wages rise." What Ricardo meant was that profits depend on the cost of wages estimated in labour. Hence improvements in the production of articles habitually consumed by the labourer may increase profits without diminishing the real remuneration of the labourer. The last essay is on the definition and method of political economy, a subject later and more maturely treated in the author's *System of Logic*.

In 1848 Mill published his *Principles of Political Economy, with some of their Applications to Social Philosophy*. This title, though, as we shall see, open to criticism, indicated on the part of the author a less narrow and formal conception of the field of the science than had been common amongst his predecessors. He aimed, in fact, at producing a work which might replace in ordinary use the *Wealth of Nations*, which in his opinion was "in many parts obsolete and in all imperfect." Adam Smith had invariably associated the general principles of the subject with their applications, and in treating those applications had perpetually appealed to other and often far larger considerations than pure political economy affords. And in the same spirit Mill desired, whilst incorporating all the results arrived at in the special science by Smith's successors, to exhibit purely economic phenomena in relation to the most advanced conceptions of his own time on the general philosophy of society, as Smith had done in reference to the philosophy of the eighteenth century.[1]

---

[1] Curiously, in an otherwise well-executed Abridgment of Mill's work, published in the United States (1886) by J. Laurence Laughlin, as a text-book for colleges, all that "should properly be classed under the head of Sociology" has been omitted, Mill's own conception being thus set aside, and his book made to conform to the common type.

This design he certainly failed to realise. His book is very far indeed from being a "modern Adam Smith." It is an admirably lucid and even elegant exposition of the Ricardian economics, the Malthusian theory being of course incorporated with these, but, notwithstanding the introduction of many minor novelties, it· is, in its scientific substance, little or nothing more. When Cliffe Leslie says that Mill so qualified and amended the doctrines of Ricardo that the latter could scarcely have recognised them, he certainly goes a great deal too far; Senior really did more in that direction. Mill's effort is usually to vindicate his master where others have censured him, and to palliate his admitted laxities of expression. Already his profound esteem for Ricardo's services to economics had been manifest in his *Essays*, where he says of him, with some injustice to Smith, that, "having a science to create," he could not "occupy himself with more than the leading principles," and adds that "no one who has thoroughly entered into his discoveries" will find any difficulty in working out "even the minutiæ of the science." James Mill, too, had been essentially an expounder of Ricardo; and the son, whilst greatly superior to his father in the attractiveness of his expository style, is, in regard to his economic doctrine, substantially at the same point of view. It is in their general philosophical conceptions and their views of social aims and ideals that the elder and younger Mill occupy quite different positions in the line of progress. The latter could not, for example, in his adult period have put forward as a theory of government the shallow sophistries which the plain good sense of Macaulay sufficed to expose in the writings of the former; and he had a nobleness of feeling which, in relation to the higher social questions, raised him far above the ordinary coarse utilitarianism of the Benthamites.

The larger and more philosophic spirit in which Mill dealt with social subjects was undoubtedly in great measure due to the influence of Comte, to whom, as Mr. Bain justly says, he was under greater obligations than he himself was disposed to admit. Had he more completely undergone that influence, we are sometimes tempted to think he might have wrought the reform in economics which still remains to be achieved, emancipating the science from the *a priori* system, and founding a genuine theory of industrial life on observation in the broadest sense. But probably the time was not ripe for such a construction, and it is possible that Mill's native intellectual defects might have made him unfit for the task, for, as Roscher has said, "ein historischer Kopf war er nicht." However this might have been, the effects of his early train- ing, in which positive were largely alloyed with metaphysical elements, sufficed in fact to prevent his attaining a perfectly normal mental attitude. He never altogether overcame the vicious direction which he had received from the teaching of his father, and the influence of the Benthamite group in which he was brought up. Hence it was that, according to the striking expression of Roscher, his whole view of life was "zu wenig aus Einem Gusse." The incongruous mixture of the narrow dogmas of his youthful period with the larger ideas of a later stage gave a wavering and indeterminate character to his entire philosophy. He is, on every side, eminently "un-final;" he represents tendencies to new forms of opinion, and opens new vistas in various directions, but founds scarcely anything, and remains indeed, so far as his own position is concerned, not merely incomplete but inco- herent.[1] It is, however, precisely this dubious position which seems to us to give a special interest to his career, by fitting him in a peculiar degree to prepare and facilitate transitions.

What he himself thought to be "the chief merit of his treatise" was the marked distinction drawn between the theory of production and that of distribution, the laws of

[1] Mr. John Morley ("Mill on Religion," in *Critical Miscellanies*, 2d ser., 1877) betrays something like consternation at finding in Mill's posthumous writings statements of opinion distinctly at variance with philosophic doctrines he had energetically maintained during his whole life.

the former being based on unalterable natural facts, whilst the course of distribution is modified from time to time by the changing ordinances of society. This distinction, we may remark, must not be too absolutely stated, for the organisation of production changes with social growth, and, as Lauderdale long ago showed, the nature of the distribution in a community reacts on production. But there is a substantial truth in the distinction, and the recognition of it tends to concentrate attention on the question—How can we improve the existing distribution of wealth? The study of this problem led Mill, as he advanced in years, further and further in the direction of socialism; and, whilst to the end of his life his book, however otherwise altered, continued to deduce the Ricardian doctrines from the principle of enlightened selfishness, he was looking forward to an order of things in which synergy should be founded on sympathy.

The gradual modification of his views in relation to the economic constitution of society is set forth in his *Autobiography*. In his earlier days, he tells us, he "had seen little further than the *old school*" (note this significant title) "of political economy into the possibilities of fundamental improvement in social arrangements. Private property, as now understood, and inheritance appeared the *dernier mot* of legislation." The notion of proceeding to any radical redress of the injustice "involved in the fact that some are born to riches and the vast majority to poverty" he had then reckoned chimerical. But now his views were such as would "class him decidedly under the general designation of socialist;" he had been led to believe that the whole contemporary framework of economic life was merely temporary and provisional, and that a time would come when "the division of the produce of labour, instead of depending, as in so great a degree it now does, on the accident of birth, would be made by concert on an acknowledged principle of justice." "The social problem of the future" he considered to be "how to unite the greatest individual liberty of action," which was often compromised in socialistic schemes, "with a common ownership in the raw material of the globe, and an equal participation in all the benefits of combined labour." These ideas, he says, were scarcely indicated in the first edition of the *Political Economy*, rather more clearly and fully in the second, and quite unequivocally in the third,—the French Revolution of 1848 having made the public more open to the reception of novelties in opinion.

Whilst thus looking forward to a new economic order, he yet thinks its advent very remote, and believes that the inducements of private interest will in the meantime be indispensable.[1] On the spiritual side he maintains a similar attitude of expectancy. He anticipates the ultimate disappearance of theism, and the substitution of a purely human religion, but believes that the existing doctrine will long be necessary as a stimulus and a control. He thus saps existing foundations without providing anything to take their place, and maintains the necessity of conserving for indefinite periods what he has radically discredited. Nay, even whilst sowing the seeds of change in the direction of a socialistic organisation of society, he favours present or proximate arrangements which would urge the industrial world towards other issues. The system of peasant proprietorship of land is distinctly individualistic in its whole tendency ; yet he extravagantly praises it in the earlier part of his book, only receding from that laudation when he comes to the chapter on the future of the labouring classes. And the system of so-called co-operation in production which he so warmly commended in the later editions of his work, and led some of his followers to preach as the one thing needful, would inevitably strengthen the principle of personal property, and, whilst professing at most to substitute the competition of associations for that of individuals, would by no means exclude the latter.

The elevation of the working classes he bound up too

---

[1] See also his *Chapters on Socialism*, in *Fortnightly Review*, 1879.

exclusively with the Malthusian ethics, on which he laid quite
an extravagant stress, though, as Mr. Bain has observed, it is
not easy to make out his exact views, any more than his
father's, on this subject. We have no reason to think that he
ever changed his opinion as to the necessity of a restriction on
population; yet that element seems foreign to the socialistic
idea to which he increasingly leaned. It is at least difficult
to see how, apart from individual responsibility for the support of a family, what Malthus called moral restraint could
be adequately enforced. This difficulty is indeed the fatal
flaw which, in Malthus's own opinion, vitiated the scheme of
Godwin.

Mill's openness to new ideas and his enthusiasm for improvement cannot be too much admired. But there appears
to have been combined with these fine traits in his mental
constitution a certain want of practical sense, a failure to
recognise and acquiesce in the necessary conditions of human
life, and a craving for "better bread than can be made of
wheat." He entertained strangely exaggeratèd, or rather perverted, notions of the "subjection," the capacities, and the
rights of women. He encourages a spirit of revolt on the part
of working men against their perpetual condemnation, as a
class, to the lot of living by wages, without giving satisfactory
proof that this state of things is capable of change, and without showing that such a lot, duly regulated by law and
morality, is inconsistent with their real happiness. He also
insists on the "independence" of the working class—which,
according to him, *farà da se*—in such a way as to obscure, if
not to controvert, the truths that superior rank and wealth are
naturally invested with social power, and are bound in duty
to exercise it for the benefit of the community at large, and
especially of its less favoured members. And he attaches a
quite undue importance to mechanical and, indeed, illusory
expedients, such as the limitation of the power of bequest and
the confiscation of the "unearned increment" of rent.

With respect to economic method also, he shifted his posi-

tion; yet to the end occupied uncertain ground. In the fifth
of his early essays he asserted that the method *a priori* is the
only mode of investigation in the social sciences, and that the
method *a posteriori* " is altogether inefficacious in those sciences,
as a means of arriving at any considerable body of valuable
truth." When he wrote his *Logic*, he had learned from
Comte that the *a posteriori* method—in the form which he
chose to call "inverse deduction"—was the only mode of
arriving at truth in general sociology; and his admission of
this at once renders the essay obsolete. But, unwilling to
relinquish the *a priori* method of his youth, he tries to establish a distinction of two sorts of economic inquiry, one of
which, though not the other, can be handled by that method.
Sometimes he speaks of political economy as a department
"carved out of the general body of the science of society;"
whilst on the other hand the title of his systematic work implies a doubt whether political economy is a part of "social
philosophy" at all, and not rather a study preparatory and
auxiliary to it. Thus, on the logical as well as the dogmatic
side, he halts between two opinions. Notwithstanding his
misgivings and even disclaimers, he yet remained, as to method,
a member of the old school, and never passed into the new or
"historical" school, to which the future belongs.

The question of economic method was also taken up by the
ablest of his disciples, John Elliott Cairnes (1824–75), who
devoted a volume to the subject (*Logical Method of Political
Economy*, 1857; 2d ed., 1875). Professor Walker has spoken
of the method advocated by Cairnes as being different from
that put forward by Mill, and has even represented the former
as similar to, if not identical with, that of the German historical school. But this is certainly an error. Cairnes, notwithstanding some apparent vacillation of view and certain
concessions more formal than real, maintains the utmost rigour
of the deductive method; he distinctly affirms that in political
economy there is no room for induction at all, "the economist
starting with a knowledge of ultimate causes," and being thus,

"at the outset of his enterprise, at the position which the physicist only attains after ages of laborious research." He does not, indeed, seem to be advanced beyond the point of view of Senior, who professed to deduce all economic truth from four elementary propositions. Whilst Mill in his *Logic* represents verification as an essential part of the process of demonstration of economic laws, Cairnes holds that, as they "are not assertions respecting the character or sequence of phenomena" (though what else can a scientific law be ?), "they can neither be established nor refuted by statistical or documentary evidence." A proposition which affirms nothing respecting phenomena cannot be controlled by being confronted with phenomena. Notwithstanding the unquestionable ability of his book, it appears to mark, in some respects, a retrogression in methodology, and can for the future possess only an historical interest.

Regarded in that light, the labours of Mill and Cairnes on the method of the science, though intrinsically unsound, had an important negative effect. They let down the old political economy from its traditional position, and reduced its extravagant pretensions by two modifications of commonly accepted views. First, whilst Ricardo had never doubted that in all his reasonings he was dealing with human beings as they actually exist, they showed that the science must be regarded as a purely hypothetic one. Its deductions are based on unreal, or at least one-sided, assumptions, the most essential of which is that of the existence of the so-called " economic man," a being who is influenced by two motives only, that of acquiring wealth and that of avoiding exertion ; and only so far as the premises framed on this conception correspond with fact can the conclusions be depended on in practice. Senior in vain protested against such a view of the science, which, as he saw, compromised its social efficacy ; whilst Torrens, who had previously combated the doctrines of Ricardo, hailed Mill's new presentation of political economy as enabling him, whilst in one sense rejecting those doctrines, in another sense to

accept them.   Secondly, beside economic science, it had often
been said, stands an economic art,—the former ascertaining
truths respecting the laws of economic phenomena, the latter
prescribing the right kind of economic action ; and many had
assumed that, the former being given, the latter is also in our
possession—that, in fact, we have only to convert theorems
into precepts, and the work is done.   But Mill and Cairnes
made it plain that this statement could not be accepted, that
action can no more in the economic world than in any other
province of life be regulated by considerations borrowed from
one department of things only ; that economics can suggest
ideas which are to be kept in view, but that, standing alone,
it cannot direct conduct—an office for which a wider prospect
of human affairs is required.   This matter is best elucidated
by a reference to Comte's classification, or rather hierarchical
arrangement, of the sciences.   Beginning with the least complex, mathematics, we rise successively to astronomy, physics,
chemistry, thence to biology, and from it again to sociology.
In the course of this ascent we come upon all the great
laws which regulate the phenomena of the inorganic world,
of organised beings, and of society.   A further step, however,
remains to be taken—namely, to morals ; and at this point
the provinces of theory and practice tend to coincide, because
every element of conduct has to be considered in relation
to the general good.   In the final synthesis all the previous
analyses have to be used as instrumental, in order to determine
how every real quality of things or men may be made to
converge to the welfare of Humanity.

Cairnes's most important economic publication was his last,
entitled *Some Leading Principles of Political Economy newly
Expounded*, 1874.   In this work, which does not profess to
be a complete treatise on the science, he criticises and emends
the statements which preceding writers had given of some of
its principal doctrines, and treats elaborately of the limitations
with which they are to be understood, and the exceptions to
them which may be produced by special circumstances.   Whilst

marked by great ability, it affords evidence of what has been justly observed as a weakness in Cairnes's mental constitution —his "deficiency in intellectual sympathy," and consequent frequent inability to see more than one side of a truth.

The three divisions of the book relate respectively to (1) value, (2) labour and capital, and (3) international trade.   In the first he begins by elucidating the meaning of the word "value," and under this head controverts the view of Jevons that the exchange value of anything depends entirely on its utility, without, perhaps, distinctly apprehending what Jevons meant by this proposition.   On supply and demand he shows, as Say had done before, that these, regarded as aggregates, are not independent, but strictly connected and mutually depen- dent phenomena—identical, indeed, under a system of barter, but, under a money system, conceivable as distinct.   Supply and demand with respect to particular commodities must be understood to mean supply and demand at a given price ; and thus we are introduced to the ideas of market price and normal price (as, following Cherbuliez, he terms what Smith less happily called natural price).   Normal price again leads to the consideration of cost of production, and here, against Mill and others, he denies that profit and wages enter into cost of pro- duction ; in other words, he asserts what Senior (whom he does not name) had said before him, though he had not con- sistently carried out the nomenclature, that cost of production is the sum of labour and abstinence necessary to production, wages and profits being the remuneration of sacrifice and not elements of it.   But, it may well be asked, How can an amount of labour be added to an amount of abstinence ? Must not wages and profits be taken as "measures of cost " ?   By adhering to the conception of "sacrifice," he exposes the emptiness of the assertion that " dear labour is the great obstacle to the extension of British trade "—a sentence in which "British trade " means capitalists' profits.   At this point we are introduced to a doctrine now first elaborated, though there are indications of it in Mill, of whose theory of international values it is in fact an extension. In foreign trade cost of production, in Cairnes's sense, does not regulate values, because it cannot perform that function except under a régime of effective competition, and between different countries effective competition does not exist. But, Cairnes asks, to what extent does it exist in domestic industries? So far as capital is concerned, he thinks the condition is sufficiently fulfilled over the whole field—a position, let it be said in passing, which he does not seem to make out, if we consider the practical immobility of most invested, as distinct from disposable, capital. But in the case of labour the requisite competition takes place only within certain social, or rather industrial, strata. The world of industry may be divided into a series of superposed groups, and these groups are practically "non-competing," the disposable labour in any one of them being rarely capable of choosing its field in a higher.[1] The law that cost of production determines price cannot, therefore, be absolutely stated respecting domestic any more than respecting international exchange; as it fails for the latter universally, so it fails for the former as between non-competing groups. The law that holds between these is similar to that governing international values, which may be called the equation of reciprocal demand. Such a state of relative prices will establish itself amongst the products of these groups as shall enable that portion of the products of each group which is applied to the purchase of the products of all other groups to discharge its liabilities towards those other groups. The reciprocal demand of the groups determines the "average relative level" of prices within each group; whilst cost of

[1] Economists are fond of comparing the rate of profit or wages in one *nation* (using this word in its economic sense) to a single fluid surface which is continually disturbed by transient influences and continually tending to recover its level. We must compare these rates in different nations to reservoirs which, not communicating with each other, stand always at different, though variable, levels. And the latter comparison will apply also to the rates (at least of wages) in different economic "groups," or strata, within the same community.

production regulates the distribution of price among the individual products of each group. This theorem is perhaps of no great practical value; but the tendency of the whole investigation is to attenuate the importance of cost of production as a regulator of normal price, and so to show that yet another of the accepted doctrines of the science had been propounded in too rigid and absolute a form. As to market price, the formula by which Mill had defined it as the price which equalises demand and supply Cairnes shows to be an identical proposition, and he defines it as the price which most advantageously adjusts the existing supply to the existing demand pending the coming forward of fresh supplies from the sources of production.

His second part is chiefly remarkable for his defence of what is known as the wages fund doctrine, to which we adverted when speaking of Senior. Mill had given up this doctrine, having been convinced by Thornton that it was erroneous; but Cairnes refused to follow his leader, who, as he believes, ought not to have been convinced.[1] After having given what is certainly a fallacious reply to Longe's criticism of the expression "average rate of wages," he proceeds to vindicate the doctrine in question by the consideration that the amount of a nation's wealth devoted at any time to the payment of wages—if the character of the national industries and the methods of production employed remain the same— is in a definite relation to the amount of its general capital; the latter being given, the former is also given. In illustrating his view of the subject, he insists on the principle (true in the main, but too absolutely formulated by Mill) that "demand for commodities is not demand for labour." It is not necessary here to follow his investigation, for his reasoning has not satisfied his successors, with the exception of

[1] Jevons strangely says, in the Preface to his *Theory of Political Economy*, 2d ed., that the wage fund doctrine "has been abandoned by most English economists owing to the attacks," amongst others, "of Cairnes." Cairnes was, in truth, a supporter of the doctrine.

Fawcett, and the question of wages is now commonly treated without reference to a supposed determinate wages fund. Cairnes next studies trades-unionism in relation to wages, and arrives in substance at the conclusion that the only way in which it can affect their rate is by accelerating an advance which must ultimately have taken place independently of its action. He also takes occasion to refute Mr. (now Lord) Brassey's supposed law of a uniform cost of labour in every part of the world. Turning to consider the material prospects of the working classes, he examines the question of the changes which may be expected in the amount and partition of the fund out of which abstinence and labour are remunerated. He here enunciates the principle (which had been, however, stated before him by Ricardo and Senior) that the increased productiveness of industry will not affect either profit or wages unless it cheapen the commodities which the labourer consumes. These latter being mostly commodities of which raw produce is the only or principal element, their cost of production, notwithstanding improvements in knowledge and art, will increase unless the numbers of the labouring class be steadily kept in check; and hence the possibility of elevating the condition of the labourer is confined within very narrow limits, if he continues to be a labourer only. The condition of any substantial and permanent improvement in his lot is that he should cease to be a mere labourer—that profits should be brought to reinforce the wages fund, which has a tendency, in the course of industrial progress, to decline relatively to the general capital of a country. And hence Cairnes—abandoning the purely theoretic attitude which he elsewhere represents as the only proper one for the economist—recommends the system of so-called co-operation (that is, in fact, the abolition of the large capitalist) as offering to the working classes "the sole means of escape from a harsh and hopeless destiny," and puts aside rather contemptuously the opposition of the Positivists to this solution, which yet many besides the Positivists, as, for example, Leslie and F. A. Walker, regard as chimerical.

The third part is devoted mainly to an exposition of Ricardo's doctrine of the conditions of international trade and Mill's theory of international values. The former Cairnes modifies by introducing his idea of the partial influence of reciprocal demand, as distinguished from cost of production, on the regulation of domestic prices, and founds on this rectification an interesting account of the connection between the wages prevailing in a country and the character and course of its external trade. He emends Mill's statement, which represented the produce of a country as exchanging for that of other countries at such values "as are required in order that the whole of her exports may exactly pay for the whole of her imports" by substituting for the latter phrase the condition that each country should by means of her exports discharge all her foreign liabilities—in other words, by introducing the consideration of the balance of debts. This idea was not new; it had been indicated by John Leslie Foster as early as 1804,[1] and was touched on by Mill himself; but Cairnes expounds it well; and it is important as clearing away common misconceptions, and sometimes removing groundless alarms.[2] Passing to the question of free trade, he disposes of some often-repeated protectionist arguments, and in particular refutes the American allegation of the inability of the highly-paid labour of that country to compete with the "pauper labour" of Europe. He is not so successful in meeting the "political argument," founded on the admitted importance for civilisation of developing diversified national industries; and he meets only by one of the highly questionable commonplaces of the doctrinaire economists Mill's proposition that protection may foster nascent industries really adapted to a country till they have struck root and are able to endure the stress of foreign competition.

We have dwelt at some length on this work of Cairnes, not only because it presents the latest forms of several accepted

[1] In his *Essay on the Principle of Commercial Exchanges.*

[2] On this whole subject see Professor C. F. Bastable's *Theory of International Trade*, 1887.

L

economic doctrines, but also because it is, and, we believe, will remain, the last important product of the old English school. The author at the outset expresses the hope that it will strengthen, and add consistence to, the scientific fabric "built up by the labours of Adam Smith, Malthus, Ricardo, and Mill." Whilst recognising with him the great merits of Smith, and the real abilities and services of his three successors here named, we cannot entertain the same opinion as Cairnes respecting the permanence of the fabric they constructed. We hold that a new edifice is required, incorporating indeed many of the materials of the old, but planned on different ideas and in some respects with a view to different ends —above all, resting on different philosophic foundations, and having relation in its whole design to the more comprehensive structure of which it will form but one department, namely, the general science of society.

We shall hereafter have occasion to refer to Cairnes's *Essays in Political Economy*, 1873. His *Slave Power* (1862) was the most valuable work which appeared on the subject of the great American conflict.

FRANCE.

All the later European schools presuppose—in part adopting, in part criticising—the work of the English economists from Smith[1] to Ricardo and the Epigoni. The German school has had in a greater degree than any other a movement of its own

---

[1] The first French translation of the *Wealth of Nations*, by Blavet, appeared in the *Journal de l'Agriculture, du Commerce, des Finances, et des Arts*, 1779–80; new editions of it were published in 1781, 1788, and 1800; it was also printed at Amsterdam in 1784. Smith himself recommended it in his third edition of the original as excellent. In 1790 appeared the translation by Roucher, to which Condorcet had intended to add notes, and in 1802 that by Count Germain Garnier, executed during his exile in England, which is now considered the standard version, and has been reproduced, with notes by Say, Sismondi, Blanqui, &c., in the *Collection des Principaux Économistes*.

—following, at least in its more recent period, an original method, and tending to special and characteristic conclusions. The French school, on the other hand,—if we omit the socialists, who do not here come under consideration,—has in the main reproduced the doctrines of the leading English thinkers,—stopping short, however, in general of the extremes of Ricardo and his disciples. In the field of exposition the French are unrivalled; and in political economy they have produced a series of more or less remarkable systematic treatises, text books, and compendiums, at the head of which stands the celebrated work of J. B. Say. But the number of seminal minds which have appeared in French economic literature—of writers who have contributed important truths, introduced improvements of method, or presented the phenomena under new lights—has not been large. Sismondi, Dunoyer, and Bastiat will deserve our attention, as being the most important of those who occupy independent positions (whether permanently tenable or not), if we pass over for the present the great philosophical renovation of Auguste Comte, which comprehended actually or potentially all the branches of sociological inquiry. Before estimating the labours of Bastiat, we shall find it desirable to examine the views of Carey, the most renowned of American economists, with which the latest teachings of the ingenious and eloquent Frenchman are, up to a certain point, in remarkable agreement. Cournot, too, must find a place among the French writers of this period, as the chief representative of the conception of a mathematical method in political economy.

Of Jean Baptiste Say (1767–1832) Ricardo says—"He was the first, or among the first, of Continental writers who justly appreciated and applied the principles of Smith, and has done more than all other Continental writers taken together to recommend that enlightened and beneficial system to the nations of Europe." The *Wealth of Nations* in the original language was placed in Say's hands by Clavière, afterwards minister, then director of the assurance society of which

Say was a clerk ; and the book made a powerful impression on him. Long afterwards, when Dupont de Nemours complained of his injustice to the physiocrats, and claimed him as, through Smith, a spiritual grandson of Quesnay and nephew of Turgot, he replied that he had learned to read in the writings of the mercantile school, had learned to think in those of Quesnay and his followers, but that it was in Smith that he had learned to seek the causes and the effects of social phenomena in the nature of things, and to arrive at this last by a scrupulous analysis. His *Traité d'Économie Politique* (1803) was essentially founded on Smith's work, but he aimed at arranging the materials in a more logical and instructive order.[1] He has the French art of easy and lucid exposition, though his facility sometimes degenerates into superficiality ; and hence his book became popular, both directly and through translations obtained a wide circulation, and diffused rapidly through the civilised world the doctrines of the master. Say's knowledge of common life, says Roscher, was equal to Smith's ; but he falls far·below him in living insight into larger political phenomena, and he carefully eschews historical and philosophical explanations. He is sometimes strangely shallow, as when he says that "the best tax is that smallest in amount." He appears not to have much claim to the position of an original thinker in political economy. Ricardo, indeed, speaks of him as having " enriched the science, by several discussions, original, accurate, and profound." What he had specially in view in using these words was what is, perhaps rather pretentiously, called Say's *théorie des débouchés*, with his connected disproof of the possibility of a universal glut. The theory amounts simply to this, that buying is also selling, and that it is by producing that we are enabled to purchase the products of others. Several distinguished economists, especially

---

[1] He grossly exaggerated Smith's faults of method. Thus he says— " L'ouvrage de Smith n'est qu'un assemblage confus des principes les plus sains de l'Économie politique . . . son livre est un vaste chaos d'idées justes " (*Discours Préliminaire*).

Malthus and Sismondi, in consequence chiefly of a misinterpretation of the phenomena of commercial crises, maintained that there might be general over-supply or excess of all commodities above the demand. This Say rightly denied. A particular branch of production may, it must indeed be admitted, exceed the existing capabilities of the market; but, if we remember that supply is demand, that commodities are purchasing power, we cannot accept the doctrine of the possibility of a universal glut without holding that we can have too much of everything—that "all men can be so fully provided with the precise articles they desire as to afford no market for each other's superfluities." Whatever services, however, Say may have rendered by original ideas on those or other subjects, his great merit is certainly that of a propagandist and populariser.

The imperial police would not permit a second edition of his work to be issued without the introduction of changes which, with noble independence, he refused to make; and that edition did not therefore appear till 1814.   Three other editions were published during the life of the author—in 1817, 1819, and 1826.   In 1828 Say published a second treatise, *Cours complet d'Économie Politique pratique*, which contained the substance of his lectures at the Conservatoire des Arts et Métiers and at the Collége de France.   Whilst in his earlier treatise he had kept within the narrow limits of strict economics, in his later work he enlarged the sphere of discussion, introducing in particular many considerations respecting the economic influence of social institutions.

Jean Charles L. Simonde de Sismondi (1773–1842), author of the *Histoire des Républiques Italiennes du moyen âge*, represents in the economic field a protest, founded mainly on humanitarian sentiment, against the dominant doctrines. He wrote first a treatise *De la Richesse Commerciale* (1803), in which he followed strictly the principles of Adam Smith. But he afterwards came to regard these principles as insufficient and requiring modification. He contributed an article on political economy to the *Edinburgh Encyclopædia*, in which his new views were partially indicated. They were fully developed in his principal economic work, *Nouveaux Principes d'Économie Politique, ou de la Richesse dans ses rapports avec la Population* (1819; 2d ed., 1827). This work, as he tells us, was not received with favour by economists, a fact which he explains by the consideration that he had "attacked an orthodoxy—an enterprise dangerous in philosophy as in religion." According to his view, the science, as commonly understood, was too much of a mere chrematistic: it studied too exclusively the means of increasing wealth, and not sufficiently the use of this wealth for producing general happiness. The practical system founded on it tended, as he believed, not only to make the rich richer, but to make the poor poorer and more dependent; and he desired to fix attention on the question of distribution as by far the most important, especially in the social circumstances of recent times.

The personal union in Sismondi of three nationalities, the Italian, the French, and the Swiss, and his comprehensive historical studies, gave him a special largeness of view; and he was filled with a noble sympathy for the suffering members of society. He stands nearer to socialism than any other French economist proper, but it is only in sentiment, not in opinion, that he approximates to it; he does not recommend any socialistic scheme. On the contrary, he declares in a memorable passage that, whilst he sees where justice lies, he must confess himself unable to suggest the means of realising it in practice; the division of the fruits of industry between those who are united in their production appears to him vicious; but it is, in his judgment, almost beyond human power to conceive any system of property absolutely different from that which is known to us by experience. He goes no further than protesting, in view of the great evils which he saw around him, against the doctrine of *laisser faire*, and invoking, somewhat vaguely, the intervention of Governments

to "regulate the progress of wealth" and to protect the weaker
members of the community.

His frank confession of impotence, far wiser and more
honourable than the suggestion of precipitate and dangerous
remedies, or of a recurrence to outworn mediæval institutions,
has not affected the reputation of the work. A prejudice was
indeed early created against it in consequence of its partial
harmony of tone, though, as we have seen, not of policy, with
socialism, which was then beginning to show its strength, as
well as by the rude way in which his descriptions of the
modern industrial system, especially as it existed in England,
disturbed the complacent optimism of some members of the
so-called orthodox school. These treated the book with ill-
disguised contempt, and Bastiat spoke of it as preaching an
économie politique à rebours. But it has held its place in the
literature of the science, and is now even more interesting
than when it first appeared, because in our time there is a
more general disposition, instead of denying or glossing over
the serious evils of industrial society, to face and remove or at
least mitigate them. The *laisser faire* doctrine, too, has been
discredited in theory and abandoned in practice ; and we are
ready to admit Sismondi's view of the State as a power not
merely intrusted with the maintenance of peace, but charged
also with the mission of extending the benefits of the social
union and of modern progress as widely as possible through
all classes of the community. Yet the impression which his
treatise leaves behind it is a discouraging one ; and this because he regards as essentially evil many things which seem
to be the necessary results of the development of industry.
The growth of a wealthy capitalist class and of manufacture
on the great scale, the rise of a vast body of workers who live
by their labour alone, the extended application of machines,
large landed properties cultivated with the aid of the most
advanced appliances—all these he dislikes and deprecates ;
but they appear to be inevitable. The problem is, how to
regulate and moralise the system they imply ; but we must

surely accept it in principle, unless we aim at a thorough social revolution. Sismondi may be regarded as the precursor of the German economists known under the inexact designation of "Socialists of the Chair;" but their writings are much more hopeful and inspiring.

To the subject of population he devotes special care, as of great importance for the welfare of the working classes. So far as agriculturists are concerned, he thinks the system of what he calls patriarchal exploitation, where the cultivator is also proprietor, and is aided by his family in tilling the land —a law of equal division among the natural heirs being apparently presupposed—the one which is most efficacious in preventing an undue increase of the population. The father is, in such a case, able distinctly to estimate the resources available for his children, and to determine the stage of subdivision which would necessitate the descent of the family from the material and social position it had previously occupied. When children beyond this limit are born, they do not marry, or they choose amongst their number one to continue the race. This is the view which, adopted by J. S. Mill, makes so great a figure in the too favourable presentation by that writer of the system of peasant proprietors.

In no French economic writer is greater force or general solidity of thought to be found than in Charles Dunoyer (1786–1862), author of *La Liberté du Travail* (1845 ; the substance of the first volume had appeared under a different title in 1825), honourably known for his integrity and independence under the régime of the Restoration. What makes him of special importance in the history of the science is his view of its philosophical constitution and method. With respect to method, he strikes the keynote at the very outset in the words "rechercher expérimentalement," and in professing to build on "les données de l'observation et de l'expérience." He shows a marked tendency to widen economics into a general science of society, expressly describing political economy as having for its province the whole order of things which results from the exercise and development of the social forces.   This larger study is indeed better named Sociology; and economic studies are better regarded as forming one department of it. But the essential circumstance is that, in Dunoyer's treatment of his great subject, the widest intellectual, moral, and political considerations are inseparably combined with purely economic ideas. It must not be supposed that by liberty, in the title of his work, is meant merely freedom from legal restraint or administrative interference ; he uses it to express whatever tends to give increased efficiency to labour. He is thus led to discuss all the causes of human progress, and to exhibit them in their historical working.

Treating, in the first part, of the influence of external conditions, of race, and of culture on liberty in this wider sense, he proceeds to divide all productive effort into two great classes, according as the action is exercised on things or on men, and censures the economists for having restricted their attention to the former. He studies in his second and third parts respectively the conditions of the efficiency of these two forms of human exertion.   In treating of economic life, strictly so called, he introduces his fourfold division of material industry, in part adopted by J. S. Mill, as " (1) extractive, (2) voiturière, (3) manufacturière, (4) agricole," a division which is useful for physical economics, but will always, when the larger social aspect of things is considered, be inferior to the more commonly accepted one into agricultural, manufacturing, and commercial industry, banking being supposed as common president and regulator.   Dunoyer, having in view only action on material objects, relegates banking, as well as commerce proper, to the separate head of exchange, which, along with association and gratuitous transmission (whether *inter vivos* or *mortis causa*), he classes apart as being, not industries, in the same sense with the occupations named, but yet functions essential to the social economy.   The industries which act on man he divides according as they occupy themselves with (1) the amelioration of our physical nature, (2)

the culture of our imagination and sentiments, (3) the education of our intelligence, and (4) the improvement of our
moral habits; and he proceeds accordingly to study the social
offices of the physician, the artist, the educator, and the priest.
We meet in Dunoyer the ideas afterwards emphasised by
Bastiat that the real subjects of human exchange are services;
that all value is due to human activity; that the powers of
nature always render a gratuitous assistance to the labour of
man; and that the rent of land is really a form of interest on
invested capital.   Though he had disclaimed the task of a
practical adviser in the often-quoted sentence—"Je n'impose
rien; je ne propose même rien; j'expose," he finds himself,
like all economists, unable to abstain from offering counsel.
And his policy is opposed to any state interference with industry.   Indeed he preaches in its extreme rigour the *laisser
faire* doctrine, which he maintains principally on the ground
that the spontaneous efforts of the individual for the improvement of his condition, by developing foresight, energy, and
perseverance, are the most efficient means of social culture.
But he certainly goes too far when he represents the action
of Governments as normally always repressive and never
directive.   He was doubtless led into this exaggeration by
his opposition to the artificial organisations of labour proposed
by so many of his contemporaries, against which he had to
vindicate the principle of competition; but his criticism of
these schemes took, as Comte remarks, too absolute a character,
tending to the perpetual interdiction of a true systematisation
of industry.[1]

AMERICA.

At this point it will be convenient to turn aside and notice
the doctrines of the American economist Carey.   Not much
had been done before him in the science by citizens of the
United States.   Benjamin Franklin, otherwise of world-wide

---

[1] The French economists are continued on page 175.

renown, was author of a number of tracts, in most of which he merely enforces practical lessons of industry and thrift, but in some throws out interesting theoretic ideas. Thus, fifty years before Smith, he suggested (as Petty, however, had already done) human labour as the true measure of value (*Modest Inquiry into the Nature and Necessity of a Paper Currency,* 1721), and in his *Observations concerning the Increase of Mankind* (1751) he expresses views akin to those of Malthus. Alexander Hamilton, secretary of the treasury, in 1791 presented in his official capacity to the House of Representatives of the United States a Report on the measures by which home manufactures could be promoted.[1] In this document he gives a critical account of the theory of the subject, represents Smith's system of free trade as possible in practice only if adopted by all nations simultaneously, ascribes to manufactures a greater productiveness than to agriculture, and seeks to refute the objections against the development of the former in America founded on the want of capital, the high rate of wages, and the low price of land. The conclusion at which he arrives is that for the creation of American manufactures a system of moderate protective duties was necessary, and he proceeds to describe the particular features of such a system. There is some reason to believe that the German economist List, of whom we shall speak hereafter, was influenced by Hamilton's work, having, during his exile from his native country, resided in the United States.

Henry Charles Carey (1793–1879), son of an American citizen who had emigrated from Ireland, represents a reaction against the dispiriting character which the Smithian doctrines had assumed in the hands of Malthus and Ricardo. His aim was, whilst adhering to the individualistic economy, to place it on a higher and surer basis, and fortify it against the assaults of socialism, to which some of the Ricardian tenets had exposed it. The most comprehensive as well as mature exposition of his views is contained in his *Principles of Social*

---

[1] Hamilton's Works, edited by H. C. Lodge, vol. iii. p. 294.

Science (1859). Inspired with the optimistic sentiment natural to a young and rising nation with abundant undeveloped resources and an unbounded outlook towards the future, he seeks to show that there exists, independently of human wills, a natural system of economic laws, which is essentially beneficent, and of which the increasing prosperity of the whole community, and especially of the working classes, is the spontaneous result,—capable of being defeated only by the ignorance or perversity of man resisting or impeding its action. He rejects the Malthusian doctrine of population, maintaining that numbers regulate themselves sufficiently in every well-governed society, and that their pressure on subsistence characterises the lower, not the more advanced, stages of civilisation. He rightly denies the universal truth, for all stages of cultivation, of the law of diminishing returns from land. His fundamental theoretic position relates to the antithesis of wealth and value.

Wealth had been by most economists confounded with the sum of exchange values; even Smith, though at first distinguishing them, afterwards allowed himself to fall into this error. Ricardo had, indeed, pointed out the difference, but only towards the end of his treatise, in the body of which value alone is considered. The later English economists had tended to regard their studies as conversant only with exchange; so far had this proceeded that Whately had proposed for the science the name of Catallactics. When wealth is considered as what it really is, the sum of useful products, we see that it has its origin in external nature as supplying both materials and physical forces, and in human labour as appropriating and adapting those natural materials and forces. Nature gives her assistance gratuitously; labour is the sole foundation of value. The less we can appropriate and employ natural forces in any production the higher the value of the product, but the less the addition to our wealth in proportion to the labour expended. Wealth, in its true sense of the sum of useful things, is the measure of the power we have acquired

over nature, whilst the value of an object expresses the
resistance of nature which labour has to overcome in order
to produce the object. Wealth steadily increases in the
course of social progress; the exchange value of objects, on
the other hand, decreases. Human intellect and faculty of
social combination secure increased command over natural
powers, and use them more largely in production, whilst less
labour is spent in achieving each result, and the value of the
product accordingly falls. The value of the article is not fixed
by its cost of production in the past; what really determines
it is the cost which is necessary for its reproduction under the
present conditions of knowledge and skill. The dependence
of value on cost, so interpreted, Carey holds to be universally
true; whilst Ricardo maintained it only with respect to objects
capable of indefinite multiplication, and in particular did not
regard it as applicable to the case of land. Ricardo saw in
the productive powers of land a free gift of nature which had
been monopolised by a certain number of persons, and which
became, with the increased demand for food, a larger and
larger value in the hands of its possessors. To this value,
however, as not being the result of labour, the owner, it might
be maintained, had no rightful claim; he could not justly
demand a payment for what was done by the " original and
indestructible powers of the soil." But Carey held that land,
as we are concerned with it in industrial life, is really an
instrument of production which has been formed as such by
man, and that its value is due to the labour expended on it
in the past,—though measured, not by the sum of that labour,
but by the labour necessary under existing conditions to bring
new land to the same stage of productiveness. He studies
the occupation and reclamation of land with peculiar advantage
as an American, for whom the traditions of first settlement
are living and fresh, and before whose eyes the process is
indeed still going on. The difficulties of adapting a primitive
soil to the work of yielding organic products for man's use
can be lightly estimated only by an inhabitant of a country

long under cultivation. It is, in Carey's view, the overcoming
of these difficulties by arduous and continued effort that entitles
the first occupier of land to his property in the soil. Its present value forms a very small proportion of the cost expended
on it, because it represents only what would be required, with
the science and appliances of our time, to bring the land
from its primitive into its present state. Property in land is
therefore only a form of invested capital—a quantity of labour
or the fruits of labour permanently incorporated with the soil;
for which, like any other capitalist, the owner is compensated
by a share of the produce. He is not rewarded for what is
done by the powers of nature, and society is in no sense
defrauded by his sole possession. The so-called Ricardian
theory of rent is a speculative fancy, contradicted by all
experience. Cultivation does not in fact, as that theory
supposes, begin with the best, and move downwards to the
poorer soils in the order of their inferiority.[1] The light and
dry higher lands are first cultivated; and only when population has become dense and capital has accumulated, are the
low-lying lands, with their greater fertility, but also with their
morasses, inundations, and miasmas, attacked and brought into
occupation. Rent, regarded as a proportion of the produce,
sinks, like all interest on capital, in process of time, but, as an
absolute amount, increases. The share of the labourer increases,
both as a proportion and an absolute amount. And thus the
interests of these different social classes are in harmony.

But, Carey proceeds to say, in order that this harmonious
progress may be realised, what is taken from the land must
be given back to it. All the articles derived from it are
really separated parts of it, which must be restored on pain of
its exhaustion. Hence the producer and the consumer must
be close to each other; the products must not be exported to
a foreign country in exchange for its manufactures, and thus
go to enrich as manure a foreign soil. In immediate exchange

---

[1] It is, however, a mistake to suppose that the assumption of this
historical order of descent is essential to the theory in question.

value the landowner may gain by such exportation, but the productive powers of the land will suffer. And thus Carey, who had set out as an earnest advocate of free trade, arrives at the doctrine of protection: the "co-ordinating power" in society must intervene to prevent private advantage from working public mischief.[1] He attributes his conversion on the question to his observation of the effects of liberal and protective tariffs respectively on American prosperity. This observation, he says, threw him back on theory, and led him to see that the intervention referred to might be necessary to remove (as he phrases it) the obstacles to the progress of younger communities created by the action of older and wealthier nations. But it seems probable that the influence of List's writings, added to his own deep-rooted and hereditary jealousy and dislike of English predominance, had something to do with his change of attitude.

The practical conclusion at which he thus arrived, though it is by no means in contradiction to the doctrine of the existence of natural economic laws, accords but ill with his optimistic scheme ; and another economist, accepting his fundamental ideas, applied himself to remove the foreign accretion, as he regarded it, and to preach the theory of spontaneous social harmonies in relation with the practice of free trade as its legitimate outcome.[2]

FRANCE—(*Continued*).

Frédéric Bastiat (1801–1850), though not a profound

---

[1] This argument seems scarcely met by Professor F. A. Walker, *Political Economy*, 50–52. But perhaps he is right in thinking that Carey exaggerates the importance of the considerations on which it is founded. Mill and Leslie remark that the transportation of agricultural products from the western to the Atlantic States has the same effect as their export to Europe, so far as this so-called "land-butchery" is concerned ; besides, some manures are obtainable from abroad.

[2] Other writings of Carey's besides his *Social Science* are his *Essay on the Rate of Wages* (1835) ; *Principles of Political Economy* (1838-1840) ; *Past, Present, and Future* (1848) ; *Unity of Law* (1872).

thinker, was a brilliant and popular writer on economic questions. Though he always had an inclination for such studies, he was first impelled to the active propagation of his views by his earnest sympathy with the English anti-corn-law agitation. Naturally of an ardent temperament, he threw himself with zeal into the free-trade controversy, through which he hoped to influence French economic policy, and published in 1845 a history of the struggle under the title of *Cobden et la Ligue.* In 1845–48 appeared his *Sophismes Économiques* (Eng. trans. by P. J. Stirling, 1873), in which he exhibited his best qualities of mind. Though Cairnes goes too far in comparing this work with the *Lettres Provinciales*, it is certainly marked by much liveliness, point, and vigour. But to expose the absurdities of the ordinary protectionism was no difficult task ; it is only in such a form as the policy assumed in the scheme of List, as purely provisional and preparatory, that it deserves and demands consideration. After the revolution of 1848, which for a time put an end to the free-trade movement in France, the efforts of Bastiat were directed against the socialists. Besides several minor pieces possessing the same sort of merit as the *Sophismes*, he produced, with a view to this controversy, his most ambitious as well as characteristic work, the *Harmonies Économiques* (Eng. trans. by P. J. Stirling, 1860). Only the first volume was published; it appeared in 1850, and its author died in the same year. Since then the notes and sketches which he had prepared as materials towards the production of the second volume have been given to the public in the collected edition of his writings (by Paillottet, with Life by Fontenay, 7 vols.), and we can thus gather what would have been the spirit and substance of the later portions of the book.

It will always be historically interesting as the last incarnation of thorough-going economic optimism. This optimism, recurring to its first origin, sets out from theological considerations, and Bastiat is commended by his English translator for treating political economy " in connection with final causes."

The spirit of the work is to represent "all principles, all motives, all springs of action, all interests, as co-operating towards a grand final result which humanity will never reach, but to which it will always increasingly tend, namely, the indefinite approximation of all classes towards a level, which steadily rises,—in other words, the equalisation of individuals in the general amelioration."

What claimed to be novel and peculiar in his scheme was principally his theory of value. Insisting on the idea that value does not denote anything inherent in the objects to which it is attributed, he endeavoured to show that it never signifies anything but the ratio of two "services." This view he develops with great variety and felicity of illustration. Only the mutual services of human beings, according to him, possess value and can claim a retribution; the assistance given by nature to the work of production is always purely gratuitous, and never enters into price. Economic progress, as, for example, the improvement and larger use of machinery, tends perpetually to transfer more and more of the elements of utility from the domain of property, and therefore of value, into that of community, or of universal and unpurchased enjoyment. It will be observed that this theory is substantially identical with Carey's, which had been earlier propounded; and the latter author in so many words alleges it to have been taken from him without acknowledgment. It has not perhaps been sufficiently attended to that very similar views are found in Dunoyer, of whose work Bastiat spoke as exercising a powerful influence on "the restoration of the science," and whom Fontenay, the biographer of Bastiat, tells us he recognised as one of his masters, Charles Comte [1] being the other.

The mode which has just been explained of conceiving industrial action and industrial progress is interesting and

[1] Charles Comte (1782–1837) was son-in-law of J. B. Say. He was associated with Dunoyer in his political writings and, like him, distinguished for his honourable independence. He was author of the *Traité de Législation*, a meritorious and useful, but not a profound work.

M

instructive so far as it is really applicable, but it was unduly generalised.   Cairnes has well pointed out that Bastiat's theoretic soundness was injuriously affected by his habit of studying doctrines with a direct view to contemporary social and political controversies.   He was thus predisposed to accept views which appeared to lend a sanction to legitimate and valuable institutions, and to reject those which seemed to him to lead to dangerous consequences.   His constant aim is, as he himself expressed it, to "break the weapons" of anti-social reasoners "in their hands," and this preoccupation interferes with the single-minded effort towards the attainment of scientific truth.   The creation or adoption of his theory of value was inspired by the wish to meet the socialistic criticism of property in land ; for the exigencies of this controversy it was desirable to be able to show that nothing is ever paid for except personal effort.   His view of rent was, therefore, so to speak, foreordained, though it may have been suggested, as indeed the editor of his posthumous fragments admits, by the writings of Carey.   He held, with the American author, that rent is purely the reward of the pains and expenditure of the landlord or his predecessors in the process of converting the natural soil into a *farm* by clearing, draining, fencing, and the other species of permanent improvements.[1]   He thus gets rid of the (so-called) Ricardian doctrine, which was accepted by the socialists, and by them used for the purpose of assailing the institution of landed property, or, at least, of supporting a claim of compensation to the community for the appropriation of the land by the concession of the "right to labour."   As Cairnes has said,[2] "what Bastiat did was this : having been at infinite pains to exclude gratuitous gifts of nature from the possible elements of value, and pointedly identified " [rather, associated] " the phenomenon with 'human effort' as its

[1] M. Leroy-Beaulieu maintains (*Essai sur la Répartition des Richesses*, 2d ed., 1882) that this, though not strictly, is approximately true—that economic forms a very small part of actual rent.

[2] *Essays in Political Economy*, p. 334.

exclusive source, he designates human effort by the term 'service,' and then employs this term to admit as sources of value those very gratuitous natural gifts the exclusion of which in this capacity constituted the essence of his doctrine." The justice of this criticism will be apparent to any one who considers the way in which Bastiat treats the question of the value of a diamond. That what is paid for in most cases of human dealings is *effort* no one can dispute. But it is surely a *reductio ad absurdum* of his theory of value, regarded as a doctrine of universal application, to represent the price of a diamond which has been accidentally found as remuneration for the effort of the finder in appropriating and transmitting it. And, with respect to land, whilst a large part of rent, in the popular sense, must be explained as interest on capital, it is plain that the native powers of the soil are capable of appropriation, and that then a price can be demanded and will be paid for their use.

Bastiat is weak on the philosophical side; he is filled with the ideas of theological teleology, and is led by these ideas to form *a priori* opinions of what existing facts and laws must necessarily be. And the *jus naturæ*, which, like metaphysical ideas generally, has its root in theology, is as much a postulate with him as with the physiocrats. Thus, in his essay on *Free Trade*, he says:—"Exchange is a natural right like property. Every citizen who has created or acquired a product ought to have the option of either applying it immediately to his own use or ceding it to whosoever on the surface of the globe consents to give him in exchange the object of his desires." Something of the same sort had been said by Turgot; and in his time this way of regarding things was excusable, and even provisionally useful; but in the middle of the 19th century it was time that it should be seen through and abandoned.

Bastiat had a real enthusiasm for a science which he thought destined to render great services to mankind, and he seems to have believed intensely the doctrines which gave a special colour to his teaching.　If his optimistic exaggerations favoured the propertied classes, they certainly were not prompted by self-interest or servility.　But they *are* exaggerations; and, amidst the modern conflicts of capital and labour, his perpetual assertion of social harmonies is the cry of "peace, peace," where there is no peace.　The freedom of industry, which he treated as a panacea, has undoubtedly brought with it great benefits; but a sufficient experience has shown that it is inadequate to solve the social problem.　How can the advocates of economic revolution be met by assuring them that everything in the natural economy is harmonious—that, in fact, all they seek for already exists?　A certain degree of spontaneous harmony does indeed exist, for society could not continue without it, but it is imperfect and precarious; the question is, How can we give to it the maximum of completeness and stability?

Augustin Cournot (1801–1877) appears to have been the first[1] who, with a competent knowledge of both subjects, endeavoured to apply mathematics to the treatment of economic questions.　His treatise entitled *Recherches sur les Principes Mathématiques de la Théorie des Richesses* was published in 1838.　He mentions in it only one previous enterprise of the same kind (though there had in fact been others)—that, namely, of Nicolas François Canard, whose book, published in 1802, was crowned by the Institute, though "its principles were radically false as well as erroneously applied."　Notwithstanding Cournot's just reputation as a writer on mathematics, the *Recherches* made little impression.　The truth seems to be that his results are in some cases of little importance, in others of questionable correctness, and that, in the abstractions to which he has recourse in order to facilitate his calculations, an essential part of the real conditions of the problem is sometimes omitted.　His pages abound in symbols

---

[1] Hermann Heinrich Gossen's work, *Entwickelung der Gesetze des menschlichen Verkehrs*, so highly praised by Jevons, *Theory of Pol. Econ.*, 2d ed., Pref., was published in 1854.

representing unknown functions, the form of the function
being left to be ascertained by observation of facts, which he
does not regard as a part of his task, or only some known
properties of the undetermined function being used as bases
for deduction.   Jevons includes in his list of works in which
a mathematical treatment of economics is adopted a second
treatise which Cournot published in 1863, with the title
Principes de la Théorie des Richesses.   But in reality, in the
work so named, which is written with great ability, and contains much forcible reasoning in opposition to the exaggerations of the ordinary economists, the mathematical method is
abandoned, and there is not an algebraical formula in the book.
The author admits that the public has always shown a repugnance to the use of mathematical symbols in economic discussion, and, though he thinks they might be of service in
facilitating exposition, fixing the ideas, and suggesting further
developments, he acknowledges that a grave danger attends
their use.   The danger, according to him, consists in the
probability that an undue value may be attached to the
abstract hypotheses from which the investigator sets out, and
which enable him to construct his formulæ.   And his practical
conclusion is that mathematical processes should be employed
only with great precaution, or even not employed at all if the
public judgment is against them, for " this judgment," he
says, " has its secret reasons, almost always more sure than
those which determine the opinions of individuals."   It is an
obvious consideration that the acceptance of unsound or one-
sided abstract principles as the premises of argument does not
depend on the use of mathematical forms, though it is possible
that the employment of the latter may by association produce
an illusion in favour of the certainty of those premises.   But
the great objection to the use of mathematics in economic
reasoning is that it is necessarily sterile.   If we examine the
attempts which have been made to employ it, we shall find
that the fundamental conceptions on which the deductions
are made to rest are vague, indeed metaphysical, in their

character. Units of animal or moral satisfaction, of utility,
and the like, are as foreign to positive science as a unit of
dormitive faculty would be; and a unit of value, unless we
understand by value the quantity of one commodity exchange-
able under given conditions for another, is an equally indefinite
idea. Mathematics can indeed formulate ratios of exchange
when they have once been observed; but it cannot by any
process of its own determine those ratios, for quantitative
conclusions imply quantitative premises, and these are wanting. There is then no future for this kind of study, and it
is only waste of intellectual power to pursue it. But the importance of mathematics as an educational introduction to all
the higher orders of research is not affected by this conclusion.
The study of the physical medium, or environment, in which
economic phenomena take place, and by which they are
affected, requires mathematics as an instrument; and nothing
can ever dispense with the didactic efficacy of that science,
as supplying the primordial type of rational investigation,
giving the lively sentiment of decisive proof, and disinclining
the mind to illusory conceptions and sophistical combinations.
And a knowledge of at least the fundamental principles of
mathematics is necessary to economists to keep them right in
their statements of doctrine, and prevent their enunciating
propositions which have no definite meaning. Even distinguished writers sometimes betray a serious deficiency in
this respect; thus they assert that one quantity "varies in-
versely as" another, when what is meant is that the sum
(not the product) of the two is constant; and they treat as
capable of numerical estimation the amount of an aggregate
of elements which, differing in kind, cannot be reduced to a
common standard. As an example of the latter error, it may
be mentioned that "quantity of labour," so often spoken of
by Ricardo, and in fact made the basis of his system, includes
such various species of exertion as will not admit of summa-
tion or comparison.

ITALY.

The first Italian translation of the *Wealth of Nations* appeared in 1780. The most distinguished Italian economist of the period here dealt with was, however, no disciple of Smith. This was Melchiorre Gioja, author, besides statistical and other writings, of a voluminous work entitled *Nuovo Prospetto delle Scienze Economiche* (6 vols., 1815-17; the work was never completed), intended to be an encyclopædia of all that had been taught by theorists, enacted by Governments, or effected by populations in the field of public and private economy. It is a learned and able treatise, but so overladen with quotations and tables as to repel rather than attract readers. Gioja admired the practical economic system of England, and enlarges on the advantages of territorial properties, manufactures, and mercantile enterprises on the large as opposed to the small scale. He defends a restrictive policy, and insists on the necessity of the action of the state as a guiding, supervising, and regulating power in the industrial world. But he is in full sympathy with the sentiment of his age against ecclesiastical domination and other mediæval survivals. We can but very briefly notice Romagnosi (d. 1835), who, by his contributions to periodical literature, and by his personal teaching, greatly influenced the course of economic thought in Italy; Antonio Scialoja (*Principii d'Economia Sociale*, 1840; and *Carestia e Governo*, 1853), an able advocate of free trade (d. 1877); Luigi Cibrario, well known as the author of *Economia Politica del medio evo* (1839; 5th ed., 1861: French trans. by Barneaud, 1859), which is in fact a view of the whole social system of that period; Girolamo Boccardo (b. 1829; *Trattato Teorico-pratico di Economia Politica*, 1853); the brilliant controversialist Francesco Ferrara, professor at Turin from 1849 to 1858 (in whose school most of the present Italian teachers of the science were, directly or indirectly, educated), a partisan of the *laisser faire* doctrine in its most extreme form, and an advocate of the peculiar opinions of Carey and Bastiat on the subject of rent; and, lastly, the Neapolitan minister Ludovico Bianchini (*Principii della Scienza del Ben Vivere Sociale*, 1845 and 1855), who is remarkable as having followed in some degree an historical direction, and asserted the principle of relativity, and who also dwelt on the relations of economics with morals, by a due attention to which the Italian economists have, indeed, in general been honourably distinguished.

SPAIN.

The *Wealth of Nations* was translated into Spanish by Ortiz in 1794. It may perhaps have influenced Gaspar de Jovellanos, who in 1795 presented to the council of Castile and printed in the same year his celebrated *Informe de la Sociedad Economica de Madrid en expediente de Ley Agraria,* which was a powerful plea for reform, especially in taxation and the laws affecting agriculture, including those relating to the systems of entail and mortmain. An English version of this memoir is given in the translation (1809) of Laborde's *Spain,* vol. iv.

GERMANY.

Roscher observes that Smith did not at first produce much impression in Germany.[1] He does not appear to have been known to Frederick the Great; he certainly exercised no influence on him. Nor did Joseph II. take notice of his work. And of the minor German princes, Karl Friedrich of Baden, as a physiocrat, would not be accessible to his doctrines. It was otherwise in the generation whose principal activity belongs to the first decade of the 19th century. The Prussian statesmen who were grouped round Stein had been formed as

---

[1] The first German version of the *Wealth of Nations* was that by Johann Friedrich Schiller, published 1776–78. The second, which is the first good one, was by Christian Garve (1794, and again 1799 and 1810). A later one by C. W. Asher (1861) is highly commended.

economists by Smith, as had also Gentz, intellectually the most important man of the Metternich régime in Austria.

The first German expositors of Smith who did more than merely reproduce his opinions were Christian Jacob Kraus (1753–1807), Georg Sartorius (1766–1828), and August Ferdinand Lüder (1760–1819). They contributed independent views from different standpoints,—the first from that of the effect of Smith's doctrine on practical government, the second from that of its bearing on history, the third from that of its relation to statistics. Somewhat later came Gottlieb Hufeland (1760–1817), Johann Friedrich Eusebius Lotz (1771–1838,) and Ludwig Heinrich von Jakob (1759–1827), who, whilst essentially of the school of Smith, apply themselves to a revision of the fundamental conceptions of the science. These authors did not exert anything like the wide influence of Say, partly on account of the less attractive form of their writings, but chiefly because Germany had not then, like France, a European audience. Julius von Soden (1754–1831) is largely founded on Smith, whom, however, he criticises with undue severity, especially in regard to his form and arrangement; the *Wealth of Nations* he describes as a series of precious fragments, and censures Smith for the absence of a comprehensive view of his whole subject, and also as onesidedly English in his tendencies.

The highest form of the Smithian doctrine in Germany is represented by four distinguished names:—Karl Heinrich Rau (1792–1870), Friedrich Nebenius (1784–1857), Friedrich Benedict Wilhelm Hermann (1795–1868), and Johann Heinrich von Thünen (1783–1850).

Rau's characteristic is "erudite thoroughness." His *Lehrbuch* (1826–32) is an encyclopædia of all that up to his time had appeared in Germany under the several heads of *Volkswirthschaftslehre*, *Volkswirthschaftspolitik*, and *Finanzwissenschaft*. His book is rich in statistical observations, and is particularly instructive on the economic effects of different geographical conditions. It is well adapted for the teaching of public servants whose duties are connected with economics, and it has in fact been the source from which the German official world down to the present time has derived its knowledge of the science. In his earlier period Rau had insisted on the necessity of a reform of economic doctrine (*Ansichten der Volkswirthschaft*, 1821), and had tended towards relativity and the historical method; but he afterwards conceived the mistaken notion that that method " only looked into the past without studying the means of improving the present," and became himself purely practical in the narrower sense of that word. He has the merit of having given a separate treatment of *Unternehmergewinn*, or " wages of management." The Prussian minister Nebenius, who was largely instrumental in the foundation of the Zollverein, was author of a highly esteemed monograph on public credit (1820). The *Staatswirthschaftliche Untersuchungen* (1832; 2d ed., 1870) of Hermann do not form a regular system, but treat a series of important special subjects. His rare technological knowledge gave him a great advantage in dealing with some economic questions. He reviewed the principal fundamental ideas of the science with great thoroughness and acuteness. " His strength," says Roscher, "lies in his clear, sharp, exhaustive distinction between the several elements of a complex conception, or the several steps comprehended in a complex act." For keen analytical power his German brethren compare him with Ricardo. But he avoids several one-sided views of the English economist. Thus he places public spirit beside egoism as an economic motor, regards price as not measured by labour only but as a product of several factors, and habitually contemplates the consumption of the labourer, not as a part of the cost of production to the capitalist, but as the main practical end of economics. Von Thünen is known principally by his remarkable work entitled *Der Isolirte Staat in Beziehung auf Landwirthschaft und Nationalökonomie* (1826; 2d ed., 1842). In this treatise, which is a classic in the political economy of agriculture, there is a rare union of exact observation with creative imagination. With a view to exhibit the natural development of agriculture, he imagines a state, isolated from the rest of the world, circular in form and of uniform fertility, without navigable rivers or canals, with a single large city at its centre, which supplies it with manufactures and receives in exchange for them its food-products, and proceeds to study the effect of distance from this central market on the agricultural economy of the several concentric spaces which compose the territory. The method, it will be seen, is highly abstract, but, though it may not be fruitful, it is quite legitimate. The author is under no illusion blinding him to the unreality of the hypothetic case. The supposition is necessary, in his view, in order to separate and consider apart one essential condition—that, namely, of situation with respect to the market. It was his intention (imperfectly realised, however) to institute afterwards several different hypotheses in relation to his isolated state, for the purpose of similarly studying other conditions which in real life are found in combination or conflict. The objection to this method lies in the difficulty of the return from the abstract study to the actual facts ; and this is probably an insuperable one in regard to most of its applications. The investigation, however, leads to trustworthy conclusions as to the conditions of the succession of different systems of land economy. The book abounds in calculations relating to agricultural expenditure and income, which diminish its interest to the general reader, though they are considered valuable to the specialist. They embody the results of the practical experience of the author on his estate of Tellow in Mecklenburg-Schwerin. Von Thünen was strongly impressed with the danger of a violent conflict between the middle class and the proletariate, and studied earnestly the question of wages, which he was one of the first to regard habitually, not merely as the price of the commodity labour, but as the means of subsistence of the mass of the community. He arrived by mathematical reasonings of some complexity at a formula which expresses the amount of "natural wages" as $= \sqrt{ap}$, where a is the necessary expenditure of the labourer for subsistence, and p is the product of his labour.   To this formula he attributed so much importance that he directed it to be engraved on his tomb.   It implies that wages ought to rise with the amount of the product; and this conclusion led him to establish on his estate a system of participation by the labourers in the profits of farming, of which some account will be found in Mr. Sedley Taylor's *Profit-sharing between Capital and Labour* (1884).   Von Thünen deserves more attention than he has received in England; both as a man and as a writer he was eminently interesting and original; and there is much in *Der Isolirte Staat* and his other works that is awakening and suggestive.

Roscher recognises what he calls a Germano-Russian (deutsch-russische) school of political economy, represented principally by Heinrich Storch (1766–1825).   Mercantilist principles had been preached by a native ("autochthonen") economist, Ivan Possoschkoff, in the time of Peter the Great. The new ideas of the Smithian system were introduced into Russia by Christian Von Schlözer (1774–1831) in his professorial lectures and in his *Anfangsgründe der Staatswirthschaft, oder die Lehre von National-reichthume* (1805–1807). Storch was instructor in economic science of the future emperor Nicholas and his brother the grand-duke Michael, and the substance of his lessons to them is contained in his *Cours d'Économie Politique* (1815).   The translation of this treatise into Russian was prevented by the censorship; Rau published a German version of it, with annotations, in 1819. It is a work of a very high order of merit.   The epithet "deutsch-russisch" seems little applicable to Storch; as Roscher himself says, he follows mainly English and French writers—Say, Sismondi, Turgot, Bentham, Steuart, and Hume, but, above all, Adam Smith.   His personal position (and the same is true of Schlözer) led him to consider economic doctrines in connection with a stage of culture different from that of the Western populations amongst which they had been formulated ; this change of the point of view opened the door to relativity, and helped to prepare the Historical method. Storch's study of the economic and moral effects of serfdom is regarded as especially valuable. The general subjects with which he has particularly connected his name are (1) the doctrine of immaterial commodities (or elements of national prosperity), such as health, talent, morality, and the like; (2) the question of "productive" and "unproductive," as characters of labour and of consumption, on which he disagreed with Smith and may have furnished indications to Dunoyer; and (3) the differences between the revenue of nations and that of individuals, on which he follows Lauderdale and is opposed to Say. The latter economist having published at Paris (1823) a new edition of Storch's *Cours*, with criticisms sometimes offensive in tone, he published by way of reply to some of Say's strictures what is considered his ripest and scientifically most important work, *Considérations sur la nature du Revenu National* (1824 ; translated into German by the author himself, 1825).

A distinct note of opposition to the Smithian economics was sounded in Germany by two writers, who, setting out from somewhat different points of view, animated by different sentiments, and favouring different practical systems, yet, so far as their criticisms are concerned, arrive at similar conclusions ; we mean Adam Müller and Friedrich List.

Adam Müller (1779–1829) was undoubtedly a man of real genius. In his principal work *Elemente der Staatskunst* (1809), and his other writings, he represents a movement of economic thought which was in relation with the (so-called) Romantic literature of the period. The reaction against Smithianism of which he was the coryphæus was founded on an attachment to the principles and social system of the Middle Ages. It is possible that the political and historical ideas which inspire him, his repugnance to contemporary liberalism, and his notions of regular organic development, especially in relation to England, were in some degree imbibed from Edmund Burke, whose *Reflections on the Revolution in France* had been translated into German by Friedrich Gentz, the friend and teacher of Müller. The association of his criticisms with mediæval prepossessions ought not to prevent our recognising the elements of truth which they contain.

He protests against the doctrine of Smith and against modern political economy in general on the ground that it presents a mechanical, atomistic, and purely material conception of society, that it reduces to nullity all moral forces and ignores the necessity of a moral order, that it is at bottom no more than a theory of private property and private interests, and takes no account of the life of the people as a whole in its national solidarity and historical continuity. Exclusive attention, he complains, is devoted to the immediate production of objects possessing exchange value and to the transitory existence of individuals; whilst to the maintenance of the collective production for future generations, to intellectual products, powers, possessions, and enjoyments, and to the State with its higher tasks and aims, scarcely a thought is given. The truth is that nations are specialised organisms with distinct principles of life, having definite individualities which determine the course of their historical development. Each is through all time one whole; and, as the present is the heir of the past, it ought to keep before it constantly the permanent good of the community in the future. The economic existence of a people is only one side or province of its entire activity, requiring to be kept in harmony with the higher ends of society; and the proper organ to effect this reconciliation is the State, which, instead of being merely an apparatus for the administration of justice, represents the totality of the national life. The division of labour, Müller holds, is imperfectly developed by Smith, who makes it to arise out of a native bent for truck or barter; whilst its dependence on capital—on the labours and accumulations of past generations—is not duly emphasised, nor is the necessary counterpoise and completion of the division of labour, in the principle of the national combination of labour, properly brought out. Smith recognises only material, not spiritual, capital ; yet the latter, represented in every nation by language, as the former by money, is a real national store of experience, wisdom, good sense, and moral feeling, transmitted with increase by each generation to its successor, and enables each generation to produce immensely more than by its own unaided powers it could possibly do. Again, the system of Smith is one-sidedly British ; if it is innocuous on the soil of England, it is because in her society the old foundations on which the spiritual and material life of the people can securely rest are preserved in the surviving spirit of feudalism and the inner connection of the whole social system—the national capital of laws, manners, reputation, and credit, which has been handed down in its integrity in consequence of the insular position of the country. For the continent of Europe a quite different system is necessary, in which, in place of the sum of the private wealth of individuals being viewed as the primary object, the real wealth of the nation and the production of national power shall be made to predominate, and along with the division of labour its national union and concentration—along with the physical, no less the intellectual and moral, capital shall be embraced. In these leading traits of Müller's thought there is much which foreshadows the more recent forms of German economic and sociological speculation, especially those characteristic of the " Historical" school.

Another element of opposition was represented by Friedrich List (1798–1846), a man of great intellectual vigour as well as practical energy, and notable as having powerfully contributed by his writings to the formation of the German Zoll-verein. His principal work is entitled *Das Nationale System der Politischen Oekonomie* (1841 ; 6th ed., 1877 : Eng. trans., 1885). Though his practical conclusions were different from Müller's, he was largely influenced by the general mode of thinking of that writer, and by his strictures on the doctrine

of Smith. It was particularly against the cosmopolitan principle in the modern economical system that he protested, and
against the absolute doctrine of free trade, which was in
harmony with that principle: He gave prominence to the
National idea, and insisted on the special requirements of
each nation according to its circumstances and especially to
the degree of its development.

He refuses to Smith's system the title of the industrial,
which he thinks more appropriate to the mercantile system,
and designates the former as "the exchange-value system."
He denies the parallelism asserted by Smith between the economic conduct proper to an individual and to a nation, and
holds that the immediate private interest of the separate
members of the community will not lead to the highest good
of the whole. The nation is an existence, standing between
the individual and Humanity, and formed into a unity by its
language, manners, historical development, culture, and constitution. This unity is the first condition of the security,
wellbeing, progress, and civilisation of the individual; and
private economic interests, like all others, must be subordinated to the maintenance, completion, and strengthening of
the nationality. The nation having a continuous life, its true
wealth consists—and this is List's fundamental doctrine—not
in the quantity of exchange-values which it possesses, but in
the full and many-sided development of its productive powers.
Its economic education, if we may so speak, is more important
than the immediate production of values, and it may be right
that the present generation should sacrifice its gain and enjoyment to secure the strength and skill of the future. In the
sound and normal condition of a nation which has attained
economic maturity, the three productive powers of agriculture,
manufactures, and commerce should be alike developed. But
the two latter factors are superior in importance, as exercising
a more effective and fruitful influence on the whole culture
of the nation, as well as on its independence. Navigation,
railways, all higher technical arts, connect themselves specially

with these factors; whilst in a purely agricultural state there is a tendency to stagnation, absence of enterprise, and the maintenance of antiquated prejudices. But for the growth of the higher forms of industry all countries are not adapted—only those of the temperate zones, whilst the torrid regions have a natural monopoly in the production of certain raw materials; and thus between these two groups of countries a division of labour and confederation of powers spontaneously takes place. List then goes on to explain his theory of the stages of economic development through which the nations of the temperate zone, which are furnished with all the necessary conditions, naturally pass, in advancing to their normal economic state. These are (1) pastoral life, (2) agriculture, (3) agriculture united with manufactures; whilst in the final stage agriculture, manufactures, and commerce are combined. The economic task of the state is to bring into existence by legislative and administrative action the conditions required for the progress of the nation through these stages. Out of this view arises List's scheme of industrial politics. Every nation, according to him, should begin with free trade, stimulating and improving its agriculture by intercourse with richer and more cultivated nations, importing foreign manufactures and exporting raw products. When it is economically so far advanced that it can manufacture for itself, then a system of protection should be employed to allow the home industries to develop themselves fully, and save them from being overpowered in their earlier efforts by the competition of more matured foreign industries in the home market. When the national industries have grown strong enough no longer to dread this competition, then the highest stage of progress has been reached; free trade should again become the rule, and the nation be thus thoroughly incorporated with the universal industrial union. In List's time, according to his view, Spain, Portugal, and Naples were purely agricultural countries; Germany and the United States of North America had arrived at the second stage, their manufactures being in process of development;

France was near the boundary of the third or highest stage, which England alone had reached. For England, therefore, as well as for the agricultural countries first-named, free trade was the right economic policy, but not for Germany or America. What a nation loses for a time in exchange-values during the protective period she much more than gains in the long run in productive power,—the temporary expenditure being strictly analogous, when we place ourselves at the point of view of the life of the nation, to the cost of the industrial education of the individual. The practical conclusion which List drew for his own country was that she needed for her economic progress an extended and conveniently bounded territory reaching to the sea-coast both on north and south, and a vigorous expansion of manufactures and commerce, and that the way to the latter lay through judicious protective legislation with a customs union comprising all German lands, and a German marine with a Navigation Act. The national German spirit, striving after independence and power through union, and the national industry, awaking from its lethargy and eager to recover lost ground, were favourable to the success of List's book, and it produced a great sensation. He ably represented the tendencies and demands of his time in his own country; his work had the effect of fixing the attention, not merely of the speculative and official classes, but of practical men generally, on questions of Political Economy; and he had without doubt an important influence on German industrial policy. So far as science is concerned, the emphasis he laid on the relative historical study of stages of civilisation as affecting economic questions, and his protest against absolute formulas, had a certain value; and the preponderance given to the national development over the immediate gains of individuals was sound in principle; though his doctrine was, both on its public and private sides, too much of a mere chrematistic. and tended in fact to set up a new form of mercantilism, rather than to aid the contemporary effort towards social reform.

Most of the writers at home or abroad hitherto mentioned continued the traditions of the school of Smith, only developing his doctrine in particular directions, sometimes not without one-sidedness or exaggeration, or correcting minor errors into which he had fallen, or seeking to give to the exposition of his principles more of order and lucidity.   Some assailed the abuse of abstraction by Smith's successors, objected to the conclusions of Ricardo and his followers their non-accordance with the actual facts of human life, or protested against the anti-social consequences which seemed to result from the application of the (so-called) orthodox formulas.   A few challenged Smith's fundamental ideas, and insisted on the necessity of altering the basis of general philosophy on which his economics ultimately rest.   But, notwithstanding various premonitory indications, nothing substantial, at least nothing effective, was done, within the field we have as yet surveyed, towards the establishment of a really new order of thinking, or new mode of proceeding, in this branch of inquiry.   Now, however, we have to describe a great and growing movement, which has already considerably changed the whole character of the study in the conceptions of many, and which promises to exercise a still more potent influence in the future.   We mean the rise of the Historical School, which we regard as marking the third epoch in the modern development of economic science.

CHAPTER VI.

THE HISTORICAL SCHOOL.

THE negative movement which filled the eighteenth century had for its watchword on the economic side the liberation of industrial effort from both feudal survivals and Governmental fetters. But in all the aspects of that movement, the economic as well as the rest, the process of demolition was historically only the necessary preliminary condition of a total renovation, towards which Western Europe was energetically tending, though with but an indistinct conception of its precise nature. The disorganisation of the body of opinion which underlay the old system outran the progress towards the establishment of new principles adequate to form a guidance in the future. The critical philosophy which had wrought the disorganisation could only repeat its formulas of absolute liberty, but was powerless for reconstruction. And hence there was seen throughout the West, after the French explosion, the remarkable spectacle of a continuous oscillation between the tendency to recur to outworn ideas and a vague impulse towards a new order in social thought and life, this impulse often taking an anarchical character.

From this state of oscillation, which has given to our century its equivocal and transitional aspect, the only possible issue was in the foundation of a scientific social doctrine which should supply a basis for the gradual convergence of opinion on human questions. The foundation of such a doctrine is the immortal service for which the world is indebted to Auguste Comte (1798–1857).

The leading features of Sociology, as he conceived it, are the following :—(1) it is essentially *one* science, in which all the elements of a social state are studied in their relations and mutual actions ; (2) it includes a dynamical as well as a statical theory of society ; (3) it thus eliminates the absolute, substituting for an imagined fixity the conception of ordered change ; (4) its principal method, though others are not excluded, is that of historical comparison ; (5) it is pervaded by moral ideas, by notions of social duty, as opposed to the individual rights which were derived as corollaries from the *jus naturæ ;* and (6) in its spirit and practical consequences it tends to the realisation of all the great ends which compose "the popular cause" ; yet (7) it aims at this through peaceful means, replacing revolution by evolution.[1] The several characteristics we have enumerated are not independent; they may be shown to be vitally connected with each other. Several of these features must now be more fully described; the others will meet us before the close of the present survey.

In the masterly exposition of sociological method which is contained in the fourth volume of the *Philosophie Positive* (1839),[2] Comte marks out the broad division between social statics and social dynamics—the former studying the laws of social coexistence, the latter those of social development. The fundamental principle of the former is the general consensus

---

[1] It would be a grave error to suppose that the subjection of social phenomena to natural laws affords any encouragement to a spirit of fatalistic quietism. On the contrary, it is the existence of such laws that is the necessary basis of all systematic action for the improvement either of our condition or of our nature, as may be seen by considering the parallel case of hygienic and therapeutic agencies. And, since the different orders of phenomena are more modifiable in proportion to their greater complexity, the social field admits of more extensive and efficacious human intervention than the inorganic or vital domain. In relation to the dynamical side of Sociology, whilst the direction and essential character of the evolution are predetermined, its rate and secondary features are capable of modification.

[2] He had already in 1822 stated his fundamental principles in an opuscule which is reproduced in the Appendix to his *Politique Positive.*

between the several social organs and functions, which, without unduly pressing a useful analogy, we may regard as resembling that which exists between the several organs and functions of an animal body. The study of dynamical is different from, and necessarily subordinated to, that of statical sociology, progress being in fact the development of order, just as the study of evolution in biology is different from, and subordinated to, that of the structures and functions which are exhibited by evolution as they exist at the several points of an ascending scale. The laws of social coexistence and movement are as much subjects for observation as the corresponding phenomena in the life of an individual organism. For the study of development in particular, a modification of the comparative method familiar to biologists will be the appropriate mode of research. The several successive stages of society will have to be systematically compared, in order to discover their laws of sequence, and to determine the filiation of their characteristic features.

Though we must take care that both in our statical and dynamical studies we do not ignore or contradict the fundamental properties of human nature, the project of deducing either species of laws from those properties independently of direct observation is one which cannot be realised. Neither the general structure of human society nor the march of its development could be so predicted. This is especially evident with respect to dynamical laws, because, in the passage of society from one phase to another, the preponderating agency is the accumulated influence of past generations, which is much too complex to be investigated deductively—a conclusion which it is important to keep steadily before us now that some of the (so-called) anthropologists are seeking to make the science of society a mere annex and derivative of biology. The principles of biology unquestionably lie at the foundation of the social science, but the latter has, and must always have, a field of research and a method of inquiry peculiar to itself. The field is history in the largest sense, including contemporary fact ; and the principal, though not exclusive, method is, as we have said, that process of sociological comparison which is most conveniently called " the historical method."

These general principles affect the economic no less than other branches of social speculation ; and with respect to that department of inquiry they lead to important results. They show that the idea of forming a true theory of the economic frame and working of society apart from its other sides is illusory. Such study is indeed provisionally indispensable, but no rational theory of the economic organs and functions of society can be constructed if they are considered as isolated from the rest. In other words, a separate economic science is, strictly speaking, an impossibility, as representing only one portion of a complex organism, all whose parts and their actions are in a constant relation of correspondence and reciprocal modification. Hence, too, it will follow that, whatever useful indications may be derived from our general knowledge of individual human nature, the economic structure of society and its mode of development cannot be deductively foreseen, but must be ascertained by direct historical investigation. We have said " its mode of development " ; for it is obvious that, as of every social element, so of the economic factor in human affairs, there must be a dynamical doctrine, a theory of the successive phases of the economic condition of society ; yet in the accepted systems this was a desideratum, nothing but some partial and fragmentary notions on this whole side of the subject being yet extant.[1] And, further, the economic structure and working of one historic stage being different from those of another, we must abandon the idea of an absolute system possessing universal validity, and substitute that of a series of such systems, in which, however,

[1] Under the influence of these views of Comte, J. S. Mill attempted in Book IV. of his *Political Economy* a treatment of Economic Dynamics ; but that appears to us one of the least satisfactory portions of his work.

the succession is not at all arbitrary, but is itself regulated by law.

Though Comte's enterprise was a constructive one, his aim being the foundation of a scientific theory of society, he could not avoid criticising the labours of those who before him had treated several branches of social inquiry. Amongst them the economists were necessarily considered; and he urged or implied, in various places of his above-named work, as well as of his *Politique Positive*, objections to their general ideas and methods of procedure essentially the same with those which we stated in speaking of Ricardo and his followers. J. S. Mill shows himself much irritated by these comments, and remarks on them as showing "how extremely superficial M. Comte" (whom he yet regards as a thinker quite comparable with Descartes and Leibnitz) " could sometimes be,"—an unfortunate observation, which he would scarcely have made if he could have foreseen the subsequent march of European thought, and the large degree in which the main points of Comte's criticism have been accepted or independently reproduced.

GERMANY.

The second manifestation of this new movement in economic science was the appearance of the German historical school. The views of this school do not appear to have arisen, like Comte's theory of sociological method, out of general philosophic ideas; they seem rather to have been suggested by an extension to the economic field of the conceptions of the historical school of jurisprudence of which Savigny was the most eminent representative. The juristic system is not a fixed social phenomenon, but is variable from one stage in the progress of society to another; it is in vital relation with the other coexistent social factors: and what is, in the jural sphere, adapted to one period of development, is often unfit for another. These ideas were seen to be applicable to the economic system also; the relative point of view was thus reached, and the absolute attitude was found to be untenable. Cosmopolitanism in theory, or the assumption of a system equally true of every country, and what has been called per-petualism, or the assumption of a system applicable to every social stage, were alike discredited. And so the German historical school appears to have taken its rise.

Omitting preparatory indications and undeveloped germs of doctrine, we must trace the origin of the school to Wilhelm Roscher. Its fundamental principles are stated, though with some hesitation, and with an unfortunate contrast of the his-torical with the "philosophical" method,[1] in his *Grundriss zu Vorlesungen über die Staatswirthschaft nach geschichtlicher Methode* (1843). The following are the leading heads in-sisted on in the preface to that work.

"The historical method exhibits itself not merely in the external form of a treatment of phenomena according to their chronological succession, but in the following fundamental ideas. (1.) The aim is to represent what nations have thought, willed, and discovered in the economic field, what they have striven after and attained, and why they have attained it. (2.) A people is not merely the mass of individuals now living; it will not suffice to observe contemporary facts. (3.) All the peoples of whom we can learn anything must be studied and compared from the economic point of view, especially the ancient peoples, whose development lies before us in its totality. (4.) We must not simply praise or blame economic institutions; few of them have been salutary or detrimental to all peoples and at all stages of culture; rather it is a principal task of science to show how and why, out of what was once reasonable and beneficent, the unwise and inexpedient has often gradually arisen." Of the principles enunciated in this paraphrase of Roscher's words a portion

[1] This phraseology was probably borrowed from the controversy on the method of jurisprudence between Thibaut on the one hand and Savigny and Hugo on the other.

of the third alone seems open to objection; the economy of
ancient peoples is not a more important subject of study than
that of the moderns; indeed, the question of the relative importance of the two is one that ought not to be raised. For
the essential condition of all sound sociological inquiry is the
comparative consideration of the entire series of the most
complete evolution known to history—that, namely, of the
group of nations forming what is known as the Occidental
Commonwealth, or, more briefly, "the West." The reasons
for choosing this social series, and for provisionally restricting
our studies almost altogether to it, have been stated with
unanswerable force by Comte in the *Philosophie Positive.*
Greece and Rome are, indeed, elements in the series; but it
is the development as a whole, not any special portions of it,
that Sociology must keep in view in order to determine the
laws of the movement,—just as, in the study of biological
evolution, no one stage of an organism can be considered as of
preponderating importance, the entire succession of changes
being the object of research. Of Roscher's further eminent
services we shall speak hereafter; he is now mentioned only
in relation to the origin of the new school.

In 1848 Bruno Hildebrand published the first volume of a
work, which, though he lived for many years after (d. 1878),
he never continued, entitled *Die Nationalökonomie der Gegenwart und Zukunft.* Hildebrand was a thinker of a really
high order; it may be doubted whether amongst German
economists there has been any endowed with a more profound
and searching intellect. He is quite free from the wordiness
and obscurity which too often characterise German writers,
and traces broad outlines with a sure and powerful hand. His
book contains a masterly criticism of the economic systems
which preceded, or belonged to, his time, including those of
Smith, Müller, List, and the socialists. But it is interesting
to us at present mainly from the general position he takes up,
and his conception of the real nature of political economy.
The object of his work, he tells us, is to open a way in the

economic domain to a thorough historical direction and method, and to transform the science into a doctrine of the laws of the economic development of nations. It is interesting to observe that the type which he sets before him in his proposed reform of political economy is not that of historical jurisprudence, but of the science of language as it has been reconstructed in the present century, a selection which indicates the comparative method as the one which he considered appropriate. In both sciences we have the presence of an ordered variation in time, and the consequent substitution of the relative for the absolute.

In 1853 appeared the work of Karl Knies, entitled *Die Politische Oekonomie vom Standpunkte der geschichtlichen Methode.* This is an elaborate exposition and defence of. the historical method in its application to economic science, and is the most systematic and complete manifesto of the new school, at least on the logical side. The fundamental propositions are that the economic constitution of society at any epoch on the one hand, and on the other the contemporary theoretic conception of economic science, are results of a definite historical development; that they are both in vital connection with the whole social organism of the period, having grown up along with it and under the same conditions of time, place, and nationality; that the economic system must therefore be regarded as passing through a series of phases correlative with the successive stages of civilisation, and can at no point of this movement be considered to have attained an entirely definitive form; that no more the present than any previous economic organisation of society is to be regarded as absolutely good and right, but only as a phase in a continuous historical evolution; and that in like manner the now prevalent economic doctrine is not to be viewed as complete and final, but only as representing a certain stage in the unfolding or progressive manifestation of the truth.

The theme of the book is handled with, perhaps, an undue degree of expansion and detail. The author exhibits much sagacity as well as learning, and criticises effectively the errors, inconsistencies, and exaggerations of his predecessors. But in characterising and vindicating the historical method he has added nothing to Comte. A second edition of his treatise was published in 1883, and in this he makes the singular confession that, when he wrote in 1852, the *Philosophie Positive*, the six volumes of which had appeared from 1830 to 1842, was entirely unknown to him and, he adds, probably to all German economists. This is not to the credit of their open-mindedness or literary vigilance, if we remember that Mill was already in correspondence with Comte in 1841, and that his eulogistic notice of him in the *Logic* appeared in 1843. When, however, Knies at a later period examined Comte's work, he was, he tells us, surprised at finding in it so many anticipations of, or " parallelisms " with, his own conclusions. And well he might; for all that is really valuable in his methodology is to be found in Comte, applied on a larger scale, and designed with the broad and commanding power which marks the *dii majores* of philosophy.

There are two points which seem to be open to criticism in the position taken by some German economists of the historical school.

1. Knies and some other writers, in maintaining the principle of relativity in economic theory, appear not to preserve the due balance in one particular. The two forms of absolutism in doctrine, cosmopolitanism and what Knies calls perpetualism, he seems to place on exactly the same footing; in other words, he considers the error of overlooking varieties of local circumstances and nationality to be quite as serious as that of neglecting differences in the stage of historical development. But this is certainly not so. In every branch of Sociology the latter is much the graver error, vitiating radically, wherever it is found, the whole of our investigations. If we ignore the fact, or mistake the direction, of the social movement, we are wrong in the most fundamental point of all—a point, too, which is involved in every question. But the variations de-

pending on difference of race, as affecting bodily and mental endowment, or on diversity of external situation, are secondary phenomena only; they must be postponed in studying the general theory of social development, and taken into account afterwards when we come to examine the modifications in the character of the development arising out of peculiar conditions. And, though the physical nature of a territory is a condition which is likely to operate with special force on economic phenomena, it is rather on the technical forms and comparative extension of the several branches of industry that it will act than on the social conduct of each branch, or the co-ordination and relative action of all, which latter are the proper subjects of the inquiries of the economist.

2. Some members of the school appear, in their anxiety to assert the relativity of the science, to fall into the error of denying economic laws altogether; they are at least unwilling to speak of "natural laws" in relation to the economic world. From a too exclusive consideration of law in the inorganic sphere, they regard this phraseology as binding them to the notion of fixity and of an invariable system of practical economy. But, if we turn our attention rather to the organic sciences, which are more kindred to the social, we shall see that the term "natural law" carries with it no such implication. As we have more than once indicated, an essential part of the idea of life is that of development, in other words, of "ordered change." And that such a development takes place in the constitution and working of society in all its elements is a fact which cannot be doubted, and which these writers themselves emphatically assert. That there exist between the several social elements such relations as make the change of one element involve or determine the change of another is equally plain; and why the name of natural laws should be denied to such constant relations of coexistence and succession it is not easy to see. These laws, being universal, admit of the construction of an abstract theory of economic development; whilst a part of the German historical school tends to

substitute for such a theory a mere description of different national economies, introducing prematurely—as we have pointed out—the action of special territorial or ethnological conditions, instead of reserving this as the ground of later modifications, in concrete cases, of the primary general laws deduced from a study of the common human evolution.

To the three writers above named, Roscher, Hildebrand, and Knies, the foundation of the German historical school of political economy belongs. It does not appear that Roscher in his own subsequent labours has been much under the influence of the method which he has in so many places admirably characterised. In his *System der Volkswirthschaft* (vol. i., *Grundlagen der Nationalökonomie*, 1854; 16th ed., 1883: Eng. transl. by J. J. Lalor, 1878; vol. ii., *N. O. des Ackerbaues*, 1860; 10th ed., 1882; vol. iii., *N. O. des Handels und Gewerbfleisses*, 4th ed., 1883) the dogmatic and the historical matter are rather juxtaposed than vitally combined. It is true that he has most usefully applied his vast learning to special historical studies, in relation especially to the progress of the science itself. His treatise *Ueber das Verhältniss der Nationalökonomie zum classischen Alterthume* (1849), his *Zur Geschichte der Englischen Volkswirthschaftslehre* (Leipsic, 1851–2), and, above all, that marvellous monument of erudition and industry, his *Geschichte der National-Oekonomik in Deutschland* (1874), to which he is said to have devoted fifteen years of study, are among the most valuable extant works of this kind, though the last by its accumulation of detail is unfitted for general study outside of Germany itself. Several interesting and useful monographs are collected in his *Ansichten der Volkswirthschaft vom geschichtlichen Standpunkte* (3d ed., 1878). His systematic treatise, too, above referred to, abounds in historical notices of the rise and development of the several doctrines of the science. But it cannot be alleged that he has done much towards the transformation of political economy which his earliest labours seemed to announce; and Cossa appears to be right in saying that his dogmatic work has not effected any substantial modification of the principles of Hermann and Rau.

The historical method has exhibited its essential features more fully in the hands of the younger generation of scientific economists in Germany, amongst whom may be reckoned Lujo Brentano, Adolf Held, Erwin Nasse, Gustav Schmoller, H. Rösler, Albert Schaffle, Hans von Scheel, Gustav Schonberg, and Adolf Wagner. Besides the general principle of an historical treatment of the science, the leading ideas which have been most strongly insisted on by this school are the following. I. The necessity of accentuating the moral element in economic study. This consideration has been urged with special emphasis by Schmoller in his *Grundfragen* (1875) and by Schäffle in his *Das gesellschaftliche System der menschlichen Wirthschaft* (3d ed., 1873). G. Kries (d. 1858) appears also to have handled the subject well in a review of J. S. Mill. According to the most advanced organs of the school, three principles of organisation are at work in practical economy; and, corresponding with these, there are three different systems or spheres of activity. The latter are (1) private economy; (2) the compulsory public economy; (3) the "caritative" sphere. In the first alone personal interest predominates; in the second the general interest of the society; in the third the benevolent impulses. Even in the first, however, the action of private interest cannot be unlimited; not to speak here of the intervention of the public power, the excesses and abuses of the fundamental principle in this department must be checked and controlled by an economic morality, which can never be left out of account in theory any more than in practical applications. In the third region above named, moral influences are of course supreme. II. The close relation which necessarily exists between economics and jurisprudence. This has been brought out by L. von Stein and H. Rösler, but is most systematically established by Wagner—who is, without doubt, one of the most eminent of living German economists —especially in his *Grundlegung*, now forming part of the

comprehensive *Lehrbuch der politischen Oekonomie* published
by him and Professor Nasse jointly. The doctrine of the
jus naturæ, on which the physiocrats, as we have seen, reared
their economic structure, has lost its hold on belief, and the
old *a priori* and absolute conceptions of personal freedom and
property have given way along with it. It is seen that the
economic position of the individual, instead of depending
merely on so-called natural rights or even on his natural
powers, is conditioned by the contemporary juristic system,
which is itself an historical product. The above-named conceptions, therefore, half economic half juristic, of freedom
and property require a fresh examination. It is principally
from this point of view that Wagner approaches economic
studies. The point, as he says, on which all turns is the old
question of the relation of the individual to the community.
Whoever with the older juristic and political philosophy and
national economy places the individual in the centre comes
necessarily to the untenable results which, in the economic
field, the physiocratic and Smithian school of free competition
has set up. Wagner on the contrary investigates, before
anything else, the conditions of the economic life of the community, and, in subordination to this, determines the sphere
of the economic freedom of the individual. III. A different
conception of the functions of the State from that entertained
by the school of Smith. The latter school has in general
followed the view of Rousseau and Kant that the sole office of
the state is the protection of the members of the community
from violence and fraud. This doctrine, which was in harmony
with those of the *jus naturæ* and the social contract, was
temporarily useful for the demolition of the old economic
system with its complicated apparatus of fetters and restrictions. But it could not stand against a rational historical
criticism, and still less against the growing practical demands
of modern civilisation. In fact, the abolition of the impolitic
and discredited system of European Governments, by bringing
to the surface the evils arising from unlimited competition,

irresistibly demonstrated the necessity of public action according to new and more enlightened methods. The German
historical school recognises the State as not merely an institution for the maintenance of order, but as the organ of the
nation for all ends which cannot be adequately effected by
voluntary individual effort. Whenever social aims can be
attained only or most advantageously through its action, that
action is justified.[1] The cases in which it can properly inter-
fere must be determined separately on their own merits and
in relation to the stage of national development. It ought
certainly to promote intellectual and æsthetic culture. It
ought to enforce provisions for public health and regulations
for the proper conduct of production and transport. It ought
to protect the weaker members of society, especially women,
children, the aged, and the destitute, at least in the absence
of family maintenance and guardianship. It ought to secure
the labourer against the worst consequences of personal injury
not due to his own negligence, to assist through legal recognition and supervision the efforts of the working classes for joint
no less than individual self-help, and to guarantee the safety
of their earnings, when intrusted to its care.

A special influence which has worked on this more recent
group is that of theoretic socialism; we shall see hereafter
that socialism as a party organisation has also affected their
practical politics. With such writers as St. Simon, Fourier,
and Proudhon, Lassalle, Marx, Engels, Marlo, and Rodbertus
(who, notwithstanding a recent denial, seems rightly described
as a socialist) we do not deal in the present treatise; but we
must recognise them as having powerfully stimulated the
younger German economists (in the strict sense of this last
word). They have even modified the scientific conclusions
of the latter, especially through criticism of the so-called
orthodox system. Schäffle and Wagner may be especially
named as having given a large space and a respectful attention

---

[1] It will in each case be necessary to examine whether the action can
best be taken by the central, or by the local, government.

to their arguments. In particular, the important consideration, to which we have already referred, that the economic position of the individual depends on the existing legal system, and notably on the existing organisation of property, was first insisted on by the socialists. They had also pointed out that the present institutions of society in relation to property, inheritance, contract, and the like, are (to use Lassalle's phrase) "historical categories which have changed, and are subject to further change," whilst in the orthodox economy they are generally assumed as a fixed order of things on the basis of which the individual creates his own position. J. S. Mill, as we have seen, called attention to the fact of the distribution of wealth depending, unlike its production, not on natural laws alone, but on the ordinances of society, but it is some of the German economists of the younger historical school who have most strongly emphasised this view. To rectify and complete the conception, however, we must bear in mind that those ordinances themselves are not arbitrarily changeable, but are conditioned by the stage of general social development.

In economic politics these writers have taken up a position between the German free-trade (or, as it is sometimes with questionable propriety called, the Manchester) party and the democratic socialists. The latter invoke the omnipotence of the State to transform radically and immediately the present economic constitution of society in the interest of the proletariate. The free-traders seek to minimise state action for any end except that of maintaining public order, and securing the safety and freedom of the individual. The members of the school of which we are now speaking, when intervening in the discussion of practical questions, have occupied an intermediate standpoint. They are opposed alike to social revolution and to rigid *laisser faire*. Whilst rejecting the socialistic programme, they call for the intervention of the State in accordance with the theoretic principles already mentioned, for the purpose of mitigating the pressure of the modern industrial system on its weaker members, and extending in greater measure to the working classes the benefits of advancing civilisation. Schäffle in his *Capitalismus und Socialismus* (1870; now absorbed into a larger work), Wagner in his *Rede über die sociale Frage* (1871), and Schönberg in his *Arbeitsämter: eine Aufgabe des deutschen Reichs* (1871) advocated this policy in relation to the question of the labourer. These expressions of opinion, with which most of the German professors of political economy sympathised, were violently assailed by the organs of the free-trade party, who found in them "a new form of socialism." Out of this arose a lively controversy; and the necessity of a closer union and a practical political organisation being felt amongst the partisans of the new direction, a congress was held at Eisenach in October 1872, for the consideration of "the social question." It was attended by almost all the professors of economic science in the German universities, by representatives of the several political parties, by leaders of the working men, and by some of the large capitalists. At this meeting the principles above explained were formulated. Those who adopted them obtained from their opponents the appellation of " Katheder-Socialisten," or " socialists of the (professorial) chair," a nickname invented by H. B. Oppenheim, and which those to whom it was applied were not unwilling to accept. Since 1873 this group has been united in the " Verein fur Socialpolitik," in which, as the controversy became mitigated, free-traders also have taken part. Within the Verein a division has shown itself. The left wing has favoured a systematic gradual modification of the law of property in such a direction as would tend to the fulfilment of the socialistic aspirations, so far as these are legitimate, whilst the majority advocate reform through state action on the basis of existing jural institutions. Schäffle goes so far as to maintain that the present " capitalistic" régime will be replaced by a socialistic organisation; but, like J. S. Mill, he adjourns this change to a more or less remote future, and expects it as the result of a natural development, or process of " social selection ; " [1] he repudiates any immediate or violent revolution, and rejects any system of life which would set up "abstract equality" against the claims of individual service and merit. The further the investigations of the German historical school have been carried, in the several lines of inquiry it has opened, the more clearly it has come to light that the one thing needful is not merely a reform of political economy, but its fusion in a complete science of society. This is the view long since insisted on by Auguste Comte ; and its justness is daily becoming more apparent. The best economists of Germany now tend strongly in this direction. Schäffle, who is largely under the influence of Comte and Herbert Spencer, has actually attempted the enterprise of widening economic into social studies. In his most important work, which had been prepared by previous publications, *Bau und Leben des socialen Körpers* (1875–78 ; new ed., 1881), he proposes to give a comprehensive plan of an anatomy, physiology, and psychology of human society. He considers social processes as analogous to those of organic bodies; and, sound and suggestive as the idea of this analogy, already used by Comte, undoubtedly is, he carries it, perhaps, to an undue degree of detail and elaboration. The same conception is adopted by P. von Lilienfeld in his *Gedanken über die Socialwissenschaft der Zukunft* (1873–79). A tendency to the fusion of economic science in Sociology is also found in Adolph Samter's *Sozial-lehre* (1875)—though the economic aspect of society is there specially studied—and in Schmoller's treatise *Ueber einige Grundfragen des Rechts und der Volkswirthschaftslehre* (1875) ; and the necessity of such a transformation is energetically asserted by H. von Scheel in the preface to his German version (1879) of an English tract [1] *On the present Position and Prospects of Political Economy.*

[1] This should be remembered by readers of M. Leroy-Beaulieu's work on Collectivism (1884), in which he treats Schäffle as the principal theoretic representative of that form of socialism.

[2] By the present writer ; being an Address to the Section of Economic Science and Statistics of the British Association at its meeting in Dublin in 1878.

The name "Realistic," which has sometimes been given to the historical school, especially in its more recent form, appears to be injudiciously chosen. It is intended to mark the contrast with the "abstract" complexion of the orthodox economics. But the error of these economics lies, not in the use, but in the abuse of abstraction. All science implies abstraction, seeking, as it does, for unity in variety; the question in every branch is as to the right constitution of the abstract theory in relation to the concrete facts. Nor is the new school quite correctly distinguished as "inductive." Deduction doubtless unduly preponderates in the investigations of the older economists; but it must be remembered that it is a legitimate process, when it sets out, not from *a priori* assumptions, but from proved generalisations. And the appropriate method of economics, as of all sociology, is not so much induction as the specialised form of induction known as comparison, especially the comparative study of "social series" (to use Mill's phrase), which is properly designated as the "historical" method. If the denominations here criticised were allowed to prevail, there would be a danger of the school assuming an unscientific character. It might occupy itself too exclusively with statistical inquiry, and forget in the detailed examination of particular provinces of economic life the necessity of large philosophic ideas and of a systematic co-ordination of principles. So long as economics remain a separate branch of study, and until they are absorbed into Sociology, the thinkers who follow the new direction will do wisely in retaining their original designation of the historical school.

The members of this and the other German schools have produced many valuable works besides those which there has been occasion to mention above. Ample notices of their contributions to the several branches of the science (including its applications) will be found dispersed through Wagner and Nasse's *Lehrbuch* and the comprehensive *Handbuch* edited by Schönberg. The following list, which does not pretend to approach to

completeness, is given for the purpose of directing the student
to a certain number of books which ought not to be overlooked in the study of the subjects to which they respectively
refer :—

Knies, *Die Eisenbahnen und ihre Wirkungen* (1853), *Der Telegraph*
(1857), *Geld und Credit* (1873-76-79) ; Rösler, *Zur Kritik der Lehre vom
Arbeitslohn*, (1861) ; Schmoller, *Zur Geschichte der deutschen Kleinge-
werbe im* 19 *Jahrh.* (1870) ; Schäffle, *Theorie der ausschliessenden Absatz-
verhältnisse* (1867), *Quintessenz des Socialismus* (6th ed., 1878), *Grundsätze
der Steuerpolitik* (1880); Nasse, *Mittelalterliche Feldgemeinschaft in England*,
(1869) ; Brentano, *On the History and Development of Gilds*, prefixed to
Toulmin Smith's *English Gilds* (1870), *Die Arbeitergilden der Gegenwart*
(1871-72), *Das Arbeitsverhältniss gemäss dem heutigen Recht* (1877), *Die
Arbeitsversicherung gemäss der heutigen Wirthschaftsordnung* (1879),
Der Arbeitsversicherungszwang (1881) ; Held (born 1844, accidentally
drowned in the Lake of Thun, 1880), *Die Einkommensteuer* (1872), *Die
deutsche Arbeiterpresse der Gegenwart* (1873), *Sozialismus, Sozialdemok-
ratie und Sozialpolitik* (1878), *Grundriss für Vorlesungen über Nationalökonomie* (2d ed., 1878) ; *Zwei Bücher zur socialen Geschichte Englands*
(posthumously published, 1881) ; Von Scheel (born 1839), *Die Theorie
der socialen Frage* (1871), *Unsere social-politischen Parteien* (1878). To
these may be added L. von Stein, *Die Verwaltungslehre* (1876-79), *Lehrbuch der Finanzwissenschaft* (4th ed., 1878). E. Dühring is the ablest
of the few German followers of Carey ; we have already mentioned (Bibl.
Note) his History of the Science. To the Russian-German school
belongs the work of T. von Bernhardi, which is written from the historical point of view, *Versuch einer Kritik der Gründe welche für grosses und
kleines Grundeigenthum angeführt werden* 1848. The free-trade school of
Germany is recognised as having rendered great practical services in that
country, especially by its systematic warfare against antiquated privileges
and restrictions. Cobden has furnished the model of its political action,
whilst, on the side of theory, it is founded chiefly on Say and Bastiat.
The members of this school whose names have been most frequently
heard by the English public are those of J. Prince Smith (d. 1874), who
may be regarded as having been its head ; H. von Treitschke, author of
Der Socialismus und seine Gönner, 1875 (directed against the Katheder-
Socialisten) ; V. Böhmert, who has advocated the participation of workmen in profits (*Die Gewinnbetheiligung*, 1878) ; A. Emminghaus, author
of *Das Armenwesen in Europäischen Staaten*, 1870, part of which has
been translated in E. B. Eastwick's *Poor Relief in Different Parts of
Europe*, 1873 ; and J. H. Schultze-Delitzsch, well known as the founder of
the German popular banks, and a strenuous supporter of the system of
"co-operation." The socialist writers, as has been already mentioned, are

not included in the present historical survey, nor do we in general notice writings of the economists (properly so called) having relation to the history of socialism or the controversy with it.[1]

The movement which created the new school in Germany, with the developments which have grown out of it, have without doubt given to that country at the present time the primacy in economic studies. German influence has been felt in the modification of opinion in other countries—most strongly, perhaps, in Italy, and least so in France. In England it has been steadily making way, though retarded by the insular indifference to the currents of foreign thought which has eminently marked our dominant school. Alongside of the influence thus exerted, a general distaste for the " orthodox " system has been spontaneously growing, partly from a suspicion that its method was unsound, partly from a profound dissatisfaction with the practice it inspired, and the detected hollowness of the policy of mere *laisser faire*. Hence everywhere a mode of thinking and a species of research have shown themselves, and come into favour, which are in harmony with the systematic conceptions of the historical economists. Thus a dualism has established itself in the economic world, a younger school advancing towards predominance, whilst the old school still defends its position, though its adherents tend more and more to modify their attitude and to admit the value of the new lights.

ITALY.

It is to be regretted that but little is known in England and America of the writings of the recent Italian economists.

[1] The most important economic work which has appeared in Germany since the above paragraph was written is undoubtedly the *System der Nationaloekonomie* of G. Cohn, of which vol. i. (1885) only has yet been published. A movement of reaction in favour of the older school is represented by C. Menger (*Untersuchungen über die Methode der Social-wissenschaften*, 1883), H. Dietzel (*Beiträge zur Methode der Wirthschafts-wissenchaft*, 1884), and E. Sax (*Das Wesen und die Aufgabe der National-oekonomie*, 1884, and *Grundlegung der theoretischen Staatswirthschaft*, 1887).

Luigi Cossa's *Guida*, which was translated at the suggestion
of Jevons,[1] has given us some notion of the character and
importance of their labours. The urgency of questions of
finance in Italy since its political renascence has turned their
researches for the most part into practical channels, and they
have produced numerous monographs on statistical and administrative questions. But they have also dealt ably with
the general doctrines of the science. Cossa pronounces Angelo
Messedaglia (b. 1820), professor at Padua, to be the foremost
of contemporary Italian economists; he has written on public
loans (1850) and on population (1858), and is regarded as
a master of the subjects of money and credit. His pupil
Fedele Lampertico (b. 1833) is author of many writings,
among which the most systematic and complete is his *Economia
dei popoli e degli stati* (1874–1884). Marco Minghetti (1818–
1886), distinguished as a minister, was author, besides other
writings, of *Economia pubblica e le sue attinenze colla morale
e col diritto* (1859). Luigi Luzzati, also known as an able
administrator, has by several publications sought to prepare
the way for reforms. The Sicilians Vito Cusumano and
Giuseppe Ricca Salerno have produced excellent works :—the
former on the history of political economy in the Middle Ages
(1876), and the economic schools of Germany in their relation to the social question (1875); the latter on the theories
of capital, wages, and public loans (1877-8-9). G. Toniolo,
E. Nazzani, and A. Loria have also ably discussed the theories
of rent and profit, as well as some of the most important
practical questions of the day. Cossa, to whom we are indebted for most of these particulars, is himself author of
several works which have established for him a high reputation, as his *Scienza delle Finanze* (1875 ; 4th ed., 1887), and
his *Primi Elementi di Economia Politica* (1875 ; 8th ed.,
1888), which latter has been translated into several European
languages.

---

[1] *Guide to the Study of Political Economy*, 1880. See also the Biblio-
graphical matter in his *Primi Elementi di E. P.*, vol. i., 8th ed., 1888.

Of greater interest than such an imperfect catalogue of writers is the fact of the appearance in Italy of the economic dualism to which we have referred as characterising our time. There also the two schools—the old or so-called orthodox and the new or historical—with their respective modified forms, are found face to face. Cossa tells us that the instructors of the younger economists in northern Italy were publicly denounced in 1874 as Germanists, socialists, and corrupters of the Italian youth. In reply to this charge Luzzati, Lampertico, and Scialoja convoked in Milan the first congress of economists (1875) with the object of proclaiming their resistance to the idea which was sought to be imposed on them "that the science was born and died with Adam Smith and his commentators." M. Émile de Laveleye's interesting *Lettres d'Italie* (1878–79) throw light on the state of economic studies in that country in still more recent years. Minghetti, presiding at the banquet at which M. de Laveleye was entertained by his Italian brethren, spoke of the "two tendencies" which had manifested themselves, and implied his own inclination to the new views. Carlo Ferraris, a pupil of Wagner, follows the same direction. Formal expositions and defences of the historical method have been produced by Schiattarella (*Del metodo in Economia Sociale*, 1875) and Cognetti de Martiis (*Delle attinenze tra l'Economia Sociale e la Storia*, 1865). A large measure of acceptance has also been given to the historical method in learned and judicious monographs by Ricca Salerno (see especially his essay *Del metodo in Econ. Pol.*, 1878). Luzzati and Forti for some time edited a periodical, the *Giornale degli Economisti*, which was the organ of the new school, but which, when Cossa wrote, had ceased to appear. Cossa himself, whilst refusing his adhesion to this school on the ground that it reduces political economy to a mere narrative of facts,—an observation which, we must be permitted to say, betrays an entire misconception of its true principles,—admits that it has been most useful in several ways, and especially as having given the signal for a salutary, though, as he thinks, an excessive, reaction against the doctrinaire exaggerations of the older theorists.

FRANCE.

In France the historical school has not made so strong an impression,—partly, no doubt, because the extreme doctrines of the Ricardian system never obtained much hold there. It was by his recognition of its freedom from those exaggerations that Jevons was led to declare that "the truth is with the French school," whilst he pronounced our English economists to have been "living in a fool's paradise." National prejudice may also have contributed to the result referred to, the ordinary Frenchman being at present disposed to ask whether any good thing can come out of Germany. But, as we have shown, the philosophic doctrines on which the whole proceeding of the historical school is founded were first enunciated by a great French thinker, to whose splendid services most of his fellow-countrymen are singularly dead. Perhaps another determining cause is to be looked for in official influences, which in France, by their action on the higher education, impede the free movement of independent conviction, as was seen notably in the temporary éclat they gave on the wider philosophic stage to the shallow eclecticism of Cousin. The tendency to the historical point of view has appeared in France, as elsewhere; but it has shown itself not so much in modifying general doctrine as in leading to a more careful study of the economic opinions and institutions of the past.

Much useful work has been done by Frenchmen (with whom Belgians may here be associated) in the history of political economy, regarded either as a body of theory or as a system—or series of systems—of policy. Blanqui's history (1837-38) is not, indeed, entitled to a very high rank, but it was serviceable as a first general draught. That of Villeneuve-Bargemont (1839) was also interesting and useful, as presenting the Catholic view of the development and tendencies of the science. C. Perin's *Les doctrines economiques depuis un siècle* (1880) is written from the same point of view. A number of valuable monographs on particular statesmen or thinkers has also been produced by Frenchmen,—as, for example, that of A. Batbie on Turgot (*Turgot Philosophe, Économiste, et Administrateur*, 1861); of A. Neymarck on the same statesman (*Turgot et ses doctrines*, 1885); of Pierre Clément on Colbert (*Histoire de Colbert et de son Administration*, 2d̨ ed., 1875); of H. Baudrillart on Bodin (*J. Bodin et son Temps ; Tableau des Théories politiques et des Idées économiques au* 16ᵉ *siècle*, 1853); of Léonce de Lavergne on the physiocrats (*Les Économistes Français du* 18ᵉ *siècle*, 1870). Works, too, of real importance have been produced on particular aspects of the industrial development, as those of L. de Lavergne on the rural economy of France (1857), and of England, Scotland, and Ireland (1854). The treatise of M. de Laveleye, *De la Propriété et de ses formes primitives* (1874 ; Eng. trans. by G. R. Marriott, 1878), is specially worthy of notice, not merely for its array of facts respecting the early forms of property, but because it co-operates strongly with the tendency of the new school to regard each stage of economic life from the relative point of view, as resulting from an historic past, harmonising with the entire body of contemporary social conditions, and bearing in its bosom the germs of a future, predetermined in its essential character, though modifiable in its secondary dispositions.

M. de Laveleye has done much to call attention to the general principles of the historical school, acting in this way most usefully as an interpreter between Germany and France. But he appears in his most recent manifesto (*Les Lois naturelles et l'objet de l'Économie Politique*, 1883) to separate himself from the best members of that school, and to fall into positive error, when he refuses to economics the character of a true science (or department of a science) as distinguished from an art, and denies the existence of economic laws or

tendencies independent of individual wills. Such a denial
seems to involve that of social laws generally, which is a singularly retrograde attitude for a thinker of our time to take
up, and one which cannot be excused since the appearance of
the *Philosophie Positive*. The use of the metaphysical phrase
"necessary laws" obscures the question; it suffices to speak
of laws which do in fact prevail. M. de Laveleye relies on
morals as supplying a parallel case, where we deal, not with
natural laws, but with "imperative prescriptions," as if these
prescriptions did not imply, as their basis, observed coexist-
ences and sequences, and as if there were no such thing as
moral evolution. He seems to be as far from the right point
of view in one direction as his opponents of the old school in
another. All that his arguments have really any tendency to
prove is the proposition, undoubtedly a true one, that economic
facts cannot be explained by a theory which leaves out of
account the other social aspects, and therefore that our studies
and expositions of economic phenomena must be kept in close
relation with the conclusions of the larger science of society.

We cannot do more than notice in a general way some of
the expository treatises of which there has been an almost
continuous series from the time of Say downwards, or indeed
from the date of Germain Garnier's *Abrégé des Principes de
l'Économie Politique* (1796). That of Destutt de Tracy forms
a portion of his *Éléments d'Idéologie* (1823). Droz brought
out especially the relations of economics to morals and of
wealth to human happiness (*Économie Politique*, 1829). Pelle-
grino Rossi,—an Italian, formed, however, as an economist by
studies in Switzerland, professing the science in Paris, and
writing in French (*Cours d'Économie Politique*, 1838–54),—
gave in classic form an exposition of the doctrines of Say,
Malthus, and Ricardo. Michel Chevalier (1806–1879), specially known in England by his tract, translated by Cobden, on
the fall in the value of gold (*La Baisse d'Or*, 1858), gives in
his *Cours d'Économie Politique* (1845–50) particularly valuable matter on the most recent industrial phenomena, and

on money and the production of the precious metals. Henri Baudrillart, author of *Les Rapports de la Morale et de l'Économie Politique* (1860; 2d ed., 1883), and of *Histoire du Luxe* (1878), published in 1857 a *Manuel d'Économie Politique* (3d ed., 1872), which Cossa calls an "admirable compendium." Joseph Garnier (*Traité de l'Économie Politique*, 1860; 8th ed., 1880) in some respects follows Dunoyer. J. G. Courcelle-Seneuil, the translator of J. S. Mill, whom Prof. F. A. Walker calls "perhaps the ablest economist writing in the French language since J. B. Say," besides a *Traite theorique et pratique des operations de Banque* and *Theorie des Enterprises Industrielles* (1856), wrote a *Traite d'Économie Politique* (1858–59; 2d ed., 1867), which is held in much esteem. Finally, the Genevese, Antoine Elise Cherbuliez (d. 1869), was author of what Cossa pronounces to be the best treatise on the science in the French language (*Précis de la Science Économique*, 1862). L. Walras, in *Éléments d'Économie Politique pure* (1874–77), and *Theorie Mathématique de la Richesse Sociale* (1883), has followed the example of Cournot in attempting a mathematical treatment of the subject.

ENGLAND.

Sacrificing the strict chronological order of the history of economics to deeper considerations, we have already spoken of Cairnes, describing him as the last original English writer who was an adherent of the old school pure and simple. Both in method and doctrine he was essentially Ricardian; though professing and really feeling profound respect for Mill, he was disposed to go behind him and attach himself rather to their common master. Mr. Sidgwick is doubtless right in believing that his *Leading Principles* did much to shake "the unique prestige which Mill's exposition had enjoyed for nearly half a generation," and in this, as in some other ways, Cairnes may have been a dissolving force, and tended towards radical change; but, if he exercised this influence, he did so unconsciously and involuntarily. Many influences had, however, for some time been silently sapping the foundations of the old system. The students of Comte had seen that its method was an erroneous one. The elevated moral teaching of Carlyle had disgusted the best minds with the low maxims of the Manchester school. Ruskin had not merely protested against the egoistic spirit of the prevalent doctrine, but had pointed to some of its real weaknesses as a scientific theory.[1] It began to be felt, and even its warmest partisans sometimes admitted, that it had done all the work, mainly a destructive one, of which it was capable. Cairnes himself declared that, whilst most educated people believed it doomed to sterility for the future, some energetic minds thought it likely to be a positive obstruction in the way of useful reform. Miss Martineau, who had in earlier life been a thorough Ricardian, came to think that political economy, as it had been elaborated by her contemporaries, was, strictly speaking, no science at all, and must undergo such essential change that future generations would owe little to it beyond the establishment of the exist- ence of general laws in one department of human affairs.[2] The instinctive repugnance of the working classes had continued, in spite of the efforts of their superiors to recommend its lessons to them—efforts which were perhaps not unfrequently dictated rather by class interest than by public spirit. All the symptoms boded impending change, but they were visible rather in general literature and in the atmosphere of social opinion than within the economic circle.[3] But when it be- came known that a great movement had taken place, especially in Germany, on new and more hopeful lines, the English econo- mists themselves began to recognise the necessity of a reform

---

[1] The remarkable book *Money and Morals*, by John Lalor, 1852, was written partly under the influence of Carlyle. There is a good mono- graph entitled *John Ruskin, Economist*, by P. Geddes, 1884.

[2] See her *Autobiography*, 2d ed., vol. ii. p. 244.

[3] A vigorous attack on the received system was made by David Syme in his *Outlines of an Industrial Science*, 1876.

and even to further its advent.   The principal agencies of this kind, in marshalling the way to a renovation of the science, have been those of Bagehot, Leslie, and Jevons,—the first limiting the sphere of the dominant system, while seeking to conserve it within narrower bounds ; the second directly assailing it and setting up the new method as the rival and destined successor of the old ; and the third acknowledging the collapse of the hitherto reigning dynasty, proclaiming the necessity of an altered régime, and admitting the younger claimant as joint possessor in the future.   Thus, in England too, the dualism which exists on the Continent has been established ; and there is reason to expect that here more speedily and decisively than in France or Italy the historical school will displace its antagonist.   It is certainly in England next after Germany that the preaching of the new views has been most vigorously and effectively begun.

Walter Bagehot (1826–1877) was author of an excellent work on the English money market and the circumstances which have determined its peculiar character (*Lombard Street*, 1873 ; 7th ed., 1878), and of several monographs on particular monetary questions, which his practical experience, combined with his scientific habits of thought, eminently fitted him to handle.   On the general principles of economics he wrote some highly important essays collected in *Economic Studies* (edited by R. H. Hutton, 1880), the object of which was to show that the traditional system of political economy—the system of Ricardo and J. S. Mill—rested on certain fundamental assumptions, which, instead of being universally true in fact, were only realised within very narrow limits of time and space.   Instead of being applicable to all states of society, it holds only in relation to those " in which commerce has largely developed, and where it has taken the form of development, or something like the form, which it has taken in England."   It is " the science of business such as business is in large and trading communities—an analysis of the great commerce by which England has become rich."   But more than this it is not; it will not explain the economic life o earlier times, nor even of other communities in our own time and for the latter reason it has remained insular; it has nevei been fully accepted in other countries as it has been at home. It is, in fact, a sort of ready reckoner, enabling us to calculate roughly what will happen under given conditions in Lombard Street, on the Stock Exchange, and in the great markets oi the world. It is a "convenient series of deductions from assumed axioms which are never quite true, which in many times and countries would be utterly untrue, but which are sufficiently near to the principal conditions of the modern" English "world to make it useful to consider them by themselves."

Mill and Cairnes had already shown that the science they taught was a hypothetic one, in the sense that it dealt not with real but with imaginary men—" economic men " who were conceived as simply "money-making animals." But Bagehot went further: he showed what those writers, though they may have indicated, had not clearly brought out,[1] that the world in which these men were supposed to act is also "a very limited and peculiar world." What marks off this special world, he tells us, is the promptness of transfer of capital and labour from one employment to another, as determined by differences in the remuneration of those several employments—a promptness about the actual existence of which in the contemporary English world he fluctuates a good deal, but which on the whole he recognises as substantially realised.

Bagehot described himself as "the last man of the ante-Mill period," having learned his economics from Ricardo; and the latter writer he appears to have to the end greatly over-estimated. But he lived long enough to gain some knowledge of the historical method, and with it he had "no quarrel, but rather much sympathy." "Rightly conceived," he said,

---

[1] Jones, whose writings were apparently unknown to Bagehot, had, as we have seen, in some degree anticipated him in this exposition.

"it is no rival to the abstract method rightly conceived."
We will not stop to criticise a second time the term "abstract
method" here applied to that of the old school, or to insist
on the truth that all science is necessarily abstract, the only
question that can arise being as to the just degree of abstraction,
or, in general, as to the right constitution of the relation between
the abstract and the concrete.   It is more apposite to remark
that Bagehot's view of the reconciliation of the two methods
is quite different from that of most "orthodox" economists.
They commonly treat the historical method with a sort of
patronising toleration as affording useful exemplifications or
illustrations of their theorems.   But, according to him, the
two methods are applicable in quite different fields.   For what
he calls the "abstract" method he reserves the narrow, but
most immediately interesting, province of modern advanced
industrial life, and hands over to the historical the economic
phenomena of all the human past and all the rest of the
human present.   He himself exhibits much capacity for such
historical research, and in particular has thrown real light
on the less-noticed economic and social effects of the institution of money, and on the creation of capital in the earlier
stages of society.   But his principal efficacy has been in
reducing, by the considerations we have mentioned, still
further than his predecessors had done, our conceptions of
the work which the *a priori* method can do.   He in fact
dispelled the idea that it can ever supply the branch of general
Sociology which deals with wealth.   As to the relations of
economics to the other sides of Sociology, he holds that the
"abstract" science rightly ignores them.   It does not consider
the differences of human wants, or the social results of their
several gratifications, except so far as these affect the production of wealth.   In its view "a pot of beer and a picture
—a book of religion and a pack of cards—are equally worthy
of regard."   It therefore leaves the ground open for a science
which will, on the one hand, study wealth as a social fact in
all its successive forms and phases, and, on the other, will

regard it in its true light as an instrument for the conservation and evolution—moral as well as material—of human societies.

Though it will involve a slight digression, it is desirable here to notice a further attenuation of the functions of the deductive method, which is well pointed out in Mr. Sidgwick's recent remarkable work on political economy. He observes that, whilst J. S. Mill declares that the method *a priori* is the true method of the science, and that "it has been so understood and taught by all its most distinguished teachers," he yet himself in the treatment of production followed an inductive method (or at least one essentially different from the deductive), obtaining his results by "merely analysing and systematising our common empirical knowledge of the facts of industry." To explain this characteristic inconsistency, Mr. Sidgwick suggests that Mill, in making his general statement as to method, had in contemplation only the statics of distribution and exchange. And in this latter field Mr. Sidgwick holds that the *a priori* method, if it be pursued with caution, if the simplified premises be well devised and the conclusions "modified by a rough conjectural allowance" for the elements omitted in the premises, is not, for the case of a developed industrial society, "essentially false or misleading." Its conclusions are hypothetically valid, though "its utility as a means of interpreting and explaining concrete facts depends on its being used with as full a knowledge as possible of the results of observation and induction." We do not think this statement need be objected to, though we should prefer to regard deduction from hypothesis as a useful occasional logical artifice, and, as such, perfectly legitimate in this as in other fields of inquiry, rather than as the main form of method in any department of economics. Mr. Sidgwick, by his limitation of deduction in distributional questions to "a state of things taken as the type to which civilised society generally approximates," seems to agree with Bagehot that for times and places which do not correspond to this type the historical method must be used—a method which, be it observed, does not exclude, but positively implies, "reflective analysis" of the facts, and their interpretation from "the motives of human agents" as well as from other determining conditions. In the dynamical study of wealth—of the changes in its distribution no less than its production—Mr. Sidgwick admits that the method *a priori* "can occupy but a very subordinate place." We should say that here also, though to a less extent, as a logical artifice it may sometimes be useful, though the hypotheses assumed ought not to be the same that are adapted to a mature industrial stage. But the essential organ must be the historical method, studying comparatively the different phases of social evolution.

Connected with the theory of modern industry is one subject which Bagehot treated, though only in an incidental way, much more satisfactorily than his predecessors,—namely, the function of the entrepreneur, who in Mill and Cairnes is scarcely recognised except as the owner of capital. It is quite singular how little, in the *Leading Principles* of the latter, his active co-operation is taken into account. Bagehot objects to the phrase "wages of superintendence," commonly used to express his "reward," as suggesting altogether erroneous ideas of the nature of his work, and well describes the large and varied range of his activity and usefulness, and the rare combination of gifts and acquirements which go to make up the perfection of his equipment. It can scarcely be doubted that a foregone conclusion in favour of the system of (so-called) co-operation has sometimes led economists to keep these important considerations in the background. They have been brought into due prominence of late in the treatises of Profs. Marshall and F. A. Walker, who, however, have scarcely made clear, and certainly have not justified, the principle on which the amount of the remuneration of the entrepreneur is determined.

We have seen that Jones had in his dogmatic teaching anticipated in some degree the attitude of the new school; important works had also been produced, notably by Thomas Tooke and William Newmarch (*History of Prices*, 1838–1857), and by James E. Thorold Rogers (*History of Agriculture and Prices in England*, 1866–82),[1] on the course of English economic history. But the first systematic statement by an English writer of the philosophic foundation of the historical method, as the appropriate organ of economic research, is to be found in an essay by T. E. Cliffe Leslie (printed in the Dublin University periodical, *Hermathena*, 1876 ; since included in his *Essays Moral and Political*, 1879). This essay was the most important publication on the logical aspect of economic science which had appeared since Mill's essay in his *Unsettled Questions*; though Cairnes had expanded and illustrated the views of Mill, he had really added little to their substance. Leslie takes up a position directly opposed to theirs. He criticises with much force and verve the principles and practice of the " orthodox " school. Those who are acquainted with what has been written on this subject by Knies and other Germans will appreciate the freshness and originality of Leslie's treatment. He points out the loose and vague character of the principle to which the classical economists profess to trace back all the phenomena with which they deal—namely, the " desire of wealth." This phrase really stands for a variety of wants, desires, and sentiments, widely different in their nature and economic effects, and undergoing important changes (as, indeed, the component elements of wealth itself also do) in the several successive stages of the social movement. The truth is that there are many different economic motors, altruistic as well as egoistic ; and they cannot all be lumped together by such a coarse generalisation. The *a priori* and purely deductive method cannot yield an explanation of the causes which regulate either the nature or the amount of wealth, nor of the varieties of distribution in different social systems, as, for example, in those of France and England. " The whole economy of every nation is the result of a long evolution in which there has been both continuity and change,

---

[1] Mr. Rogers has since continued this work, and has also published *The First Nine Years of the Bank of England*, 1887.

and of which the economical side is only a particular aspect. And the laws of which it is the result must be sought in history and the general laws of society and social evolution." The intellectual, moral, legal, political, and economic sides of social progress are indissolubly connected. Thus, juridical facts relating to property, occupation, and trade, thrown up by the social movement, are also economic facts. And, more generally, "the economic condition of English" or any other "society at this day is the outcome of the entire movement which has evolved the political constitution, the structure of the family, the forms of religion, the learned professions, the arts and sciences, the state of agriculture, manufactures, and commerce." To understand existing economic relations we must trace their historical evolution; and "the philosophical method of political economy must be one which expounds that evolution." This essay was a distinct challenge addressed to the ideas of the old school on method, and, though its conclusions have been protested against, the arguments on which they are founded have never been answered.

With respect to the dogmatic generalisations of the "orthodox" economists, Leslie thought some of them were false, and all of them required careful limitation. Early in his career he had shown the hollowness of the wage-fund theory, though he was not the first to repudiate it.[1] The doctrine of an average rate of wages and an average rate of profits he rejected except under the restrictions stated by Adam Smith, which imply a "simple and almost stationary condition" of the industrial world. He thought the glib assumption of an average rate of wages, as well as of a wage-fund, had done much harm "by hiding the real rates of wages, the real causes which govern them, and the real sources from which wages proceed." The facts, which he laboriously collected, he found

[1] That service was due to F. D. Longe (*Refutation of the Wage-Fund Theory of Modern Political Economy*, 1866). Leslie's treatment of the subject was contained in an article of *Fraser's Magazine* for July 1868, reprinted as an appendix to his *Land-Systems and Industrial Economy of Ireland, England, and Continental Countries*, 1870.

to be everywhere against the theory. In every country there is really " a great number of rates; and the real problem is, What are the causes which produce these different rates ? " As to profits, he denies that there are any means of knowing the gains and prospects of all the investments of capital, and declares it to be a mere fiction that any capitalist surveys the whole field. Bagehot, as we saw, gave up the doctrine of a national level of wages and profits except in the peculiar case of an industrial society of the contemporary English type ; Leslie denies it even for such a society. With this doctrine, that of cost of production as determining price collapses, and the principle emerges that it is not cost of production, but demand and supply, on which domestic, no less than inter- national, values depend,—though this formula will require much interpretation before it can be used safely and with advantage. Thus Leslie extends to the whole of the national industry the partial negation of the older dogma introduced by Cairnes through the idea of non-competing groups. He does not, of course, dispute the real operation of cost of pro- duction on price in the limited area within which rates of profit and wages are determinate and known; but he main- tains that its action on the large scale is too remote and un- certain to justify our treating it as regulator of price. Now, if this be so, the entire edifice which Ricardo reared on the basis of the identity of cost of production and price, with its apparent but unreal simplicity, symmetry, and completeness, disappears ; and the ground is cleared for the new structure which must take its place. Leslie predicts that, if political economy, under that name, does not bend itself to the task of rearing such a structure, the office will speedily be taken out of its hands by Sociology.

Leslie was a successful student of several special economic subjects—of agricultural economy, of taxation, of the distribu- tion of the precious metals and the history of prices, and, as has been indicated, of the movements of wages. But it is in relation to the method and fundamental doctrines of the

science that he did the most important, because the most
opportune and needful work. And, though his course was
closed too early for the interests of knowledge, and much of
what he produced was merely occasional and fragmentary, his
services will be found to have been greater than those of
many who have left behind them more systematic, elaborate,
and pretentious writings.

One of the most original of recent English writers on Political Economy was W. Stanley Jevons (1835–1882). The
combination which he presented of a predilection and aptitude
for exact statistical inquiry with sagacity and ingenuity in the
interpretation of the results was such as might remind us of
Petty. He tended strongly to bring economics into close relation with physical science. He made a marked impression
on the public mind by his attempt to take stock of our resources in the article of coal. His idea of a relation between
the recurrences of commercial crises and the period of the sun-
spots gave evidence of a fertile and bold scientific imagination,
though he cannot be said to have succeeded in establishing
such a relation. He was author of an excellent treatise on
Money and the Mechanism of Exchange (1875), and of various
essays on currency and finance, which have been collected
since his death, and contain vigorous discussions on subjects
of this nature, as on bimetallism (with a decided tendency in
favour of the single gold standard), and several valuable suggestions, as with respect to the most perfect system of currency,
domestic and international, and in particular the extension of
the paper currency in England to smaller amounts. He proposed in other writings (collected in *Methods of Social Reform*,
1883) a variety of measures, only partly economic in their
character, directed especially to the elevation of the working
classes, one of the most important being in relation to the
conditions of the labour of married women in factories. This
was one of several instances in which he repudiated the *laisser
faire* principle, which indeed, in his book on *The State in
Relation to Labour* (1882), he refuted in the clearest and

most convincing way, without changing the position he had
always maintained as an advocate of free trade. Towards the
end of his career, which was prematurely terminated, he was
more and more throwing off "the incubus of metaphysical
ideas and expressions" which still impeded the recognition or
confused the appreciation of social facts. He was, in his own
words, ever more distinctly coming to the conclusion "that
the only hope of attaining a true system of economics is to
fling aside, once and for ever, the mazy and preposterous assumptions of the Ricardian school." With respect to method,
though he declares it to be his aim to "investigate inductively
the intricate phenomena of trade and industry," his views had
not perhaps assumed a definitive shape. The editor of some of
his remains declines to undertake the determination of his
exact position with respect to the historical school. The
fullest indications we possess on that subject are to be found
in a lecture of 1876, *On the Future of Political Economy.* He
saw the importance and necessity in economics of historical
investigation, a line of study which he himself was led by
native bent to prosecute in some directions. But he scarcely
apprehended the full meaning of the historical method, which
he erroneously contrasted with the "theoretical," and apparently supposed to be concerned only with verifying and illustrating certain abstract doctrines resting on independent bases.
Hence, whilst he declared himself in favour of "thorough
reform and reconstruction," he sought to preserve the *a priori*
mode of proceeding alongside of, and concurrently with, the
historical. Political economy, in fact, he thought was breaking
up and falling into several, probably into many, different
branches of inquiry, prominent amongst which would be the
"theory" as it had descended from his best predecessors,
especially those of the French school, whilst another would
be the "historical study," as it was followed in England by
Jones, Rogers, and others, and as it had been proclaimed in
general principle by his contemporary Cliffe Leslie. This was
one of those eclectic views which have no permanent validity,

but are useful in facilitating a transition. The two methods will doubtless for a time coexist, but the historical will inevitably supplant its rival. What Jevons meant as the "theory" he wished to treat by mathematical methods (see his *Theory of Political Economy*, 1871; 2d ed., 1879). This project had, as we have seen, been entertained and partially carried into effect by others before him, though he unduly multiplies the number of such earlier essays when, for example, he mentions Ricardo and J. S. Mill as writing mathematically because they sometimes illustrated the meaning of their propositions by dealing with definite arithmetical quantities. Such illustrations, of which a specimen is supplied by Mill's treatment of the subject of international trade, have really nothing to do with the use of mathematics as an instrument for economic research, or even for the co-ordination of economic truths. We have already, in speaking of Cournot, explained why, as it seems to us, the application of mathematics in the higher sense to economics must necessarily fail, and we do not think that it succeeded in Jevons's hands. His conception of "final utility" is ingenious. But it is no more than a mode of presenting the notion of price in the case of commodities homogeneous in quality and admitting of increase by infinitesimal additions; and the expectation of being able by means of it to subject economic doctrine to a mathematical method will be found illusory. He offers[1] as the result of a hundred pages of mathematical reasoning what he calls a "curious conclusion,"[2] in which "the keystone of the whole theory of exchange and of the principal problems of economics lies." This is the proposition that "the ratio of exchange of any two commodities will be the reciprocal of the ratio of the final degrees of utility of the quantities of commodity available for consumption after the exchange is completed." Now, as long as we remain in the region of the metaphysical entities termed utilities, this theorem is unverifiable and indeed unintelligible, because we

[1] *Theory of Political Economy*, 2d ed., p. 103.
[2] *Fortnightly Review* for November 1876, p. 617.

have no means of estimating quantitatively the mental impression of final, or any other, utility. But when we translate it into the language of real life, measuring the "utility" of anything to a man by what he will give for it, the proposition is at once seen to be a truism. What Jevons calls "final utility" being simply the price per unit of quantity, the theorem states that, in an act of exchange, the product of the quantity of the commodity given by its price per unit of quantity (estimated in a third article) is the same as the corresponding product for the commodity received—a truth so obvious as to require no application of the higher mathematics to discover it. If we cannot look for results more substantial than this, there is not much encouragement to pursue such researches, which will in fact never be anything more than academic playthings, and which involve the very real evil of restoring the "metaphysical ideas and expressions" previously discarded. The reputation of Jevons as an acute and vigorous thinker, inspired with noble popular sympathies, is sufficiently established. But the attempt to represent him, in spite of himself, as a follower and continuator of Ricardo, and as one of the principal authors of the development of economic theory (meaning by "theory" the old *a priori* doctrine) can only lower him in estimation by placing his services on grounds which will not bear criticism. His name will survive in connection, not with new theoretical constructions, but with his treatment of practical problems, his fresh and lively expositions, and, as we have shown, his energetic tendency to a renovation of economic method.

Arnold Toynbee (1852–1883), who left behind him a beautiful memory, filled as he was with the love of truth and an ardent and active zeal for the public good, was author of some fragmentary or unfinished pieces, which yet well deserve attention both for their intrinsic merit and as indicating the present drift of all the highest natures, especially amongst our younger men, in the treatment of economic questions.[1] He

[1] See his *Lectures on the Industrial Revolution in England*, with Memoir by the Master of Balliol, 1884 ; 2d ed., 1887.

had a belief in the organising power of democracy which it is not easy to share, and some strange ideas due to youthful enthusiasm, such as, for example, that Mazzini is "the true teacher of our age;" and he fluctuates considerably in his opinion of the Ricardian political economy, in one place declaring it to be a detected "intellectual imposture," whilst elsewhere, apparently under the influence of Bagehot, he speaks of it as having been in recent times "only corrected, re-stated, and put into the proper relation to the science of life," meaning apparently, by this last, general sociology. He saw, however, that our great help in the future must come, as much had already come, from the historical method, to which in his own researches he gave preponderant weight. Its true character, too, he understood better than many even of those who have commended it; for he perceived that it not merely explains the action of special local or temporary conditions on economic phenomena, but seeks, by comparing the stages of social development in different countries and times, to "discover laws of universal application." If, as we are told, there exists at Oxford a rising group of men who occupy a position in regard to economic thought substantially identical with that of Toynbee, the fact is one of good omen for the future of the science.

AMERICA.

For a long time, as we have already observed, little was done by America in the field of Economics. The most obvious explanation of this fact, which holds with respect to philosophical studies generally, is the absorption of the energies of the nation in practical pursuits. Further reasons are suggested in two instructive Essays—one by Professor Charles F. Dunbar in the *North American Review*, 1876, the other by Cliffe Leslie in the *Fortnightly Review* for October 1880. We have already referred to the Report on Manufactures by Alexander Hamilton; and the memorial drawn up by Albert Gallatin (1832), and presented to Congress from the

Philadelphia Convention in favour of Tariff reform, deserves to be mentioned as an able statement of the arguments against protection. Three editions of the *Wealth of Nations* appeared in America, in 1789, 1811, and 1818, and Ricardo's principal work was reprinted there in 1819. The treatises of Daniel Raymond (1820), Thomas Cooper (1826), Willard Phillips (1828), Francis Wayland (1837), and Henry Vethake (1838) made known the principles arrived at by Adam Smith and some of his successors. Rae, a Scotchman settled in Canada, published (1834) a book entitled *New Principles of Political Economy*, which has been highly praised by J. S. Mill (bk. i. chap. 11), especially for its treatment of the causes which determine the accumulation of capital. The principal works which afterwards appeared down to the time of the Civil War were Francis Bowen's *Principles of Political Economy*, 1856, afterwards entitled *American Political Economy*, 1870 ; John Bascom's *Political Economy*, 1859 ; and Stephen Colwell's *Ways and Means of Payment*, 1859. In the period including and following the war appeared Amasa Walker's *Science of Wealth*, 1866 ; 18th ed., 1883, and A. L. Perry's *Elements of Political Economy*, 1866. A. Walker and Perry are free-traders ; Perry is a disciple of Bastiat. Of Carey we have already spoken at some length; his American followers are E. Peshine Smith (*A Manual of Political Economy*, 1853), William Elder (*Questions of the Day*, 1871), and Robert E. Thompson (*Social Science*, 1875). The name of no American economist stands higher than that of General Francis A. Walker (son of Amasa Walker), author of special works on the *Wages Question* (1876) and on *Money* (1878), as well as of an excellent general treatise on *Political Economy* (1883 ; 2d ed. 1887). The principal works on American economic history are those of A. S. Bolles, entitled *Industrial History of the United States* (1878), and *Financial History of the United States*, 1774–1885, published in 1879 and later years.

The deeper and more comprehensive study of the subject which has of late years prevailed in America, added to influences from abroad, has given rise, there also, to a division of economists into two schools—an old and a new—similar to those which we have found confronting each other elsewhere. A meeting was held at Saratoga in September 1885, at which a society was founded, called the American Economic Association. The object of this movement was to oppose the idea that the field of economic research was closed, and to promote a larger and more fruitful study of economic questions. The same spirit has led to the establishment of the *Quarterly Journal of Economics*, published at Boston for Harvard University, which promises to do excellent work. The first article in this Journal is by C. F. Dunbar, whose review of a Century of American Political Economy we have already noticed ; and in this article he sets out, in the interest of conciliation, the tendencies of the two schools.

This division of opinion has been manifested in a striking way by a discussion on the method and fundamental principles of Economics, which was conducted in the pages of the periodical entitled *Science*, and has since been reproduced in a separate form (*Science Economic Discussion*, New York, 1886). In this controversy the views of the new school were expounded and advocated with great ability. The true nature of economic method, the relativity both of economic institutions and of economic thought, arising from their dependence on varying social conditions, the close connection of economic doctrine with contemporary jurisprudence, the necessity of keeping economics in harmony with social ethics, and the importance of a study of consumption (denied by J. S. Mill and others) were all exhibited with remarkable clearness and force.[1] There is every reason to believe with Leslie that

[1] The contributors on the side of the new school were Dr. Edwin R. A. Seligman, Professor E. J. James, Professor Richard T. Ely, Henry C. Adams, Richmond Mayo Smith, and Simon N. Patten. The representatives of the old school were Professor Simon Newcomb, F. W. Taussig, and Arthur T. Hadley.

America will take an active part both in bringing to light the economic problems of the future and in working out their solution.

Contemporary English Economists.

It is no part of our plan to pass judgment on the works of contemporary English authors,—a judgment which could not in general be final, and which would be subject to the imputation of bias in a greater degree than estimates of living writers in foreign countries. But, for the information of the student, some opinions may be expressed which scarcely any competent person would dispute. The best brief exposition of political economy, substantially in accordance with Mill's treatise, is to be found in Fawcett's *Manual* (6th ed., 1884). But those who admit in part the claims of the new school will prefer Mr. and Mrs. Marshall's *Economics of Industry* (2d ed., 1881). Better, in some respects, than either is the *Political Economy* of the American writer, Francis A. Walker, to which we have already referred. Other meritorious works are J. E. T. Rogers's *Manual of Political Economy*, 1870; John Macdonell's *Survey of Political Economy*, 1871; and John L. Shadwell's *System of Political Economy*, 1877. Professor W. E. Hearn's *Plutology* (1864) contains one of the ablest extant treatments of the subject of production. Mr. Goschen's is the best work on the foreign exchanges (10th ed., 1879). Mr. Macleod, though his general economic scheme has met with no acceptance, is recognised as supplying much that is useful on the subject of banking. Professor Rogers's *Six Centuries of Work and Wages* (1884) is the most trustworthy book on the economic history of England during the period with which he deals. W. Cunningham's *Growth of English Industry and Commerce* (1882) is instructive on the mercantile system. Dr. W. Neilson Hancock has shown in a multitude of papers a most extensive and accurate knowledge of the social economy of Ireland.

We cannot here overlook a work like that of Mr. Sidgwick (1883), to which we have already referred on a special point. It is impossible not to respect and admire the conscientious and penetrating criticism which he applies to the *a priori* system of economics in its most mature form. But it is open to question whether the task was wisely undertaken. It cannot be permanently our business to go on amending and limiting the Ricardian doctrines, and asking by what special interpretations of phrases or additional qualifications they may still be admitted as having a certain value. The time for a new construction has arrived; and it is to this, or at least to the study of its conditions, that competent thinkers with the due scientific preparation should now devote themselves. It is to be feared that Mr. Sidgwick's treatise, instead of, as he hopes, " eliminating unnecessary controversy," will tend to revive the *stériles contestations* and *oiseuses disputes de mots*, which Comte censured in the earlier economists. It is interesting to observe that the part of the work which is, and has been recognised as, the most valuable is that in which, shaking off the fictions of the old school, he examines independently by the light of observation and analysis the question of the industrial action of Governments.

CHAPTER VII.

CONCLUSION.

LET us briefly consider in conclusion, by the light of the preceding historical survey, what appear to be the steps in the direction of a renovation of economic science which are now at once practicable and urgent.

I. Economic investigation has hitherto fallen for the most part into the hands of lawyers and men of letters, not into those of a genuinely scientific class. Nor have its cultivators in general had that sound preparation in the sciences of inorganic and vital nature which is necessary whether as supplying bases of doctrine or as furnishing lessons of method. Their education has usually been of a metaphysical kind. Hence political economy has retained much of the form and spirit which belonged to it in the seventeenth and eighteenth centuries, instead of advancing with the times, and assuming a truly positive character. It is homogeneous with the school logic, with the abstract unhistorical jurisprudence, with the *a priori* ethics and politics, and other similar antiquated systems of thought; and it will be found that those who insist most strongly on the maintenance of its traditional character have derived their habitual mental pabulum from those regions of obsolete speculation. We can thus understand the attitude of true men of science towards this branch of study, which they regard with ill-disguised contempt, and to whose professors they either refuse or very reluctantly concede a place in their brotherhood.

The radical vice of this unscientific character of political economy seems to lie in the too individual and subjective aspect under which it has been treated. Wealth having been conceived as what satisfies desires, the definitely determinable qualities possessed by some objects of supplying physical energy, and improving the physiological constitution, are left out of account. Everything is gauged by the standard of subjective notions and desires. All desires are viewed as equally legitimate, and all that satisfies our desires as equally wealth. Value being regarded as the result of a purely mental appreciation, the social value of things in the sense of their objective utility, which is often scientifically measurable, is passed over, and ratio of exchange is exclusively considered. The truth is, that at the bottom of all economic investigation must lie the idea of the destination of wealth for the maintenance and evolution of a society. And, if we overlook this, our economics will become a play of logic or a manual for the market, rather than a contribution to social science; whilst wearing an air of completeness, they will be in truth one-sided and superficial. Economic science is something far larger than the Catallactics to which some have wished to reduce it. A special merit of the physiocrats seems to have lain in their vague perception of the close relation of their study to that of external nature; and, so far, we must recur to their point of view, basing our economics on physics and biology as developed in our own time.[1] Further, the science must be cleared of all the theologico-metaphysical elements or tendencies which still encumber and deform it. Teleology and optimism on the one hand, and the jargon of "natural liberty" and "indefeasible rights" on the other, must be finally abandoned.

Nor can we assume as universal premises, from which economic truths can be deductively derived, the convenient

---

[1] This aspect of the subject has been ably treated in papers contributed to the Proceedings of the Royal Society of Edinburgh on several occasions during and since 1881 by Mr. P. Geddes, well known as a biologist.

formulas which have been habitually employed, such as that
all men desire wealth and dislike exertion. These vague
propositions, which profess to anticipate and supersede social
experience, and which necessarily introduce the absolute where
relativity should reign, must be laid aside. The laws of
wealth (to reverse a phrase of Buckle's) must be inferred from
the facts of wealth, not from the postulate of human selfishness. We must bend ourselves to a serious direct study of
the way in which society has actually addressed itself and now
addresses itself to its own conservation and evolution through
the supply of its material wants. What organs it has developed
for this purpose, how they operate, how they are affected by
the medium in which they act and by the coexistent organs
directed to other ends, how in their turn they react on those
latter, how they and their functions are progressively modified in process of time—these problems, whether statical or
dynamical, are all questions of fact, as capable of being studied
through observation and history as the nature and progress
of human language or religion, or any other group of social
phenomena. Such study will of course require a continued
" reflective analysis " of the results of observation ; and, whilst
eliminating all premature assumptions, we shall use ascertained
truths respecting human nature as guides in the inquiry and
aids towards the interpretation of facts. And the employment
of deliberately instituted hypotheses will be legitimate, but
only as an occasional logical artifice.

II. Economics must be constantly regarded as forming only
one department of the larger science of Sociology, in vital
connection with its other departments, and with the moral synthesis which is the crown of the whole intellectual system.
We have already sufficiently explained the philosophical
grounds for the conclusion that the economic phenomena of
society cannot be isolated, except provisionally, from the rest,—
that, in fact, all the primary social elements should be habitually regarded with respect to their mutual dependence and
reciprocal actions. Especially must we keep in view the high

moral issues to which the economic movement is subservient, and in the absence of which it could never in any great degree attract the interest or fix the attention either of eminent thinkers or of right-minded men. The individual point of view will have to be subordinated to the social; each agent will have to be regarded as an organ of the society to which he belongs and of the larger society of the race. The consideration of interests, as George Eliot has well said, must give place to that of functions. The old doctrine of right, which lay at the basis of the system of "natural liberty," has done its temporary work; a doctrine of duty will have to be substituted, fixing on positive grounds the nature of the social co-operation of each class and each member of the community, and the rules which must regulate its just and beneficial exercise.

Turning now from the question of the theoretic constitution of economics, and viewing the science with respect to its influence on public policy, we need not at the present day waste words in repudiating the idea that "non-government" in the economic sphere is the normal order of things. The *laisser faire* doctrine, coming down to us from the system of natural liberty, was long the great watchword of economic orthodoxy. It had a special acceptance and persistence in England in consequence of the political struggle for the repeal of the corn laws, which made economic discussion in this country turn almost altogether on free trade—a state of things which was continued by the effort to procure a modification of the protective policy of foreign nations. But it has now for some time lost the sacrosanct character with which it was formerly invested. This is a result not so much of scientific thought as of the pressure of practical needs—a cause which has modified the successive forms of economic opinion more than theorists are willing to acknowledge. Social exigencies will force the hands of statesmen, whatever their attachment to abstract formulas; and politicians have practically turned their backs on *laisser faire.* The State has with excellent effect proceeded a considerable way in the direction of controlling, for ends of social equity or public utility, the operations of individual interest. The economists themselves have for the most part been converted on the question; amongst theorists Mr. Herbert Spencer finds himself almost a *vox clamantis in deserto* in protesting against what he calls the "new slavery" of Governmental interference. He will protest in vain, so far as he seeks to rehabilitate the old absolute doctrine of the economic passivity of the State. But it is certainly possible that even by virtue of the force of the reaction against that doctrine there may be an excessive or precipitate tendency in the opposite direction. With the course of production or exchange considered in itself there will probably be in England little disposition to meddle. But the dangers and inconveniences which arise from the unsettled condition of the world of labour will doubtless from time to time here, as elsewhere, prompt to premature attempts at regulation. Apart, however, from the removal of evils which threaten the public peace, and from temporary palliations to ease off social pressure, the right policy of the State in this sphere will for the present be one of abstention. It is indeed certain that industrial society will not permanently remain without a systematic organisation. The mere conflict of private interests will never produce a well-ordered commonwealth of labour. *Freiheit ist keine Lösung.* Freedom is for society, as for the individual, the necessary condition precedent of the solution of practical problems, both as allowing natural forces to develop themselves and as exhibiting their spontaneous tendencies; but it is not in itself the solution. Whilst, however, an organisation of the industrial world may with certainty be expected to arise in process of time, it would be a great error to attempt to improvise one. We are now in a period of transition. Our ruling powers have still an equivocal character; they are not in real harmony with industrial life, and are in all respects imperfectly imbued with the modern spirit. Besides, the conditions of the new order are not yet sufficiently understood. The institutions of the future must be founded on sentiments and habits, and these must be the slow growth of thought and experience. The solution, indeed, must be at all times largely a moral one; it is the spiritual rather than the temporal power that is the natural agency for redressing or mitigating most of the evils associated with industrial life.[1] In fact, if there is a tendency—and we may admit that such a tendency is real or imminent—to push the State towards an extension of the normal limits of its action for the maintenance of social equity, this is doubtless in some measure due to the fact that the growing dissidence on religious questions in the most advanced communities has weakened the authority of the Churches, and deprived their influence of social universality. What is now most urgent is not legislative interference on any large scale with the industrial relations, but the formation, in both the higher and lower regions of the industrial world, of profound convictions as to social duties, and some more effective mode than at present exists of diffusing, maintaining, and applying those convictions. This is a subject into which we cannot enter here. But it may at least be said that the only parties in contemporary public life which seem rightly to conceive or adequately to appreciate the necessities of the situation are those that aim, on the one hand, at the restoration of the old spiritual power, or, on the other, at the formation of a new one. And this leads to the conclusion that there is one sort of Governmental interference which the advocates of *laisser faire* have not always discountenanced, and which yet, more than any other, tends to prevent the gradual and peaceful rise of a new industrial and social

[1] The neglect of this consideration, and the consequent undue exaltation of State action, which, though quite legitimate, is altogether insufficient, appears to be the principal danger to which the contemporary German school of economists is exposed. When Schmoller says, "The State is the grandest existing ethical institution for the education of the human race," he transfers to it the functions of the Church. The educational action of the State must be, in the main, only indirect.

system,—namely, the interference with spiritual liberty by setting up official types of philosophical doctrine, and imposing restrictions on the expression and discussion of opinions.

It will be seen that our principal conclusion respecting economic action harmonises with that relating to the theoretic study of economic phenomena. For, as we held that the latter could not be successfully pursued except as a duly subordinated branch of the wider science of Sociology, so in practical human affairs we believe that no partial synthesis is possible, but that an economic reorganisation of society implies a universal renovation, intellectual and moral no less than material. The industrial reformation for which western Europe groans and travails, and the advent of which is indicated by so many symptoms (though it will come only as the fruit of faithful and sustained effort), will be no isolated fact, but will form part of an applied art of life, modifying our whole environment, affecting our whole culture, and regulating our whole conduct—in a word, directing all our resources to the one great end of the conservation and development of Humanity.

INDEX.

THE END.

PRINTED BY BALLANTYNE, HANSON AND CO.
EDINBURGH AND LONDON.

Printed in the United States
By Bookmasters